Boundary Control

Subnational Authoritarianism in Federal Democracies

The democratization of a national government is only a first step in the diffusion of democracy throughout a country's territory. Even after a national government is democratized, subnational authoritarian "enclaves" often continue to deny rights to citizens of local jurisdictions. Edward L. Gibson offers new theoretical perspectives for the study of democratization in his exploration of this phenomenon. His theory of "boundary control" captures the conflict pattern between incumbents and oppositions when a national democratic government exists alongside authoritarian provinces (or "states"). He also reveals how federalism and the territorial organization of countries shape how subnational authoritarian regimes are built and unravel. Through a novel comparison of the late-nineteenth-century American "Solid South" with contemporary experiences in Argentina and Mexico, Gibson reveals that the mechanisms of boundary control are reproduced across countries and historical periods. As long as subnational authoritarian governments coexist with national democratic governments, boundary control will be at play.

Edward L. Gibson is Professor of Political Science at Northwestern University. He is the author of *Class and Conservative Parties: Argentina in Comparative Perspective* and editor of *Federalism and Democracy in Latin America*. He is also author of several scholarly articles on party politics, democratization, and federalism. Professor Gibson has received awards from the National Science Foundation CAREER Program, the Howard Foundation, and other institutions. He teaches courses on democratization, comparative politics, Latin American politics, and federalism and has received numerous teaching awards, including Northwestern University's McCormick Professorship of Teaching Excellence.

Cambridge Studies in Comparative Politics

General Editor
Margaret Levi *University of Washington, Seattle*

Assistant General Editors
Kathleen Thelen *Massachusetts Institute of Technology*
Erik Wibbels *Duke University*

Associate Editors
Robert H. Bates *Harvard University*
Gary Cox *Stanford University*
Stephen Hanson *The College of William and Mary*
Torben Iversen *Harvard University*
Stathis Kalyvas *Yale University*
Peter Lange *Duke University*
Helen Milner *Princeton University*
Frances Rosenbluth *Yale University*
Susan Stokes *Yale University*

Other Books in the Series
Ben W. Ansell, *From the Ballot to the Blackboard: The Redistributive Political Economy of Education*
David Austen-Smith, Jeffry A. Frieden, Miriam A. Golden, Karl Ove Moene, and Adam Przeworski, eds., *Selected Works of Michael Wallerstein: The Political Economy of Inequality, Unions, and Social Democracy*
Andy Baker, *The Market and the Masses in Latin America: Policy Reform and Consumption in Liberalizing Economies*
Lisa Baldez, *Why Women Protest: Women's Movements in Chile*
Stefano Bartolini, *The Political Mobilization of the European Left, 1860–1980: The Class Cleavage*
Robert Bates, *When Things Fell Apart: State Failure in Late-Century Africa*
Mark Beissinger, *Nationalist Mobilization and the Collapse of the Soviet State*
Pablo Beramendi, *The Political Geography of Inequality: Regions and Redistribution*
Nancy Bermeo, ed., *Unemployment in the New Europe*
Carles Boix, *Democracy and Redistribution*
Carles Boix, *Political Parties, Growth, and Equality: Conservative and Social Democratic Economic Strategies in the World Economy*
Catherine Boone, *Merchant Capital and the Roots of State Power in Senegal, 1930–1985*
Catherine Boone, *Political Topographies of the African State: Territorial Authority and Institutional Change*

(*continued after Index*)

Boundary Control

Subnational Authoritarianism
in Federal Democracies

EDWARD L. GIBSON

Northwestern University

CAMBRIDGE
UNIVERSITY PRESS

CAMBRIDGE UNIVERSITY PRESS
Cambridge, New York, Melbourne, Madrid, Cape Town,
Singapore, São Paulo, Delhi, Mexico City

Cambridge University Press
32 Avenue of the Americas, New York, NY 10013-2473, USA

www.cambridge.org
Information on this title: www.cambridge.org/9780521127332

First published 2012

Printed in the United States of America

A catalog record for this publication is available from the British Library.

Library of Congress Cataloging in Publication Data
Gibson, Edward L.
Boundary control : subnational authoritarianism in federal democracies /
Edward L. Gibson, Northwestern University.
pages cm. – (Cambridge studies in comparative politics)
Includes bibliographical references and index.
ISBN 978-0-521-19223-1 (hardback) – ISBN 978-0-521-12733-2 (paperback)
1. Federal government. 2. Subnational governments. 3. Authoritarianism.
4. Central-local government relations. I. Title.
JC355.G53   2012
320.4'049–dc23   2012012604

ISBN 978-0-521-19223-1 Hardback
ISBN 978-0-521-12733-2 Paperback

For Jennifer Dalzell Gibson
(hermanita)

Contents

I

Introduction

Our universe is not local.

– Brian Greene[1]

In 1983 the luminous December sun shone on the nation's capital as Raúl Alfonsín, the newly inaugurated Argentine president, waved to enthusiastic crowds from his open-topped car. The crowds cheered not only the man wearing the sash but also the political event he embodied – the birth of a new democracy. Furthermore, the horrors and the drama of the years leading to this event gave national and international observers alike the sense that Argentina had finally turned its back on a long legacy of authoritarian politics. This transition to democracy was for real, and the political officials getting ready to govern, with all their weaknesses and predictable missteps along the way, would never again permit authoritarian rulers to control power in the nation's capital.

At around the same time, far from the glare of the national press corps, and even farther from international scrutiny, an old political boss stepped assuredly into the gubernatorial palace of the northern province of Santiago del Estero. The surroundings were familiar to him. Carlos Arturo Juárez had first been elected governor of Santiago in 1949 and now looked forward to a third term in office. Juárez had been the province's puppet master for more than three decades. In the course of his career, he had maneuvered skillfully against challenges to his hold on the province from party rivals, including from the great Juan Perón himself. He had also prevailed against several military governments, whose occupations he waited out in comfortable exile financed by provincial construction magnates made wealthy during his terms in office. In 1983 he returned from one such period of exile, and his loyal local Peronist Party machine mobilized to hand him another election victory. As he surveyed the political landscape of a province he had not seen for seven years, Juárez

[1] Brian Greene, *The Fabric of the Cosmos: Space, Time, and the Texture of Reality* (New York: Knopf, 2004), 81.

remarked casually to a reporter, "Santiago del Estero is Carlos Arturo Juárez. I say it without vanity."[2]

Over the next 20 years, as the national democratic regime moved toward consolidation, Juárez busily secured an authoritarian regime in the province of Santiago del Estero. He isolated, co-opted, or repressed local opposition parties. Reforms of the provincial constitution expanded the governor's powers and the Peronist Party's control over provincial institutions. A vast patronage machine linked job security for most of the gainfully employed population to loyalty to the provincial *caudillo* and guaranteed wealth for local business elites who curried his favor. Where institutional control and patronage failed to neutralize opponents, outright repression filled the void. *Juarista* informants kept close watch on public sector employees, and deviant political behavior was punished with job loss or violence from vigilante groups. A feared provincial intelligence system also reported directly to the governor; it was led by a chief of police whose previous job experience included oversight of the detention, torture, and disappearance of local inhabitants during the 1976–83 military dictatorship.

The provincial *caudillo's* cult of personality was everywhere evident. Students graduating from public high schools found letters with their diplomas reminding them of their debt to the great leader for the education they had received. Announcers on the public address system of the capital city's racetrack called on sparse crowds of gamblers to give thanks to the governor for the glorious weather they were enjoying. Bricks piled on construction sites were engraved with his name (or that of his wife and political partner) by obsequious construction contractors. The 14-story luxury hotel that soared above the squat skyline of the capital city was named "Carlos V," not after some distant European monarch, but in honor of Carlos Arturo Juárez's fifth gubernatorial term.

That an authoritarian Santiago del Estero could survive and prosper in a democratic Argentina is a remarkable story, but it is far from unusual. Change the proper names in this narrative (and perhaps some of its more outrageous features), and it describes politics in any of the local authoritarian enclaves that dot the landscapes of democratic countries around the world. The field of democratization studies has tended to focus on national politics, and rightly so, given the global scope of national transitions to democracy in recent decades. The establishment of a national democratic government, however, is but one step in the long and complex process of democratic development within the nation-state. By no means does it ensure the diffusion of democratic practices and institutions throughout the many layers of polity and society, even in countries with long histories of national democratic rule. "Subnational authoritarianism" was a massive fact of political life in the United States until the middle of the twentieth century. It is also currently a fact of life in many democracies in the developing and postcommunist world. The unevenness of democratic governance across the national territory can be slight, with no more

---

[2] "El fin de un poder caudillista que duró más de medio siglo," *La Nación*, April 2, 2004, 10.

than minor differences from jurisdiction to jurisdiction in the transparency of electoral procedures or the rule of law. Yet these differences can also be dramatic, with full-blown authoritarian subnational governments depriving local inhabitants of rights and liberties enjoyed by residents of other provinces in the same country.

This phenomenon has remained largely undertheorized by political scientists. Scholars of U.S. history and political development have produced a plethora of studies about politics in the American southern states during the late 19th and early 20th centuries. However, few efforts place these states' politics in a comparative context or use them to shape the theoretical study of democracy.[3] As a result, the most extreme case of enfranchisement and disenfranchisement of citizens in the history of democracy lies largely outside the theoretical scrutiny of the comparative democratization field.

Until recently the study of subnational authoritarianism outside the United States was a rare event. A small number of prescient works brought the phenomenon to the attention of the scholarly community in the 1990s.[4] More recently a wave of scholarship in the field of comparative politics has explored the phenomenon in different cross-national contexts.[5]

Nevertheless, many of the processes that feed or starve subnational authoritarianism continue to be shrouded in mystery. Furthermore, as Jonathan Fox

[3] A notable exception is a book by Robert Mickey, which provides a theoretically framed historical analysis of transitions from single-party rule in three states of the U.S. South. See Robert Mickey, *Paths out of Dixie: The Decay of Authoritarian Enclaves in America's Deep South, 1944–1972* (Princeton, NJ: Princeton University Press. 2012). See also Stephen Tuck, "The Reversal of Voting Rights after Reconstruction," in *Democratization in America: A Comparative-Historical Analysis*, eds. Desmond King, Robert C. Lieberman, Gretchen Ritter, and Laurence Whitehead (Baltimore: Johns Hopkins University Press, 2009), 133–56.

[4] See, especially, Guillermo O'Donnell, *On the State, Democratization, and Some Conceptual Problems (A Latin American View with Glances at Some Post-Communist Countries)* (South Bend, IN: Kellogg Institute, April 1993); Jonathan Fox, "Latin America's Emerging Local Politics," *Journal of Democracy* 5 (April 1994); Frances Hagopian, *Traditional Politics and Regime Change in Brazil* (Cambridge: Cambridge University Press, 1996); Wayne Cornelius, Todd A. Eisenstadt, and Jane Hindley, eds., *Subnational Politics and Democratization in Mexico* (La Jolla: University of California Press, 1999).

[5] See, for example, Kelly McMann, *Economic Autonomy and Democracy: Hybrid Regimes in Russia and Kyrgyzstan* (Cambridge: Cambridge University Press, 2006); Vladimir Gel'man and Cameron Ross, eds. *The Politics of Sub-National Authoritarianism in Russia* (London: Ashgrave Press, 2010); Jacqueline Behrend, "The Unevenness of Democracy at the Subnational Level: Provincial Closed Games in Argentina," *Latin American Research Review* 46, no. 1 (2011); Allyson Lucinda Benton, "Bottom-Up Challenges to National Democracy: Mexico's (Legal) Subnational Authoritarian Enclaves," *Comparative Politics* 44, no. 3 (2012). Augustina Giraudy, "Subnational Undemocratic Regime Continuity after Democratization: Argentina and Mexico in Comparative Perspective." Ph.D. Dissertation, University of North Carolina, 2009; Carlos Gervasoni, "A Rentier Theory of Subnational Regimes," *World Politics* 62, no. 2 (2010); Special Issue, "Subnational Authoritarianism and Democratization in Latin America" (Edward L. Gibson, guest editor), *Journal of Politics in Latin America* 2, no. 2 (2010); and Special Issue, "Subnational Democracy" (Michael Bernhard and Byron Moraski, guest editors), *American Political Science Association Comparative Democratization Section Newsletter* 10, no. 1 (2012).

put it well nearly 20 years ago, "analysts of national politics tend to treat authoritarian enclaves as exceptions, while analysts of local politics rarely put them in national context."[6] Seen as a phenomenon confined to the physical peripheries of nations, its study has long been relegated to the figurative peripheries of comparative politics. Subnational authoritarian enclaves are often viewed as remote aberrations, lying physically beyond the reach of the legal and political authority of the national state, in regions impenetrable by central authority, and whose deviation from national democratic norms increases as one moves farther from metropolitan centers. Subnational authoritarianism in the nationally democratic state is thus seen as a result of intrinsic characteristics of the authoritarian enclaves (a term that lends an air of isolation and uniqueness to the phenomenon) combined with the limited ability of central authorities to extend their influence across territory. This view is evocative of Jeffrey Herbst's reflections about state-building problems in Africa, where state builders find themselves unable to effectively "broadcast power" across large physical distances.[7]

Evidence from the Western Hemisphere, however, suggests a different interpretation. Subnational authoritarianism in this region exists and often flourishes not in inchoate nation-states but in highly institutionalized countries. The U.S. central government effectively "broadcast" its power across a continent in the 19th and 20th centuries. It developed infrastructure networks, conquered territory held by other countries, successfully waged a civil war against secessionism, fought and won two world wars, and became a global superpower with proclaimed aspirations to spread democracy around the world. The democratic national government of the United States held sway over the planet, but did not challenge authoritarian political systems within its own borders until the second half of the 20th century. In Latin America subnational authoritarianism exists in comparatively well-developed states, which have unquestioned sovereignty within well-defined borders and often the ability to crush local challenges with dispatch.

In these institutional contexts, the persistence of local authoritarianism has little to do with the physical difficulties of controlling territory or the remoteness of authoritarian jurisdictions. It is part and parcel of everyday politics within the modern nation-state. It results from strategies of territorial control by local elites and from strategies of governance and coalition-building by national democratically elected leaders. A first step in demystifying the phenomenon thus involves exposing the territorial dimensions of power within modern nation-states. This requires mapping how political institutions are organized across territory, how they distribute power between political actors, and how they shape political preferences and coalition-building. It also involves opening the black box of subnational jurisdictions, shedding light on institutional strategies of political control and how they are linked to the national territorial system.

---

[6] Jonathan Fox, "Latin America's Emerging Local Politics," 109.
[7] Jeffrey Herbst, *States and Power in Africa* (Princeton, NJ: Princeton University Press, 2000).

In this way we can gain a nuanced view of the layered dynamics of political control in the democratic nation-state. We can also gain insights into how these dynamics often yield models of political governance in which, to quote one author, "the authoritarian dimension intermixes complexly and powerfully with the democratic one."[8]

Charting the institutional dynamics of subnational authoritarianism can also reveal ways in which it can unravel. The cross-national scholarship on democratization has revealed myriad ways in which conflict patterns in authoritarian countries lead to democratic openings, but understanding how these transitions might take place in subnational jurisdictions requires some modification of the theoretical lenses traditionally used at the national level. The institutional entanglement that exists between the national and the subnational in any territorial system, with regular and substantial interaction between central and local governments, adds layers of complexity and meaning to subnational democratization processes rarely found in conflicts over national democratization.

The existence of a democratic national government alongside an authoritarian subnational government creates a situation of regime juxtaposition. Two levels of government with jurisdiction over the same territory operate under different regimes, understood as the set of norms, rules, and practices that govern the selection and behavior of state leaders. Regime juxtaposition creates ongoing tensions between local and national arenas and presents strategic challenges for subnational authoritarian elites (as well as opportunities for local oppositions) that do not exist when national and subnational regime types coincide. In these contexts political pressures from national politics are potential catalysts for subnational change. Authoritarian incumbents dedicate major efforts to insulate their jurisdictions from such pressures and to limit access by local oppositions to national allies and resources. These "boundary control" efforts involve institutional strategies in multiple territorial arenas. Continuity or change in subnational authoritarianism is thus driven not by local causes alone but also by interactions between local politics and the national territorial system in which they are embedded.

This is a book about subnational authoritarianism and democratization. It explores strategic and institutional dynamics that perpetuate subnational authoritarian regimes as well as the political mechanisms that undermine them. The point of departure is the situation of regime juxtaposition within the nation-state, in which a national democratic government exists alongside authoritarian subnational governments. The book addresses three core questions:

1. What political factors explain the existence of subnational authoritarian jurisdictions in the democratic nation-state?

[8] O'Donnell, *On the State, Democratization, and Some Conceptual Problems.*

2. What regular and observable conflict patterns does this situation of regime juxtaposition generate?
3. What explains varying patterns of subnational authoritarianism and subnational democratization across time and space?

The answers that are developed in the book's chapters can be summarized as follows. First, the maintenance of subnational authoritarian enclaves in a nationally democratic country is driven by strategic interactions between local and national politics. Social, economic, or cultural factors intrinsic to the jurisdictions may contribute to the local authoritarian situation, but in the face of a democratized central government, subnational authoritarian enclaves must be nurtured and maintained by politics. The endurance of subnational authoritarianism is thus driven by active strategies of institutional and political control by local incumbents, as well as by strategic interactions and coalition-building between local and (often "democratic") national leaders.

The answer to the second question is that the situation of regime juxtaposition creates an ongoing struggle between provincial incumbents and oppositions to control the scope of provincial conflict. This is the fundamental conflict pattern created by regime juxtaposition, and it is referred to in this book as "boundary control." In struggles over boundary control, authoritarian incumbents prevail when the scope of conflict is localized. They are threatened when provincial conflict becomes nationalized. Fights over subnational democratization are thus characterized by struggles between "boundary-opening" and "boundary-closing" agents to shape the territorial reach of political action and the number of actors who are party to local conflicts.

Finally, any theory of subnational democratization must be rooted in theories of territorial politics. The book thus develops theory about how countries are organized territorially. It also argues that the territorial organization of countries has major effects on patterns of subnational authoritarianism and democratization. Through comparative case studies of three federal countries it reveals how institutional variations in "territorial regimes" affect how subnational authoritarian regimes are made and unmade.

Chapter 2 is dedicated to theory-building. It situates the subject of subnational democratization within the broader literatures on comparative politics and democratization. It makes the case that conflicts over subnational democratization are distinct from those at the national level, and it provides conceptual and theoretical ideas for analyzing the political terrain on which these conflicts unfold. It also develops a theory of subnational authoritarianism and democratization and identifies constituent mechanisms that are reproduced across countries and historical periods. These mechanisms are fleshed out in three illustrative case studies of federal countries in the Western Hemisphere. Chapter 3 examines the most spectacular case of subnational authoritarianism in the history of democracy: the rise and maintenance of the "Solid South" in the United States in the late 19th and early 20th centuries. Chapters 4 and 5 examine two contemporary cases from Latin America, Argentina and

Mexico, where subnational authoritarianism has persisted well after the countries' national governments became democratized. A comparative analysis in the conclusion addresses the differences and commonalities of the three experiences and reflects on their connections to federalism and to power relationships between political actors on both sides of the boundary-control divide. In this way, through theory-building and detailed empirical comparisons, the book offers readers new insights into how democracy spreads (or does not spread) *within* the nation-state.

ACKNOWLEDGMENTS

During the many years of writing this book, I benefited from intellectual exchanges with several people who generously gave insights, advice, and logistical help. A first round of thanks goes to my colleagues at Northwestern University, many of whom carefully read and commented on the manuscript in its various stages. I am indebted to Jeffrey Winters for the many hours of reading, thought, and conversation he dedicated to my research project. I am also grateful to James Farr, Daniel Galvin, Kenneth Janda, James Mahoney, Will Reno, Ben Ross Schneider, and Kathleen Thelen. My students (well, some of them are now prominent professors, but old habits die hard) nurtured and pushed me forward when my energy sagged. Julieta Suarez Cao has read every word and vetted (and sometimes vetoed) every idea in this book. Ernesto Calvo, Teri Caraway, and Tulia Falleti – trusted friends and colleagues – were there from the project's inception. Salma Al Shami was an incisive theoretical critic. I am also indebted to Mariana Borges, Jennifer Cyr, Gustavo Duncan, Carlos Freytes, Claudia López, Juan Cruz Olmeda, Sylvia Otero, and Alvaro Villagrán. Northwestern University, the Howard Foundation of Brown University, and the Searle Kinship Foundation generously provided me with leave time and resources to complete this project at critical points along the way.

In Argentina the late novelist, playwright, and democracy activist, Raúl Dargoltz, as well as Horacio Cao, enriched my understanding of Santiago del Estero's politics beyond measure, giving me intimate views of its most inaccessible political and physical spaces. Enrique Zuleta Puceiro was an invaluable advisor during my many field research trips to Argentina. I am also indebted to Jacqueline Behrend, Carlos Gervasoni, and Augustina Giraudy, who are each producing cutting-edge scholarship on problems of subnational democracy. I am grateful to Blanca Heredia, Carlos Elizondo, and Ivana de la Cruz for intellectual and logistical support during many visits to Mexico. I am also indebted to Vicente de la Cruz, Isidoro Yescas Martínez, Fausto Díaz Montes, and Victor Raúl Martínez Vázquez – scholars and political actors in Oaxaca working on the frontlines of democratization struggles in their state.

I wrote two chapters of this book in the congenial and stimulating intellectual environment of Nuffield College, Oxford University, in spring 2011. I am particularly grateful to Laurence Whitehead and Desmond King for making that stay possible and for their close engagement with my work. I am also grateful to Oxford scholars Nancy Bermeo, Giovanni Cappoccia, Enrique Posada Carbó, Leigh Payne, Timothy J. Power, Cindy Skatch, and Maya Tudor for hospitality and intellectual exchange.

Robert Mickey enriched my understanding of U.S. southern politics enormously and was a valued interlocutor about the comparative significance of the region's turbulent experiences with democratic politics. I am also grateful to Diana Beliard, Allyson Benton, Catherine Boone, Ana Grzymala Busse, Devin Caughey, David Collier, Jorge Dominguez, Julián Durazo Herrmann, Robert Kaufman, Steven Levitsky, Scott Mainwaring, María Victoria Murillo, the late Guillermo O'Donnell, Hector Schamis, Richard Snyder, Alfred Stepan, Evelyn Huber Stephens, Susan Stokes, and Deborah Yashar.

I was fortunate to work with Lewis Bateman, Senior Editor at Cambridge University Press. Lew's confidence in this project when it was only half-written motivated me greatly as I pushed ahead toward completion. Gail Chalew was the best copy editor an author could hope for. Peggy Rote of Aptara, Inc., managed the production process impeccably and with good cheer.

And now to the help of loved ones . . . Patrick Gibson, Alex Gibson, and Henry Gibson kept me focused on the real-world implications of my work through their skeptical and often illuminating questions. Judy Gibson was ever supportive throughout this process. My father, Eduardo Gibson, was a meticulous reader of drafts. I only wish he were here today to see the final product. My mother, Rita Gibson, and my sister Jennifer (to whom this book is dedicated), gave me a sanctuary in Cape Cod for writing, thinking, eating gluten-free food, and making key breakthroughs when the project felt hopelessly stalled.

Caryn Tomasiewicz supported me with patience, wit, and love during the final years of writing. Gracias, polaquita. I will also remember the Highlands Ranch Public Library in Colorado very fondly, for offering spacious and cozy facilities (with a fireplace!) for writing large parts of this book.

2

Territorial Politics and Subnational Democratization

Charting the Theoretical Landscape

All of my maps have been overthrown.

Jeff Tweedy[1]

To ordinary individuals the pains and trials of authoritarianism delivered by local authorities may be hard to distinguish from those delivered by national authorities. "National" versus "subnational" authoritarianism may be inconsequential distinctions to people experiencing the dreary poverty of rights of autocratic rule. Yet the territorial source of authoritarian rule *is* consequential – it is consequential for politics and it is consequential for theory. Political actors in struggles for local democratization face strategic and institutional challenges that are quite different from those faced by protagonists of national democratization struggles. Similarly, social scientists seeking to understand subnational authoritarianism's dynamics must address hierarchies and mechanisms that are unique to the internal territorial organization of countries.

A focus on subnational processes of authoritarianism and democratization demands not only a shift in the scale of observation but also a new set of theoretical lenses that help us see political dynamics invisible to those focusing on national units. Thus the study of subnational democratization should not be seen as a theoretical derivative of national democratization, wherein the main challenge lies in identifying which theories developed for the study of countries can be transferred to the study of provinces. It is a field with theoretical and empirical challenges that, although overlapping in many ways with its "parent" field, are unique to the subnational level of analysis. Subnational democratization is not democratization in short pants.

Therefore, this chapter's objectives are to map the political terrain on which conflicts over subnational democratization unfold and to reveal their unique patterns and mechanisms of political action. After reviewing unit-of-analysis

[1] Wilco, "You Are My Face," lyrics by Jeff Tweedy, music by Jeff Tweedy and Nels Cline, *Sky Blue Sky*, compact disk, Nonesuch, 2006.

issues in the study of democratization, the chapter turns to theory-building. It first builds on theories of "territorial politics" to reveal strategic and institutional conflict patterns within nation-states. It then links these patterns to a theory of subnational authoritarianism and democratization.

I. UNIT-OF-ANALYSIS ISSUES IN THE STUDY OF DEMOCRATIZATION

Democratization and the Nation Fixation

The national orientation of democratization studies was well reflected in the title of a pioneering article in the contemporary wave of scholarship. In 1984, Samuel Huntington titled the article as follows: "Will More Countries Become Democratic?"[2] It was a reasonable question to ask at the time. In a period when national authoritarian governments were giving way to democratically elected governments in much of the world, it would indeed have been odd if he had not focused on the national dynamics of regime change. However, even then, writers with a nuanced understanding of domestic politics might have rephrased Huntington's question as something that captured better what he was really asking. This rephrasing might have gone something like this: "Will More *National Governments* Become Democratic?" A scholar with a keen sense of the internal territorial heterogeneity of countries might have opted for a cumbersome but even more accurate phrasing: "Will the *Best-Known Places* of More Countries Become Democratic?" It is unlikely that articles framed in this way would have resonated very much with scholarly audiences at the time (let alone survived the average journal peer-review process), but at least their authors would have had the consolation of knowing that they were framing their questions accurately and perhaps were ahead of their time.

Yet such authors would have run afoul of what might be termed a "nation fixation" in democratization studies – the tendency to look to national units of analysis to measure and to explain the spread (or nonspread) of democracy. Conceptually, the nation fixation meant that democracy and democratization were perceived as national phenomena: the nation-state was the unit of analysis at which they could be apprehended. Inevitably the concept was operationalized as the democratization of the national government.[3]

We see this nation fixation in influential contemporary cross-national measurements of democracy. Freedom House, coding Argentina's political regime according to national political rights and civil liberties in the late 1980s, classified the country as "Free" during the very period in which authoritarian rule

---

[2] Samuel Huntington, "Will More Countries Become Democratic?" *Political Science Quarterly* 99, no. 2 (Summer 1984): 193–218.

[3] Richard Snyder provided a comprehensive critique of national biases in the study of comparative politics in his article, "Scaling Down: The Subnational Comparative Method," *Studies in Comparative International Development* 36, no. 1 (Spring 2001): 93–110.

was in full bloom in several provinces. Similarly, it scored Mexico as "Free" in all years following the 2000 national defeat of the *Partido Revolucionario Institucional* (PRI), even though experts on Mexico produced ample documentation of the continuity and even resurgence of authoritarianism in various Mexican states.[4] Freedom House did not measure the quality or extent of rights and liberties provided by subnational governments for those years nor did it include that information in the summary statistics on the quality of democracy in a particular country.[5] Nor can we find such measurements in any of the other influential democracy indices used by scholars in comparative cross-national research on democracy.[6]

At one level this is a measurement problem – the problem of measurement incompleteness. A complex political system is interpreted and classified in light of measurements of only one part of that system. At another level the nation fixation leads to a form of fallacious reasoning that Richard Snyder refers to as an "invalid part to whole mapping," which happens when "traits or processes specific to a well-studied region or other subnational unit are improperly elevated to the status of a national paradigm."[7]

The nation fixation unsurprisingly affects theory development. Identifying internal variations in the practice of democracy becomes difficult if democratization is conceived and measured only in relation to the national government (or to the "best known place" of a country). If our conceptual frameworks prevent us from perceiving the internal unevenness of democracy within a country, we cannot even begin to ask questions about it, let alone wonder about political processes that bring it about. We are theoretically oblivious to phenomena occurring before our eyes.

---

[4] See Wayne Cornelius, Todd A. Eisenstadt, and Jane Hindley, eds., *Subnational Politics and Democratization in Mexico* (La Jolla: University of California Press, 1999).

[5] The weight of national government measurements in the Freedom House index through 2006 can be seen in the wording of the "checklist questions" for the "Political Rights" component of the index. Regarding "Electoral Processes," the two lead checklist questions are phrased as follows: "1. Is the head of government or other chief national authority elected through free and fair elections? 2. Are the national legislative representatives elected through free and fair elections?" The other checklist questions and the many subquestions are also limited to national arenas. An important step forward was made in the 2007 index, when two new subquestions about *subnational* elections were added to the checklist guidelines for the "Electoral Processes" section of Political Rights. These subquestions ask whether the conduct of these elections constitutes "an opening toward improved political rights in the country, or, alternatively, a worsening of political rights." However, their place in the hierarchy of questions in the ranking (they are not "checklist questions" but only part of "checklist guidelines," and they are one out of ten subquestions in each category) gives them an undetectable effect on the total score. See Freedomhouse.org, *Freedom in the World*, at http://www.freedomhouse.org/template.cfm?page=15.

[6] In Munck and Verkuilen's exhaustive study of more than ten democracy measurement indices and data sets, all relied exclusively on national measurement indicators. See Guillermo Munck and Jay Verkuilen, "Conceptualizing and Measuring Democracy: Evaluating Alternative Indices," *Comparative Political Studies* 35, no. 1 (2002): 5–34.

[7] Richard Snyder, "Scaling Down," 99.

Democratization: National versus Subnational, and Why Does It Matter?

Why should it matter to the study of democratization that the jurisdictions in question are subnational? Writing on party politics, Giovanni Sartori warned some time ago about the "unit-jump fallacy," whereby "a sub-state, i.e., a member of a federal state, is made equal to a sovereign state."[8] Yet what, concretely, would the arguments be for calling this a fallacy? These arguments would have to do more than make the case that the subnational unit is "different" from the national unit (we already knew that). They would also have to make the case that there are theoretical costs to not recognizing it as such.

A first argument is that sovereignty matters. A subnational jurisdiction's relationship with a national government is not analogous to a country's relationship with the international system. Within countries, central governments intervene *regularly* and *substantively* in the affairs of provincial governments. This creates a systemic vertical interaction between national and subnational levels of government. Details of this interaction are codified in national constitutions and institutional arrangements that coordinate, finance, and regulate relations among levels of government. In the international system we find very few comparable cases of this regular and substantive intervention in the domestic politics of a sovereign country. Furthermore, although in national territorial politics such intervention is legitimate, in the international system it is far more problematic. Processes of change in subnational politics, therefore, are inseparable from the regular and substantive interaction between national and subnational governments.

Adding to this vertical interaction among levels of government are the vertical interactions among nongovernmental institutions. Take political parties, for example. A party competing in a province is usually not a stand-alone entity, but likely is linked systemically to a national party system and institutionally to a national party or coalition of parties. These partisan networks, with their flows of money, information, and infrastructural resources, link national and subnational politics in intricate institutional ways – and in ways not reproduced in the international state system. Similar arguments could be made about vertical interactions among private civil society organizations.

In addition to these vertical interactions are *horizontal* interactions among the subnational political units of countries. Provinces are linked to one another by partisan and intergovernmental networks that affect political action and create coalition-building scenarios that have few analogs in the international system.

Furthermore, provincial politics in a country is embedded in a territorial system, and there is considerable variation across territorial systems in their centralization, decentralization, and distribution of prerogatives among provinces.

---

[8] Giovanni Sartori, *Parties and Party Systems: A Framework for Analysis* (New York: Cambridge University Press, 1976), 83.

Is the country federal? Is it unitary? Is it somewhere in between? These features create differing strategic contexts across countries for political actors. In addition, they affect processes of local democratization differently from country to country. Our theoretical understanding of the movement from subnational authoritarianism to subnational democracy might thus be far more nuanced if we recognize the distinctive challenges of subnational analysis, rather than assume equivalence between the internal politics of national and subnational units.

What Kind of Authoritarianism?

Subnational authoritarianism in a nationally democratic country will bear a close resemblance to national patterns that Andreas Schedler labels "Electoral Authoritarianism," or Steven Levitsky and Lucan Way call "Competitive Authoritarianism."[9] In these situations, authoritarianism is exercised through the manipulation or subversion of democratic institutions rather than their elimination. Meaningful competitive threats against incumbents can exist, and representative institutions such as legislatures and political parties can serve as genuine sites of power and decision-making. However, the key to the jurisdiction's authoritarian status lies in the systematic violation of democratic rights by incumbents through the legal and illegal manipulation of representative institutions. The competitive process is systematically rigged in favor of incumbents. The playing field is, in Levitsky and Way's terminology, "uneven."[10]

There are a number of reasons for this particular institutional configuration of authoritarian rule, and they all result from the subnational status of the jurisdiction. When the larger political system is governed by a democratic regime, there are limits to the institutional forms that local authoritarian rule can take. Decorum is one reason for these limitations. A subnational political regime that violates all institutional forms of a democratic regime would likely be intolerable to national authorities and public opinion. There are also legal constraints. National laws usually have sway over subnational jurisdictions. National constitutions, particularly in federal countries, may give wide latitude to local authorities in the design of local regime institutions. However, even in the most decentralized cases these constitutions will nevertheless stipulate that subnational jurisdictions adopt "republican" forms of government. In fact, most federal constitutions further stipulate that the national government will

---

[9] Andreas Schedler, "Authoritarianism's Last Line of Defense," *Journal of Democracy* 21, no. 1 (2010); Steven Levitsky and Lucan Way, *Competitive Authoritarianism: Hybrid Regimes after the Cold War*, Problems of International Politics. New York: Cambridge University Press, 2010. The conceptualizations advanced by the authors are similar in many respects. One key difference is that Levitsky and Way consider "competitive authoritarian" regimes to be a regime type distinct from authoritarianism and democracy, whereas Schedler tends to treat "electoral authoritarianism" as a subtype of authoritarianism.

[10] Steven Levitsky and Lucan Way, *Competitive Authoritarianism*, 9–13.

guarantee the existence of republican forms of government in the constituent units of the federations.[11]

However, more compelling causes of these institutional forms of local authoritarianism can be found in the functional requirements of systemic interactions between subnational and national political systems. The subnational authoritarian polity is institutionally connected to the national democratic polity. It is represented in national politics via institutions that straddle national and subnational arenas. Financial, political, and other resources flow between arenas through institutional channels that require compatible political institutions on both sides of jurisdictional boundaries. Representative institutions, such as legislatures and political parties, are vital to the existence of such channels. In fact, linkage between subnational and national political systems in a nationally democratic country is unthinkable in the absence of common representative institutions. Thus, whatever the authoritarian predilections of local incumbents, they are condemned to republican forms of government by their jurisdiction's subnational status in a national democratic polity.

Given the complexity that this situation adds to local regime classification, I adopt a simple approach. I distinguish a democratic regime from an authoritarian regime not by its formal institutions, but by the effective exercise of political rights by populations in the jurisdiction governed by those institutions. The systematic violation of either the right of political contestation or the right of political participation (the two defining features of "polyarchies" in Robert Dahl's work) suffices to classify a case as authoritarian.[12] This approach de-links the classification of a regime from the presence or absence of specific institutions or procedures and asks whether they facilitate or obstruct the exercise of *rights* by citizens of the subnational jurisdiction. Political parties, elections, and legislatures can either abridge such rights or make them effective, depending on how they are designed and operated by power holders.[13]

Competitive threats are thus a permanent reality for incumbents of a subnational authoritarian government. The threats can be distant and effectively neutralized by the "menus of institutional manipulation" employed by

---

[11] For example, the constitutions of the United States, Mexico, and Argentina, the three federal countries analyzed in this book, contain such a stipulation.

[12] Robert Dahl, *Polyarchy; Participation and Opposition*, New Haven: Yale University Press, 1971.

[13] I eschew the term "hybrid" to define subnational authoritarian regimes because advocates of the concept tend to see "hybrid" regimes as distinctive regime types. I prefer to see them as a subtype of authoritarianism. For examples of scholarly work that applies the "hybrid" concept to subnational politics, see Kelly McMann, *Economic Autonomy and Democracy: Hybrid Regimes in Russia and Kyrgyzstan* (Cambridge: Cambridge University Press, 2006); Jacqueline Behrend, "The Unevenness of Democracy at the Subnational Level: Provincial Closed Games in Argentina," *Latin American Research Review* 46, no. 1 (2011); and Carlos Gervasoni, "A Rentier Theory of Subnational Regimes," *World Politics* 62, no. 2 (2010).

incumbents.[14] Competitive threats can also be imminent. In this sense, such regimes are no different from the national regimes identified by the literature on "electoral authoritarianism" or "competitive authoritarianism." However, subnational authoritarian incumbents differ from their national counterparts in a key way. They face a dual competitive threat, from oppositions in the local political system and from potential adversaries in the national political system. No matter how effective their strategies of local control, subnational incumbents face competitive threats from the national democratic polity as a structural fact of political life. Processes of subnational authoritarianism and democratization are thus uniquely shaped by the multilayered dynamics of territorial politics.

II. TERRITORY AND POLITICS: DEFINING TERRITORIAL POLITICS

Any theory of subnational authoritarianism and democratization must be rooted in theories of territorial politics. Sidney Tarrow was among the first to provide a workable definition of "territorial politics." According to Tarrow, it "is not *about* territory, but is about how politics is fought out *across* territory."[15] This definition can be rendered even more useful with the addition of an organizational dimension, because it is the institutional structure overlaid on territory that creates meaningful strategic contexts for political actors. For example, the usefulness of mayoralties or governorships to politicians with national ambitions varies depending on whether the political system is federal or unitary or is centralized or decentralized. Thus this book's definition of territorial politics builds on Tarrow's formulation by grafting an organizational dimension onto his conflict dimension: *territorial politics is about how politics is organized and fought out across territory.*

III. POLITICS FOUGHT OUT ACROSS TERRITORY: POLITICAL ACTION IN TERRITORIAL SYSTEMS

All conflict in national polities takes place in a hierarchy of territorial organizations and arenas. In any large-scale system of territorial governance, political institutions are entangled across space. Strategies of political control are thus seldom limited to any single arena. Although they may involve strategies that are specific to certain arenas (e.g., local strategies of political control), the final outcome – the success or failure of these strategies of territorial control – hinges on the interconnections among all levels of the national territorial system. As

---

[14] The phrase is Andreas Schedler's. See "Authoritarianism's last line of defense," p. 71. For an extensive analysis of manipulation in electoral politics, see Alberto Simpser, *Why Governments and Parties Manipulate Elections: Theory, Practice, and Implications*, forthcoming, Cambridge University Press.

[15] Sidney Tarrow et al., *Territorial Politics in Industrial Nations* (New York: Praeger, 1978), 1. See also Sidney Tarrow, *Between Center and Periphery: Grassroots Politicians in Italy and France* (New Haven, CT: Yale University Press, 1977).

political geographer Ronan Paddison notes, the state, viewed in territorial terms, is indeed a "fragmented state."[16] It is fragmented horizontally – divided spatially into jurisdictions – and is fragmented vertically, among levels of government with differing scopes of territorial authority. However, this is not an atomized fragmentation: the political arenas are interdependent.

A *territorial system* can thus be defined as the ensemble of interacting national and subnational jurisdictions. The use of the term "system" here is deliberate. In any kind of system the component parts are both autonomous and interactive, and their patterns of interaction shape the operation of the system as a whole. In territorial politics the interaction between governments in national and subnational arenas has a continuing impact on national political outcomes. The object and effects of political action, therefore, are seldom limited to one territorial arena.

One implication of these observations is that goals pursued in one geographic location are often means toward objectives in other locations. Political geographer Robert Sack defines territoriality as "a spatial strategy to affect, influence, or control resources and people, by controlling area."[17] "Controlling area" in subnational politics often means monopolizing power in the local political arena, but it also means manipulating levers of power in other arenas as well. It requires both controlling linkages between levels of territorial organization and exercising influence in national political arenas.

We can map such strategies along two dimensions: the *site* of political action and the *scale* of political action. The site of political action refers to the territorial arena (e.g., national or local) in which the political action is located. The scale of political action refers to the territorial reach of the political action's effects (or intended effects). The effects can be national, that is, felt in multiple territorial arenas (the national government or several provinces). They can also be exclusively local.

Figure 2.1 provides specific examples organized along this abstract scheme. In some cases, the site and the scope of political action are the same. When a political boss puts pressure on a local legislature or local judge for the sake of advancing a local policy objective, the site and scale of the action are local. In other cases, the site is local, but the scope of the action is national. For example, the same political boss ensures the election to the national legislature of local candidates who belong to his national party. He effectively "delivers" the local vote to increase the party's national majority. The resources he has used are largely local (for example, the provincial electoral machine or local patronage networks). However, the effects of the action are national. In another scenario, a national legislator gains power in a congressional appropriations committee in order to control fiscal transfers to his or her province. The site of the action

---

[16] Ronan Paddison, *The Fragmented State: The Political Geography of Power* (New York: St. Martin's Press, 1983).

[17] Robert Sack, *Human Territoriality: Its Theory and History* (Cambridge: Cambridge University Press, 1986), 1.

Scale of Political Action
(Its Territorial Effects)

		Subnational	**National**
	Subnational	Control local judges	Deliver local votes to national party
Site of Political Action ***(Its Location)***			
	National	Control fiscal appropriations to province	Reform national constitution. Build regional coalitions

FIGURE 2.1. Site and Scale of Political Action: Examples of Territorial Strategies

is national, but its effects are local. Building coalitions of provinces to defend regional interests or launching amendments to the national constitution would constitute cases of political action that are national both in site and in scale. They are pursued in multiple jurisdictions or in the national government and are intended to affect national outcomes. Site and scale are basic elements of any theory that situates political action within a territorial system.

IV. POLITICS ORGANIZED ACROSS TERRITORY:
TERRITORIAL REGIMES

The structure and hierarchies of a national territorial system are mapped by the territorial regime. The concept "territorial regime" may make intuitive sense, but its precise meaning and relationship to the organization of the state require clarification. Looking at any national constitution, one notes that, regardless of the number of issues that it covers, at its core there are provisions specifying two distinct regimes: the *political regime* and the *territorial regime*. The political regime governs interactions between individuals and the state, as well as the selection and behavior of public authorities. The territorial regime governs the interactions among territorial units of the state (e.g., its states, provinces, or municipalities) and specifies the division of powers between governments of subnational territorial units and the national government. Whereas the political regime tends to regulate individual rights and behavior, the territorial regime tends to regulate territorially organized collectivities. At a very general level, two *political* regime types are democracy and authoritarianism, each with many institutional variations. *Territorial* regimes can be divided into federalism or unitarism, again with considerable institutional variation within these categories.

I address these variations by asking two overarching sets of questions. First, how does the territorial regime shape the power of provinces in the national territorial system? This question addresses the territorial system as a two-level system comprising a national government and subnational governments (provinces or states).[18] The second question peers into the provincial jurisdiction itself: How does the territorial regime shape power hierarchies between provincial governments and municipal governments? Is the territorial regime province-empowering or is it municipal-empowering?

The Province in National Politics: Peripheralized and Nonperipheralized Territorial Regimes

How do territorial regimes shape the power of provinces in a national territorial system? One way to answer this question is to compare territorial regimes along two analytical dimensions: *intergovernmental* and *interprovincial*. The intergovernmental dimension refers to the degree of centralization or decentralization between national and provincial governments. This is the most frequently studied dimension in territorial politics and has tended to dominate the classification and analysis of federal systems. A decentralized territorial system maximizes the degree of autonomy enjoyed by subnational governments.[19] The ability of the central government or national actors to intervene in the local affairs of states or provinces is circumscribed when their subsystemic autonomy is high, which has obvious implications for change and continuity in subnational politics.

A less studied dimension of territorial regimes is the distribution of rights and prerogatives among the subnational units themselves. Territorial regimes can render the distribution of rights and prerogatives relatively equal among provinces. For example, all provincial governments may enjoy the same scope of authority over policy within their jurisdictions. Alternatively, territorial regimes can grant rights and prerogatives asymmetrically, with some jurisdictions enjoying greater autonomy and prerogatives than others.[20] In addition, certain provinces can be overrepresented in national political institutions, thereby given greater influence in national politics than they would have by virtue of their population size or economic weight.

---

[18] This is the classic conceptualization of federal systems, in which the subnational unit is the province. See, for example, William H. Riker. *Federalism: Origin, Operation, Significance* (Boston: Little, Brown, 1964).

[19] Centralization and decentralization can be ambiguous concepts. Tulia Falleti unpacked the concept very usefully into three dimensions: political, fiscal, and administrative. See Tulia Falleti, *Decentralization and Subnational Politics in Latin America* (Cambridge: Cambridge University Press, 2010). In this book I refer primarily to political decentralization.

[20] We often see such asymmetrical arrangements in multinational countries. See Alfred Stepan, "Electorally Generated Veto Players in Unitary and Federal Systems," in *Federalism and Democracy in Latin America*, ed. Edward L. Gibson (Baltimore: John Hopkins University Press, 2004), 323–62.

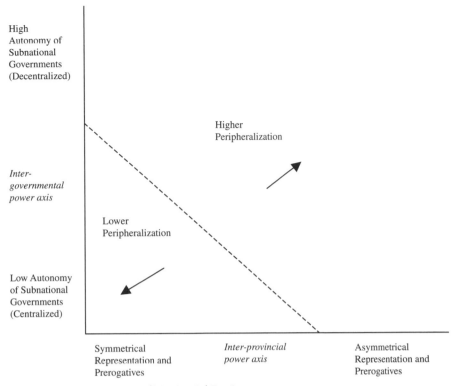

FIGURE 2.2. Dimensions of Territorial Regimes

Figure 2.2 displays the intergovernmental and interprovincial dimensions. It also shows how their interaction shapes power within a national territorial system. The vertical axis captures, appropriately, the vertical distribution of power among levels of government. It represents a centralization–decentralization continuum: the higher up on the vertical axis, the greater the degree of subsystemic autonomy enjoyed by subnational governments vis-à-vis the national government. The horizontal axis represents the distribution of rights and prerogatives among the subnational units themselves. It maps how uniformly policy-making prerogatives are distributed among subnational units, as well as how equally their populations are represented in the national political system. The more the system is characterized by an uneven distribution of prerogatives or by the institutional overrepresentation of certain provinces, the more "asymmetrical" the territorial system is along the interregional power axis. Taking these dimensions jointly, we can assess the level of *peripheralization* of the national territorial regime.

As we move outwardly on either axis we enter an area of "high peripheralization."[21] Subnational governments may be granted high levels of

---

[21] Some semantic confusion may be inevitable in the choice of terms. In his classic work on federalism, William Riker uses "peripheralized" as a synonym for "decentralized." William Riker,

subsystemic autonomy, prerogatives and national representation may be distributed unevenly between states and provinces, or a combination of both situations may exist. Movement along the dimensions of the territorial regime alters the utility of political strategies in the territorial system. An important implication is that the value of local arenas for strategies of political action tends to increase as the peripheralization of the system increases. In such contexts, "controlling area" at the subnational level provides larger payoffs, not only for local politics but also for the achievement of objectives in national arenas.

Power within the Province: Province-Empowering and Municipal-Empowering Territorial Regimes

A more complete conceptualization of territorial regimes requires that we move beyond the two-level of government model to incorporate municipal (and urban) politics into the picture. Here we are looking at the balance of power between *subnational* governmental units and asking which subnational level of government – the province or the municipality – is empowered by the national territorial regime. Is the territorial regime municipal-empowering or is it province-empowering?[22] Does the territorial regime make it possible for one subnational level of government to overawe the other, or does it provide for a balanced relationship between the two? All territorial regimes recognize municipalities as a distinct level of government. However, the autonomy and prerogatives granted to municipal governments vary widely, and in federal systems provinces have the edge. Whether federal constitutions grant significant autonomy and prerogatives to municipalities is thus of fundamental importance to how politics is organized and fought out across territory.[23]

Federalism: Origin, Operation, Significance (Boston: Little, Brown, 1964). He thus classifies federal systems according to a "centralized" and "peripheralized" dichotomy. It is not clear, however, what the value of substituting "peripheralized" for "decentralized" is for Riker's purposes. In this book I use "peripheralized" to denote more complex situations – combinations of decentralization with different scenarios of rights and prerogative distributions between subnational jurisdictions.

[22] I use the term "municipal" as a generic term to denote political jurisdictions below the provincial level, acknowledging that in federal systems in the Western Hemisphere the names of such "second-tier" geographic divisions vary. In Mexico the immediate division below the state is the municipality (whether rural or urban). In the United States it is named "county," whereas municipal governments are incorporated within counties to govern population centers. In Argentina the immediate division below the province in Argentina is usually named "department," with "municipalities" occupying the same place in the hierarchy as in the United States. Because in federal politics the formal powers of urban hubs are critical to intergovernmental conflicts, the use of the term "municipality" for second-tier jurisdictions, although denotatively not always accurate, draws attention to the salience of urban politics in the conflicts under study.

[23] The province-empowering/municipal-empowering dichotomy can be viewed as an element of centralization or decentralization between national governments and provincial governments. If municipalities are to enjoy formal autonomy, this autonomy must be spelled out and guaranteed nationally, usually in the national constitution. This is an attribute of

Whether a territorial regime is municipal-empowering or province-empowering also has important consequences for party politics and subnational democratization. Under a municipal-empowering federal system, urban municipalities are important prizes in electoral competition between parties. This creates both strong incentives for party-building at the province's most local levels and a more competitive environment for province-wide party systems.

Territorial regimes provide structure to the strategic environment in which actors in a territorial system operate. They thus provide a vital starting point for analyzing the relationship between the organization of the state and democratization. Theoretically, the choice of a territorial regime can be independent of the choice of a political regime, and there are many sequential scenarios.[24] However, once they are formally incorporated into the legal-political framework of a national state, the territorial and political regimes will inevitably influence one another. Political actors will thus pursue changes in the institutional architecture of territorial regimes as a key national strategy in conflicts about subnational democratization.

V. TERRITORIAL DEMOCRATIZATION

A final conceptual distinction is now in order. Once a national government has attained the minimum criteria for being considered a democracy, we can conceive of two distinct scenarios for the continued expansion of political rights within the nation-state: *substantive democratization* and *territorial democratization*. Substantive democratization is the granting of rights that had not been previously granted in the country, either a new concept of rights or the extension of existing rights to new categories of people regardless of where they live. Suffrage is an obvious example. The extension of the vote to previously disenfranchised categories of people (nonproperty owners, illiterates, women, minorities, etc.) is a manifestation of continuing or deepening democratization.[25]

Territorial democratization is another scenario. It involves the granting of rights *already available* to inhabitants of one part of a country to inhabitants of other parts of the country. It is the expansion of clusters of rights or democratic practices across a country's political jurisdictions. The extension of full

centralization. If municipal autonomy is not spelled out nationally and is left to provincial authorities, it is a form of political decentralization. However, it is heuristically useful to separate the province-empowering/municipal-empowering distinction from the national–provincial centralization dimension and view it in terms of subnational intergovernmental relations. We thus shift our attention to the significance of this feature for politics within the province.

24 See Edward L. Gibson and Tulia Falleti, "Unity by the Stick: Regional Conflict and the Origins of Federalism in Argentina," in *Federalism and Democracy in Latin America*, ed. Edward L. Gibson (Baltimore: John Hopkins University Press, 2004), 226–54.

25 Although these examples are at the national level, substantive democratization can occur at subnational levels as well.

representation in the national congress to inhabitants of Washington, D.C., or the granting of full rights of citizenship to inhabitants of territories (not states) would be one set of examples. The struggles that ended Jim Crow and single-party rule in the U.S. South would be another.[26]

As with substantive democratization, territorial democratization is not inevitable or unidirectional. It can be marked by ebb and flow patterns that are shaped continuously by local political dynamics and their interactions with the national polity. In contrast to substantive democratization, however, the mechanisms driving these movements remain a theoretical mystery.

This chapter so far has provided a basic mapping of institutional and conflict patterns across territory within the nation-state. We now build on these insights by linking them to theories about territorial democratization. We will see how the institutional and strategic dynamics outlined earlier create distinctive patterns of conflict and control in struggles between local authoritarian incumbents and their opponents. We will also gain a fuller sense of why, in conflicts over subnational democratization, our universe is not local.

VI. BOUNDARY CONTROL: A THEORY OF SUBNATIONAL AUTHORITARIANISM AND DEMOCRATIZATION

> *Una comarca embrujada de sol*
> *no puede ser nunca de un conquistador.*
>
> Peteco Carabajal[27]

The daily *El Liberal* was the oldest and most prestigious newspaper of the Argentine province of Santiago del Estero. In the late 1990s the province was firmly under the control of Carlos Arturo Juárez and his wife, Mercedes (Nina) Aragonés de Juárez. The ruling couple's relationship with the newspaper had not been close, but *El Liberal* had never posed a threat to the *Juarista* political system. The newspaper's owners were members of the provincial socioeconomic elite. In the parochial confines of provincial political life, this meant that

---

[26] There is obviously overlap between substantive and territorial democratization. For example, legislation in the United States granting new rights to black citizens could be seen as a substantive form of democratization, because the category benefiting from it is not by definition territorial. Yet in the context of late-19th-century and early-20th-century U.S. politics, certain regions were disproportionately affected, and the legislation was part and parcel of a strategy to democratize a particular region. As we see in Chapter 3, these efforts were part of an effort by political leaders in the national government to advance territorial democratization within the United States.

[27] "A place bewitched by the sun can never belong to a conqueror." Peteco Carabajal, "Los Santiagueños," *Ayer y Hoy* (Buenos Aires: Distribuidora Belgrano Norte, 2005), compact disk. Carabajal is a noted folkloric music composer and performer from the Argentine province of Santiago del Estero and was Minister of Culture of that province during the federal occupation of 2003–5.

they were integrated into the web of political, social, and economic relationships controlled by the *Juarista* establishment.

In the late 1990s, however, the newspaper shifted to an oppositional stance. The provincial leadership at first tolerated critical local reporting, relying for rebuttals on the media outlets it controlled. However, to its consternation the newspaper began to reprint articles from national newspapers that were critical of the provincial administration. One outside newspaper that devoted significant critical coverage to Santiago politics was *La Voz del Interior*, published in the neighboring province of Córdoba. The newspaper's resources and location in one of the country's most important provinces gave it considerable influence across the provinces of Argentina's interior regions. In 2000 *La Voz del Interior* published a critical article about the "Women's' Branch" (*La Rama Femenina*) of the Santiago Peronist Party.

Although the *Rama Femenina* was officially a women's caucus in the Peronist Party, many of its members served as shock troops for the governor's wife, Nina Aragonés de Juárez. It was one of the province's most intimidating organizations. Its members constituted a "who's who" of influential women – provincial legislators, party activists, and judges. Indeed, it was difficult for a politically ambitious woman to prosper without ties to the *Rama Femenina*. Yet it also had a significant grassroots membership of mid- and low-level supervisors and employees of the provincial public sector. They monitored public employees' political behavior, kept a watch on the political activities or sympathies of neighborhood residents, and promoted a cult of personality around the governor's wife. Mobs of *rameras*, as they were known, were occasionally dispatched to wreak violence against regime critics, delivering their leaders' wrath with blows from canes, umbrellas, and rock-filled purses.

The 2000 article by *La Voz del Interior* was reprinted verbatim in an edition of *El Liberal*. This collusion between the local paper and a nationally influential outside paper was too much for the *Juarista* leadership. Nina Aragonés de Juárez publicly accused *El Liberal* of libeling the members of the *Rama Femenina*. She expressed outrage at the paper's reprinting of the term "*ramera*," which, although used regularly by *Rama Femenina* members themselves, can also be used to denote a prostitute. The First Lady's indignation soon resulted in hundreds of "spontaneous" lawsuits against the local newspaper from similarly outraged members of the *Rama Femenina*. Provincial judges duly processed the cascade of lawsuits, with their demands for monetary compensation. No legal action was taken in national courts against the national paper that had originated the allegedly libelous article. The site and the scale of the political action were local.

Faced with financial ruin, the newspaper negotiated its way out of its mess with the *Juarista* regime. The lawsuits were dropped, and the newspaper thereafter ceased reprinting outside coverage of provincial politics. In the words of one dismayed observer, "slowly and steadily, *El Liberal*, the only opposition member of the local mass media, extinguished its critical spotlights and sterilized its editorial work, ultimately returning to the stagnant condition of official mouthpiece that had characterized it in previous periods."[28]

This episode captures a basic pattern of political action by incumbents in authoritarian jurisdictions in a democratic country. The local newspaper's opposition stance was problematic to local authorities, but what made it intolerable was the paper's institutional coordination of opposition activities with outside newspapers. The editors of *El Liberal* had committed the cardinal sin of nationalizing reporting on provincial affairs. By giving a national institutional critic a platform within the province, the editors added a new actor to the local political fray. Worse still, they threatened to institutionalize an opposition media alliance that transcended the *Juarista* leadership's jurisdictional reach. Its first order of business was thus to sever this national–subnational institutional connection and relocalize political reporting on the province. Once this was accomplished, the provincial government could deal with the local newspaper at its leisure.[29] The Juárez government's severing of *El Liberal's* connections to the outside was a successful example of boundary control.

Controlling the Scope of Political Conflict: Boundary Control and Subnational Authoritarianism

In his critical study of American democracy, *The Semi-Sovereign People*, E. E. Schattschneider lays out a general logic of political conflict that can be applied fruitfully to the study of subnational politics. Schattschneider notes that in any political conflict between two unequally matched parties, the stronger party's main incentive is to keep the conflict as isolated and private as possible. Doing so maintains the unequal power match between the two, enabling the stronger party to prevail in the conflict. In contrast, the weaker party has every incentive to expand the number of participants in the conflict. Bringing in third parties – expanding the scope of the conflict – alters the balance of power between the two original parties. Weaker parties in a private conflict, therefore, have an interest in what Schattschneider calls the "socialization" of that conflict.[30]

This situation has its analog in territorial politics. In authoritarian provinces, incumbents have an interest in keeping conflicts localized, whereas oppositions have an interest in nationalizing local conflict. Power contenders, therefore, are engaged constantly in strategies of boundary control. Incumbents seek to

---

[28] Sergio Carreras, *El reino de los Juárez: Medio siglo de miseria, terror, y desmesura en Santiago del Estero* (Buenos Aires: Aguilar, Altea, Taurus, Alfaguara, S.A., 2004), 70. Sergio Carreras wrote the *Voz del Interior's* article on the *Rama Femenina* and was one of Argentina's most relentless investigators of Santiago's murky politics during the heyday of the *Juarista* regime.

[29] Details of the incident were confirmed to the author in discussions with reporters and political observers during field research in the province of Santiago del Estero in 2004.

[30] E. E. Schattschneider, *The Semisovereign People: A Realist's View of Democracy in America* (Hinsdale, IL: Dryden Press, 1960).

National
Democratization → Boundary Control attempts by local incumbents → Conflict remains localized → Status quo prevails

Provincial conflict nationalized: → Continuity of authoritarian rule
threatened

FIGURE 2.3. Conflict and Political Change in Authoritarian Provinces Where National
Government is Democratized

maximize their influence over local politics and deprive oppositions of access
to national allies and resources. The opposition does just the opposite, looking
for ways to breach provincial borders and bring national actors into the local
conflict. The struggle between authoritarian incumbents and their opponents to
control the scope of local conflict is the basic conflict pattern that is generated
by the situation of regime juxtaposition in nationally democratic countries. The
outcome of this struggle is vital to patterns of subnational political change. The
process is displayed schematically in Figure 2.3.

Boundary control strategies can take a variety of institutional and coalitional forms. The sites and territorial scale of such strategies can also vary.
However, the fundamental objective remains the same: to control the number
of actors involved in local struggles for power. Keeping conflict localized min-
imizes the number of actors and preserves extant power asymmetries between
incumbents and oppositions. Nationalizing local conflict multiplies the number of actors, increases coalitional possibilities for oppositions, and increases
their probabilities of upsetting the provincial authoritarian leadership. The
institutional embeddedness of national and subnational political arenas creates a permanent challenge to local incumbents and ongoing opportunities
for local oppositions. In this context of institutional embeddedness, the diffusion or nondiffusion of democracy across territorial jurisdictions is closely
tied to how effectively incumbents and oppositions control the scope of local
conflict.

This abstract model provides the basis for building a detailed theoretical
framework that situates provincial conflict in a national territorial system, identifies specific institutional strategies of boundary control, and specifies the likely
political actors on either side of the territorial democratization divide. Stein
Rokkan and Derek Urwin note that in studies of center–periphery conflicts "the
degree to which the political, economic, and cultural boundaries of a periphery can be penetrated has important consequences.... In any such inquiry we
have to distinguish between boundary-opening and boundary-strengthening
groups or agencies within the periphery."[31] In this spirit the following section maps out common strategies and processes of boundary control. I first
examine how subnational authoritarian regimes are built and maintained by
boundary-strengthening activities of local incumbents. A discussion follows of

---

[31] Stein Rokkan and Derek Urwin, *Economy, Territory, Identity: Politics of West European
Peripheries* (Beverly Hills: Sage Publications, 1983), 4.

boundary-opening strategies by oppositions and of scenarios for the democratization of subnational authoritarian enclaves.

VII. STRATEGIES OF BOUNDARY CONTROL IN NATIONAL TERRITORIAL SYSTEMS

Maintaining Subnational Authoritarian Regimes: Boundary Strengthening by Incumbents

Boundary control by subnational authoritarian incumbents is played out in three sites of political action – subnational arenas, national arenas, and the institutional links between them – using three strategies: (1) the parochialization of power, (2) the nationalization of influence, and (3) the monopolization of national–subnational linkages.

Local Strategies, Local Goals: The Parochialization of Power

The first obvious unit of analysis is the area actually being controlled. The "parochialization of power" thus refers to local strategies of political control. The site of such strategies is local, and where the unit of analysis is a province, such strategies seek to maximize gubernatorial hegemony over the subnational territorial system. This system includes provincial government institutions as well as municipalities and lower orders of government. However, when the national polity is democratic, there are limits to how naked authoritarian rule can be. A provincial military government would be very difficult to sustain in a nationally democratic country, except in extreme situations of civil conflict.

In nationally democratic countries, authoritarian provincial incumbents thus face two apparently contradictory tasks: they must exercise authoritarian control over the local polity, and they must link it institutionally to the national democratic polity. Because local authoritarianism must be institutionally compatible with national democracy, party politics is at the heart of boundary control by incumbents.

In his studies of the state-level political systems of the mid-20th century American South, V. O. Key observed that one effective institutional mechanism for organizing subnational authoritarian rule was the state-level "one-party" system. Key suggested that this institutional form was very effective for exercising local domination because of "the extreme difficulty of maintaining an organized opposition." He also suggested that it was equally important as "an arrangement for national affairs" – that is, as an institutional form that integrated local politics with the national political system.[32]

---

[32] V. O. Key, *Southern Politics in State and Nation* (Knoxville: University of Tennessee Press, 1949), 16, 71–72. Where national party institutionalization is weak, however, the parochialization of power could include such institutional alternatives as bureaucratic control. See Kathryn Stoner-Weiss, *Local Heroes: The Political Economy of Russian Regional Governance* (Princeton: Princeton University Press, 1997).

This pattern can be generalized to cases of provincial authoritarianism in other parts of the world. Where national party institutionalization is a reality, there are strong incentives to exercise local control through party institutions. This requires strategies to bend local institutional arrangements toward the goal of building and maintaining subnational hegemonic parties. Such parties are the most important institutional manifestation of subnational authoritarianism in nationally democratic countries.

A terminological clarification is thus in order. This study uses the term "hegemonic party" to refer to subnational authoritarianism rather than such terms as "one party" or "single party" that are commonly used in the literature. The concept is taken from Giovanni Sartori's work on national party systems, in which he distinguishes between "predominant parties" and "hegemonic parties." In the predominant party system one party wins majorities on a regular basis, but as a result of free competition. In hegemonic party systems, hegemonic parties win by design – power holders, through legal and illegal means, ensure the victory of the dominant party.[33] Although Sartori was only addressing national party systems, this power scenario is applicable to the subnational scenarios discussed earlier.[34] It also captures the competitive context in which local authoritarian incumbents operate. The hegemonic party aims not only to organize domination in a noncompetitive context but also to counter or neutralize competitive threats.[35] Furthermore, in subnational politics these threats come from two fronts: the local jurisdiction and national politics.

The construction and maintenance of the subnational hegemonic party are in many ways local activities. However, the local strategic and institutional options available to incumbents are influenced heavily by the national territorial regime, particularly those features that affect the subsystemic autonomy of subnational jurisdictions. An important attribute of subsystemic autonomy is the power by local authorities to design local constitutions and electoral rules.

[33] See, in particular, his discussion of Mexico's *Partido Revolucionario Institutional* (PRI), 232–35. "Hegemonic" and "Predominant" party systems include opposition parties, and are thus distinct from "One-Party" systems in Sartori's classification scheme.

[34] Sartori may have held back theoretical work on subnational party politics when he dismissed the possibility that national competitive party systems could coexist with subnational hegemonic party systems. The subnational level, he noted, does not possess the "subsystemic autonomy" required to make such a situation possible. In a direct criticism of V. O. Key, Sartori asserts that "Southern politics has little to do with establishing or disestablishing a democracy." See Sartori, *Parties and Party Systems* (1976), 83. For a detailed theoretical critique of Sartori's work on these issues, see Edward L. Gibson and Julieta Suarez Cao, "Federalized Party Systems: Theory and an Empirical Application to Argentina," *Comparative Politics* 43, no. 1 (October 2010).

[35] Sartori's work does not address processes of change in hegemonic party systems. Thus, dynamics of competition over time in such systems do not figure in his theory. Beatriz Magaloni, however, provides extensive theoretical and empirical treatment of change and continuity in hegemonic parties and party systems in her book, *Voting for Autocracy: Hegemonic Party Survival and its Demise in Mexico*, New York and Cambridge, UK: Cambridge University Press (2006).

Throughout this book I place particular emphasis on this political attribute. Subsystemic autonomy is highest where local authorities have complete freedom to design local constitutions and laws governing elections for national and local offices. Subsystemic autonomy is lowest where the content of such institutions is determined by national authorities and enforced across all jurisdictions of the country.

At this point we can advance a hypothesis about the effects of this variable on the construction of party hegemony: where subsystemic autonomy is high, the construction of party hegemony will rely heavily on legal and formal institutional rules. Where subsystemic autonomy on this dimension is low, it will rely on illegal and informal arrangements. As we see later, these scenarios are important not only for how authoritarianism is maintained but also for how it comes apart.

National Strategies, Local Goals: The Nationalization of Influence

The nationalization of influence refers to the pursuit of national strategies or political positions to influence national decisions that affect the local jurisdiction. This pursuit is indispensible to local boundary control because national influence is central to the successful management of local politics. That is why successful subnational authoritarian leaders are players on the national stage. They may be low-key national players who occupy national positions for the sole purpose of buttressing their control at the provincial level; for example, former governors serving time in the senate to influence legislation or fiscal appropriations relating to their provinces. They may also include sitting governors who control the province's delegation in the national congress.

However, such leaders' participation in national arenas may reflect their national ambitions. In federal systems governors are uniquely positioned to use local power as a springboard to national office. Complacent assumptions about the territorially contained nature of "backwater" politics are thus often shattered when the periphery catapults its authoritarian progeny to the pinnacles of national power.

The subnational hegemonic party is also important to the nationalization of influence. As "an arrangement for national affairs," it maximizes the leverage of local incumbents in the national congress. The greater the number of national legislators who respond to the governor, the more leverage the governor has over national politicians. A subnational hegemonic party also increases the governor's influence in factional competition within the national party. When the governor is able to deliver more votes to particular national party leaders, he or she has more leverage in a national party faction.

Such a national presence, however, can be double-edged. Although necessary for effective local control, it is also the Achilles' heel for subnational authoritarian regimes. When provincial political leaders become national leaders, they also become embroiled in the conflicts of national politics. Provincial leaders can thus become targets of national leaders who, although totally unconcerned about politics in their adversaries' province, know that the only way to eliminate them is to undermine the local power structure that supports them. The virtuous cycle of subnational democratization can sometimes be set in motion by nothing more than a vile political dispute between national leaders.

Straddling the Local and the National: The Monopolization of National–Subnational Linkages

Linkages between the arenas of a national territorial system are crucial to the organization of power at all levels of territorial organization. However, "linkage" is somewhat vague as a concept. The one definition among many that seems to work best is as follows: "a connecting part, *whether in material or immaterial sense*; a thing (occas. a person) serving to establish or maintain a connexion; . . . a means of connexion or communication."[36]

Allowing that a link can be either material (an institution, for example) or immaterial (a relation, affinity, or communication flow) helps us get a handle on the actual objects of struggle between actors in a national territorial system. Linkages can include institutions established to regulate interprovincial and national–subnational governmental relations, institutions or persons to monitor provincial activities and expenditures, and institutions to organize the representation of provincial interests before the center. They can include revenue flows from center to periphery, communication flows, and service delivery between levels of government. They can also include relationships between national and local parties, between national and local unions, and between nongovernmental organizations. And finally, they can involve procedures for nominating local representatives to national institutions.[37] In territorial politics, whoever controls linkages controls power.

The goal of boundary control by local incumbents is invariable: to control outside involvement in local politics. As we have seen, however, the strategies that constitute it vary both in their territorial location and territorial reach. We can get a fuller sense of the spatial dynamics of boundary control by mapping these strategies according to the "site" and "scale" dimensions of territorial political action introduced earlier. Figure 2.4 displays the modal strategies according to the location in which they generally take place and the intended territorial scale of their effects. It also links them to specific institutional and strategic activities that support the goal of boundary control.

---

[36] *Oxford English Dictionary* (Oxford: Clarendon Press, 2001), Vol. VIII, 995, emphasis added.

[37] Tarrow describes these links as "networks of exchange" between center and periphery in Sidney Tarrow et al., *Territorial Politics in Industrial Nations* (New York: Praeger, 1978), 3.

	Scale of Political Action (Its Territorial Effects)	
Site of Political Action (Its Location)	Subnational	National
Subnational	**Parochialization of Power:** Design local electoral rules. **Linkage Monopolization:** Governor receives all national fiscal flows to the province	**Parochialization of Power:** "Deliver" votes to national party. **Linkage Monopolization:** Control local nominations for national offices.
National	**Nationalization of Influence:** Control national legislative agenda on issues affecting province. **Linkage Monopolization:** Control legislative committees appropriating fiscal transfers to province.	**Nationalization of Influence:** Reform national constitution. Build regional coalitions of provinces.

FIGURE 2.4. Boundary Control by Subnational Incumbents: Examples of Site and Scale of Political Strategies

Undermining Subnational Authoritarian Regimes: Boundary Opening by Oppositions

A provincial conflict is "nationalized" when extraprovincial actors ally with local oppositions, invest resources in the jurisdiction, and become participants in the local struggle for power. A first step in such a process is likely to be a local crisis in which provincial oppositions bring their conflict to the attention of external actors and succeed in linking the local conflict to the political or territorial interests of such actors.[38] Local actors are likely to include provincial opposition parties or civil society organizations. Internal factionalism in provincial hegemonic parties is also a likely source of organized challenges to incumbents.

---

[38] A reverse scenario is where national actors intervene unilaterally. However, odds for success are obviously low without mobilized local interlocutors.

Local crisis → Local opposition mobilization → Site shift: externalization of opposition grievances

→ National-subnational interest linkage → National actors join the local conflict

FIGURE 2.5. The Nationalization of Subnational Conflict by Local Oppositions: Constituent Mechanisms

The nationalization of local conflict is driven by several mechanisms, the first of which is the activation or mobilization of local opposition forces. However, where incumbent boundary control has been successful, local mobilization by itself is unlikely to overcome existing power asymmetries. Local oppositions must shift the scale of their political action: they must bring their local claims or grievances to the attention of national actors and, even more importantly, link them to the territorial interests of such actors. The constituent mechanisms of this process are displayed in Figure 2.5.

Identifying potential *national* boundary-opening agents requires that the "center" be seen not as a unitary actor (as often happens when the center-periphery dichotomy is employed) but as constellations of institutional actors with particular territorial interests and preferences. Where local party conflicts coincide with national partisan interests, national party leaders can be important boundary-opening agents in provincial politics. However, partisan interests of party leaders may conflict with bureaucratic or territorial interests of presidents, and the latter's interests may conflict with the institutional interests of national legislative leaders. These conflicts may constrain action by particular actors or may spark intervention in unexpected ways. Features of the national territorial regime may also hinder intervention by certain national actors and propitiate action by others. National interventions in subnational politics may thus not follow as predictable a pattern as those reading action off partisan affiliations might anticipate. Explaining or predicting patterns of national intervention thus requires a sense of how national actors are connected to one another, how these connections coincide with subnational conflict patterns, and how the national territorial regime creates opportunities for the nationalization of provincial conflict.

Paths from Subnational Authoritarianism: Two Types of Democratic Transition

Transitions from subnational authoritarian rule can thus have different sequential scenarios,[39] but one feature that all share is the nationalization of local conflict. Yet what are the paths that transitions from subnational authoritarian

---

[39] The notion of subnational "democratic transition" used here is that employed by O'Donnell and Schmitter for national contexts. It is a process in which authoritarian rule is challenged, and the ensuing nature of the subnational political regime is uncertain. It assumes no particular regime outcome. It can end in an authoritarian victory or the installation of a local democratic political regime. See Guillermo O'Donnell and Philippe Schmitter, *Transitions from Authoritarian Rule* (Baltimore: Johns Hopkins University Press, 1986).

Local crisis → Local opposition mobilization → National parties strengthen local opposition

parties → Continuity of local hegemonic rule challenged.

FIGURE 2.6. The Nationalization of Conflict by National Actors: The Party-Led Transition

rule are likely to take? Here I propose two scenarios: *party-led transitions* and *center-led transitions*.[40]

Description of a party-led transition is straightforward: it is subnational democratization via party competition. Its national protagonists are leaders of national political parties who ally with local opposition parties and invest resources in the jurisdiction to defeat the incumbent party. This electoral challenge is carried out *within the existing local rules of the game*. The intervention by national actors strengthens local opposition parties' institutional and material capabilities to challenge local incumbents. The strengthening of local party capabilities by national parties is the primary mechanism that shifts the local power balance. Political parties, in sum, alter local competitive dynamics autonomously.

In contrast, a center-led transition is one initiated by intervention from national state authorities (executive, judicial, or legislative). This intervention *transforms the local rules of the game*. It can be followed by a competitive party challenge, but the struggle to move from a local authoritarian regime to a democratic regime is sparked by action from central state authorities that altered the rules under which that challenge subsequently took place. The exogenous reorganization of the local rules is the mechanism that shifts the local power balance. The site of the center's actions can be local, such as an intervention ordered by the national executive that removes incumbents from power and changes local electoral rules. It can also be national, such as a decision by national courts that changes the subsystemic autonomy granted by the territorial regime and strikes at the institutional foundations of local hegemonic rule.

The defining features separating these transition types, therefore, are the national actors participating in them and the fact that one takes place under the local institutional status quo, whereas the other alters it. The processes of each transition type can be viewed schematically in Figures 2.6 and 2.7.

At this point we can venture a hypothesis about how the national territorial regime affects the process. Where the national territorial regime grants high autonomy to provinces, it is more likely that a regime transition will be center-led. Where subsystemic autonomy is low, it is more likely that the transition will be party-led.

In conditions of high subsystemic autonomy, local constitutions and electoral laws will make it difficult, if not impossible, for party challenges to defeat the incumbent party. As they shift the scale of their political mobilization to

---

[40] There are undoubtedly a greater variety of potential transition types, but these two are general enough for us to expect that others will be subsumed by them.

Local crisis → Local opposition mobilization → Central government intervention: exogenous change
   of local rules → Continuity of local hegemonic rule challenged.

FIGURE 2.7. The Nationalization of Conflict by National Actors: The Center-Led Transition

nationalize the local conflict, oppositions will be more likely to encourage central government authorities or national judiciaries to remove the legal and institutional impediments to local contestation. Where local autonomy is low, local and national opposition forces will be more able to challenge incumbents through the rough and tumble of partisan coalition-building – via subnational coalitions that destabilize the partisan arrangements that shield incumbents from national competitive pressures.

CONCLUSION

The situation this book analyzes is the existence of a provincial authoritarian government in a country with a national democratic government. The book's objective is to explain why and how such situations exist, endure, and come apart. The overarching argument of the book is that provincial authoritarian governments in democratic countries are entities that are made and unmade. Regardless of endogenous socioeconomic or cultural characteristics that propitiate local hegemony, such governments are ultimately products of strategic and institutional action by local incumbents. These incumbents are confronted by the overwhelming fact of having to interact, on a daily basis, with a democratic national political system. The keys to authoritarian continuity lie in the political responses of the jurisdiction's rulers to the reality of regime juxtaposition.

At the most general level, conflicts over subnational democratization are a struggle to determine the scope of local political conflict. By exerting boundary control, incumbents seek to keep conflict local, depriving opponents of access to outside allies and resources. Opposition forces seek to alter the local power balance by nationalizing local conflict. They reach across jurisdictional boundaries to bring outside forces into the fray. This chapter outlined the constitutive mechanisms of this process and how the territorial organization of the national state shapes strategic options available to actors on both sides of the boundary-control divide.

In the following chapters we leave this abstract terrain and plunge into concrete historical experiences. Chapter 3 on the United States explores the most dramatic instance of subnational authoritarianism in the history of democracy – the rise of the "Solid South" in the 19th century. It charts changing patterns of boundary control as the federal territorial regime made the transition from high centralization during the period known as "Reconstruction" to a highly peripheralized system after Reconstruction. The Latin American cases shift our sights to contemporary politics, addressing subnational authoritarianism and democratization in contrasting territorial regime contexts – Argentina under a federal system that resembles U.S. federalism after Reconstruction, and Mexico under a system that approximates U.S. federalism in key respects during Reconstruction. Three historical explorations thus yield a methodological bonus of four territorial regimes and a fruitful comparative pairing of cases of boundary control: under peripheralized federalism in Argentina and post-Reconstruction United States, and under nonperipheralized federalism in Mexico and Reconstruction United States.

Vast contextual and historical differences separate these cases. However, this theoretical chapter has provided navigational tools to make sense of the complexities we come across along the way. As we emerge from this exploration, it should be clear that, regardless of the messy idiosyncrasies of our historical cases, the mechanisms of boundary control reproduce themselves consistently across time and space. As long as subnational authoritarian governments exist alongside national democratic governments, boundary control will be at play.

3

Subnational Authoritarianism in the United States

Boundary Control and the "Solid South"

> On the fundamental issue, only the Federal Government was to be feared.
>
> V. O. Key[1]

THE UNITED STATES AS A COMPARATIVE CASE

In the years following the Civil War of 1861–65, the United States experienced a "transition to democracy." Sweeping national legislation granted full citizenship to four million people and enfranchised more than a million. However, this was not a transition to democracy in the sense used traditionally by democratization scholars. The national government had been democratic for more than 80 years, and most men living in the country already enjoyed these rights.[2] What the United States experienced during that period was the most extensive case of territorial democratization in history. Clusters of voting and civil rights long available to inhabitants of other jurisdictions of the country were extended to inhabitants of a group of states that held more than one-third of the national population. Most of these had been slaveholding states before the Civil War and had formed part of the short-lived secessionist experiment known as the Confederate States of America (Figure 3.1). As a result, competitive state-party systems, linked to a national competitive party system, emerged throughout the region.

The subnational democracies born of this transition, however, suffered the fate of many of their national counterparts: they failed. By the turn of the century they were replaced by a phenomenon known as the "Solid South," a regional bloc of authoritarian states that was firmly integrated into the structure of national political life. The political regimes of these states were unambiguously undemocratic by any definition of the concept. Political competition was severely restricted, and so was voting.

[1] V. O. Key, *Southern Politics in State and Nation* (New York: Alfred A. Knopf, 1949), 9.
[2] Women in the United States were given the right to vote in 1920.

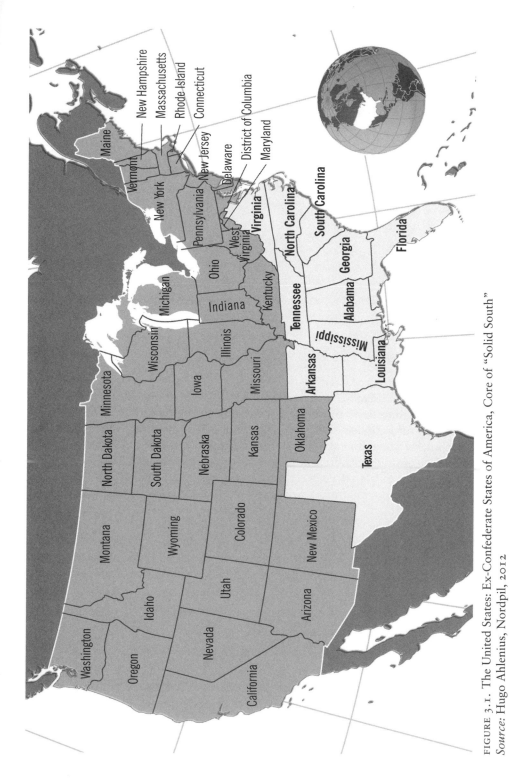

FIGURE 3.1. The United States: Ex-Confederate States of America, Core of "Solid South"

Source: Hugo Ahlenius, Nordpil, 2012

In the late 19th century, all 11 states from the former Confederacy were governed by what V. O. Key labeled "one-party" state-level systems, in which local Democratic parties exercised hegemony over political life.[3] Voting was restricted on a huge scale. Almost all inhabitants of African descent, as well as a substantial proportion of poor whites, were denied the right to vote.

This situation of regime juxtaposition, in which a large and unambiguously authoritarian assemblage of state governments coexisted with a national democratic government, lasted for the better part of a century. It would take another democratic transition in the middle of the 20th century, one that mobilized and traumatized the country's entire political system, to bring territorial democratization to the southern states.

It is tempting to assume that the authoritarian Solid South was a natural or likely outcome of local structural factors – the level of economic development, class structure, or their related sociopolitical legacies. The 11 formerly secessionist states were among the poorest in the country. They were burdened by multiple social and political curses from their slaveholding history. They were also dominated by a plantation aristocracy in the fertile "Black Belt" regions of the South that was committed to reasserting the social power relations of the antebellum period.[4] Even the most casual reader of the democratization literature knows that these structural characteristics are considered to be hostile to the emergence of democracy.

However, both theory and observation suggest a different perspective on the dynamics of southern political development. The southern states were not sovereign countries (the unit of analysis normally addressed by democratization theorists). They were subnational jurisdictions integrated into a national political system and subject to its regular and substantive interventions. In the late 19th century many of the national interventions were designed to dismantle local oligarchic orders and replace them with competitive political regimes.

Furthermore, in the decades after the Civil War, competitive political regimes *did* emerge in the southern states, and vigorously so.[5] This competitive situation persisted long after the end of the 1866–77 period of national occupation known as Reconstruction. Even after the national government withdrew

[3] A smaller number of "border states," such as Kentucky, West Virginia, Oklahoma, and Missouri, which had not formed part of the Confederate States, shared Solid South political features and formed part of the regional political block at different stages of its existence.

[4] "Black Belt" refers to the plantation-dominated southern regions. These were regions with majority black populations, although the term refers to the rich dark soils of the areas rather than their majority populations.

[5] This has been well documented by historians. See, for example, Eric Foner, *Reconstruction: America's Unfinished Revolution, 1863–1877* (New York: Harper & Row, 1988); C. Vann Woodward, *Reunion and Reaction: The Compromise of 1877 and the End of Reconstruction* (Boston: Little, Brown, 1951) and *Origins of the New South, 1877–1913* (Baton Rouge: Louisiana State University Press, 1951); and J. Morgan Kousser, *The Shaping of Southern Politics: Suffrage Restriction and the Establishment of the One-Party South, 1880–1910* (New Haven: Yale University Press, 1974).

and returned power to the prewar political elite, the southern states had a large number of active newly enfranchised voters. Their politics was shaped profoundly by the legacies of Reconstruction and opposition party-building, and they gave up their rights dearly.

The story of the authoritarian Solid South is thus not a story of natural evolution. It is a story of how authoritarian leaders in state after state responded to the massive challenges to their hegemony in the decades after the Civil War. These challenges were national and local, and the responses to them were similarly national and local. The crafting of subnational authoritarian regimes in the late-19th-century American South constitutes the most spectacular case of boundary control seen anywhere in the world.

This blemish on U.S. political history sets another record in the global history of democracy. Once rights are granted to massive numbers of people, they are not taken away under a democratic regime. At least that has been the assumption since Alexis de Tocqueville elevated it to the status of a law in his classic work, *Democracy in America:* "There is no more invariable rule in the history of society: the further electoral rights are extended, the greater is the need of extending them; for after each concession the strength of the democracy increases... concession follows concession, and no stop can be made short of universal suffrage."[6]

The United States provides a glaring historical counterexample to de Tocqueville's law. The enfranchisement of southern blacks and poor whites in the 1860s and 1870s and their wholesale disenfranchisement shortly thereafter took place under a national democratic regime. Never before or since in a national democracy (absent a coup or regime change) has this feat been matched.[7] As a comparative case the United States reveals just how consequential subnational authoritarianism can be for political development and just how costly ignorance of its mechanisms can be to our theoretical understanding of democratization. Any serious effort to shed light on the comparative dynamics of subnational authoritarianism, therefore, must start with the United States.

The greatest disenfranchisement in the history of democracy did not happen immediately, nor did the state-level hegemonic party systems that followed spring up overnight: both resulted from nearly three decades of improvisation and institutional innovation. The architects of the Solid South had no blueprints from other historical cases of national democratic regimes to draw from. They were, without a doubt, pioneers in the design of subnational authoritarian institutions. Examining this experience, therefore, has considerable comparative value. Many of the institutional methods of boundary control discovered and developed in the late-19th-century U.S. South are present in the contemporary world. Although few (if any) contemporary cases come close to the Solid South in its scope and complexity, its features reappear, imparting

---

[6] Alexis de Tocqueville, *Democracy in America*, Vol. 1 (New York: Alfred A. Knopf, 1945), 59.
[7] Vallely, *The Two Reconstructions*.

disturbing family resemblances to succeeding generations of national democracies.

This chapter explores the rise and maintenance of state-level authoritarian regimes in the American South in the 19th and 20th centuries. The story of authoritarian regime construction is divided analytically into two phases. The first is about a *national* struggle, launched by boundary openers in the immediate post–Civil War years and waged to reshape federalism, the national territorial regime. At stake was the definition of the powers of the national government to reshape the political regimes of southern states. Would federalism become a sword with which to strike down the southern antebellum political order and democratize the states, or would it be a shield to protect subnational incumbents from national pressures for local democratization? This was a complicated fight, with partisan, statutory, and jurisprudential dimensions. At its core, however, was a struggle to shape the institutional terrain that would define strategic options for actors on both sides of the boundary-control divide.

The second phase shifts the spotlight to political action by southern boundary closers after the Supreme Court struck down Reconstruction era statutes and reaffirmed 19th-century federal doctrines of subsystemic autonomy ("states' rights"). With the national territorial regime now structured in favor of boundary closers' agendas, home rule was established in the South. Local incumbents turned their attention to institutional boundary control in local and national arenas and eventually gave structure and stability to the Solid South in American politics.

I. OF SWORDS AND SHIELDS: THE CENTER-LED DEMOCRATIC TRANSITION OF 1866–1877

The First Boundary-Control Struggle: Actors and Territorial Interests

After the northern states' victory in the Civil War, a "nationalist" coalition in the Republican Party, committed to the expansion of central government powers, controlled the national congress.[8] The bastions of states' rights, the southern states, were physically destroyed and politically subjugated. The terms of their reincorporation into the union were the overriding concerns of the immediate postwar years. At one level there was the basic issue of territorial reunification. However, there was also an issue with more profound implications: the nature of the political regimes of the reincorporated states. Would the reincorporation of the ex-Confederate states be delinked from questions about the democratic or authoritarian character of their political systems? Or would it require a territorial democratization of enormous proportions within the boundaries of the reassembled American State?

---

[8] For a detailed analysis of the electoral and political economy dynamics of this Republican Party coalition, see Richard F. Bensel, *Yankee Leviathan: The Origins of Central State Authority in America, 1859–1877* (Cambridge University Press, 1990).

To the "Radical Republicans" in the national congress, the answer was clear. They had major plans for the democratic transformation of the southern states. Whether these designs had normative inspirations (democratizing the region, destroying the Black Belt aristocracy, granting full citizenship to blacks) or strategic inspirations (building a southern Republican Party) is immaterial.[9] Fulfilling either set of inspirations required the democratization of the states, widespread enfranchisement, and the enforcement of civil and voting rights. The Radical Republicans were thus the main national boundary openers of the moment, and territorial democratization was their vision for postwar American political development.

At the local level, boundary-opening allies in the South were organizationally underdeveloped at the close of the Civil War. Most were also new to politics. Yet they provided a broad base for party-building and actively sought help from national Republicans. Eric Foner reports that the end of the war was followed by a political mobilization of blacks throughout the South, in which they "organized a seemingly unending series of mass meetings, parades, and petitions demanding civil equality and the suffrage as indispensable corollaries of emancipation."[10] Mobilization was greatest in the cities, where a fair number of educated blacks lived, and in those rural areas long occupied by Union troops, where political activity had begun even before the end of the war.

Yet politically mobilized blacks faced a major obstacle from the outset. Their political awakening was matched with equal speed by the imposition of new forms of subjugation by local authorities. Black political activities were repressed across the states, laws creating new forms of labor servitude were put on the books, and black demands for redress to state authorities and local courts fell on deaf ears.

Black activists thus shifted their sights to the national sphere. With state and local authorities arrayed against them, they externalized their grievances toward the national government. Immediately after the war the most visible institutions of the national government operating in the South were the Union Army and the Freedmen's Bureau, an agency established by the national government to provide material and political support to ex-slaves. Blacks brought their grievances against local power holders to the Army and the Freedmen's Bureau on a regular basis, and these institutions became an important linkage

---

[9] The motivations of Republican leaders are a subject of debate among historians of the period. For example, Eric Foner tends to emphasize the ideological motivations of the Radical coalition, whereas such authors as C. Vann Woodward, Richard Vallely, and Stanley Hirshon emphasize electoral strategy. Richard Bensel and others in the American Political Development school stress the interaction between Republican economic policies and electoral objectives in the South, whereas Foner suggests that "generally, Congressional Radicals viewed economic issues as secondary to those of Reconstruction." Foner, *Reconstruction: America's Unfinished Revolution*, 233. All of these scenarios are consistent with a view of a national Republican Party committed to the democratization of southern politics immediately after the war.

[10] Ibid., 110.

between state and national arenas. They also created a protective shell for the organizational activities of local black activists.[11]

Just as significantly, black activists targeted the national Republican Party, particularly the leaders of its Radical wing.[12] Statements by church leaders and black-led publications, as well as "colored" political conventions held in several states in 1865 and 1866, took on an undeniably partisan tone. They called on Republican leaders in the national congress to pass legislation guaranteeing full legal equality for blacks and universal suffrage. Black activists also offered themselves as leaders and constituents for Republican party-building in the South. Attendees at black state political conventions voted to affiliate themselves with the national Republican Party, and blacks attended local meetings and state-wide Republican congresses in overwhelming numbers.[13] The message from this newly mobilized constituency to the national Republican leadership was clear: it stood ready to staff and lead a southern Republican Party and to vote for it in overwhelming numbers, if the national party put its full weight behind the transformation of southern politics.[14]

The Republican Party could also count on potential white leaders and constituents in the South. Ex-leaders of the Whig Party and prewar southern Unionists were potential local leaders of a new southern Republican Party.[15] Urban financial and commercial elites in the South, enticed by the potential bounty of expanded ties with northern commercial interests, constituted a potential economic core constituency in the region. "Upland" and poor whites, harboring long-standing resentments against a Black Belt aristocracy that had marginalized them economically and forced them into a devastating war that many of them did not support, were also potential members of a Republican mass base.[16]

---

[11] As Foner writes, "the flourishing network of [black] churches and fraternal societies provided a springboard for organization, and the Army and Freedmen's Bureau stood ready to offer protection." Ibid., 111.

[12] Ibid., 118.

[13] Ibid., 110–18.

[14] Richard Valelly states that when Radical Republicans launched party-building activities in the South "a regionwide network of black male activists already existed.... Republican party and electoral politics had a potential black male staff, as it were, waiting in the wings to make suffrage work.... The new coalition, in short, could work on both ends. The party insiders in Washington could count on a staff of black activists on the ground in the former Confederate states, and vice-versa." Richard M. Vallely, *The Two Reconstructions*, 38.

[15] C. Vann Woodward provides detailed accounts of Whig and unionist politics in the region. C. Vann Woodward, *Reunion and Reaction* and *Origins of the New South*. See also Thomas B. Alexander, "Persistent Whiggery in the Confederate South, 1860–1877," *Journal of Southern History* 27 (August 1961).

[16] Richard Bensel's *Sectionalism and American Political Development: 1880–1980* (Madison: University of Wisconsin Press, 1984), 378. For distinctions between "core constituency" and "mass base" dynamics in party formation, see Edward L. Gibson, *Class and Conservative Parties: Argentina in Comparative Perspective* (Baltimore: Johns Hopkins University Press, 1996).

The opportunities for action by the national party were matched also by the potential costs of inaction. The reincorporation of an unreconstructed and politically cohesive region that was implacably hostile to the Republican Party posed a weighty threat to its hold on national political institutions. Furthermore, the abolition of slavery gave the southern region an ironic bonus in congressional (and Electoral College) representation. Former slaves, once worth three-fifths of a white inhabitant for the purposes of congressional apportionment, were now counted in full as freedmen. If they were not enfranchised, southern Democrats would reap the gains in representation from the abolition of slavery while denying its beneficiaries (and likely Republican voters) the right to vote.[17] Enfranchising black citizens was thus a strategic priority for Republican Party leaders.

The national Democratic Party also needed a strong presence in the South to compete against Republicans elsewhere in the country. Locally, it relied on the support of the prewar political elite and the Black Belt aristocracy. Nationally it controlled a formidable political institution: the presidency of the United States. Andrew Johnson, a Democrat and former southern Unionist from the state of Tennessee, was Abraham Lincoln's vice president and assumed the presidency after Lincoln's assassination. President Johnson was, by most historical accounts, unenthusiastic about black enfranchisement. He also saw the reincorporation of southern states controlled by the prewar elite as critical to his party's fortunes.[18] His personal predispositions and partisan interests, therefore, placed him squarely in alliance with local boundary closers bent on preventing the emergence of competitive political systems in the southern states.

The immediate postwar battle over territorial democratization in the South was thus strongly driven by partisan interests of the two national political parties. However, it was very much a center-led transition because Republican party-building in the South could not be carried out without intervention by the national government. National intervention was needed to refashion local laws and constitutional orders. It was also needed to provide the enforcement – military, political, and legal – to render those new rules effective. As Richard Vallely has written, "An infrastructure for the process of electoral inclusion had to be made, and making it as fast as possible in a hostile environment was very hard."[19] The prewar southern political elite may have been weakened by

---

[17] Republican fears at the time were well captured in an 1865 statement by Thaddeus Stevens, a Republican congressman from Pennsylvania: "The eighty-three southern members with the Democrats that will in the best time be elected from the North will *always* give them a majority in Congress and in the Electoral College. They will at the very first election take possession of the White House and the halls of Congress. I need not depict the ruin that would follow." Quoted in Vallely, *The Two Reconstructions*, 29.

[18] According to Eric Foner, had southern states been reincorporated on Johnson's terms, it "would have created an unassailable political coalition capable of reuniting the Union, winning him a triumphant reelection, and determining the contours of American politics for a generation or more." Foner, *Reconstruction: America's Unfinished Revolution*, 184.

[19] Vallely, *The Two Reconstructions*, 97.

military defeat, but it wielded enormous power over its provincial dominions. "Only outside intervention," as Eric Foner put it, "could assure the freedmen a modicum of justice."[20]

However, a major institutional obstacle stood in the way of a center-led transition: 19th-century federalism. If these doctrines of federalism were to govern the reincorporation of southern states, the national government would lack the powers to recast state-level political regimes. In the moment of great institutional uncertainty wrought by the Civil War's end, Radical Republicans in the national congress saw their opportunity to redesign the powers of the national government over the states. The first boundary-control battle for the American South was thus to be a battle over the national territorial regime.

Mapping the Institutional Topography of U.S. Federalism

In the 19th century, U.S. federalism was considerably more peripheralized than it is today. On the intergovernmental dimension, state governments enjoyed high levels of discretion in the regulation of social and political life, the design of political institutions, and the granting of political rights to their citizens. Indeed, until the 1860s, state governments had complete discretion in deciding which categories of human beings could be recognized as citizens, and in several states the enslavement of people of African descent was a legal and economically important institution. Even after an amendment to the national constitution outlawed slavery throughout the land, there were few rights guaranteed by the national government that state governments were compelled to incorporate into their state constitutions. This feature of the territorial regime would have enormous implications for the civil and voting rights of blacks, most dramatically in southern states, but also in the North and West.[21]

On the interregional dimension, U.S. federalism was asymmetrical in the representation of states in national political institutions (as it is today). The national senate gave each state two seats in the chamber regardless of population size. Thus, demographically small states enjoyed considerable clout in that chamber. Given its power in the legislative branch, the senate was a valuable arena for regional blocs to influence legislation affecting their regions. An Electoral College that gave disproportionate weight to smaller states had similarly beneficial effects for them in presidential politics.

U.S. federalism was also highly province-empowering. State governments are the primary subnational governmental unit of U.S. federalism, and the constitution subordinates local governments to state governments. State law, not

---

[20] Foner, *Reconstruction: America's Unfinished Revolution*, 216.
[21] For an analysis of the nonsouthern dimensions of a national white supremacy agenda, see Desmond King and Stephen Tuck, "De-centering the South: America's Nationwide White Supremacist Order after Reconstruction," *Past and Present* 194 (February 2007), 213–54.

federal law, determines the powers and prerogatives of county and municipal governments.[22] In the mid- and late 19th century this feature would have a
particularly strong effect on political development in the southern states. Urban
municipalities had few resources to challenge the hegemony of state authorities over local polities. Their formal status in the intergovernmental hierarchy of U.S. federalism gave them little political autonomy. Furthermore,
the 19th-century southern political economy and the limited role then played
by fiscal flows from the national government to southern local governments
gave them little economic autonomy.[23] Thus, as sites of social heterogeneity
and political contestation, their potential democratizing effects on southern
politics were tempered by the political and economic arrangements of federalism.

The southern states took full advantage of the peripheralized features of U.S.
federalism, both before and after the Civil War of 1861–5. Political decentralization enhanced the protection of their "peculiar" institutions, namely slaveholding before the war. Overrepresentation in national political institutions,
combined with the successful coordination of sectional strategies in national
politics, provided leverage in national arenas for the same ends.[24] Immediately
after the war, preservation of the peripheralized federal system was a matter of
political survival for southern Democrats and their allies in the national party.
A cross-regional partisan alliance of Democrats, therefore, united to thwart
Republican plans for territorial regime transformation.

To make matters more difficult for reformers, the U.S. territorial regime
is one of the hardest to change in the universe of federal countries. Arend
Lijphart classifies the constitution of the United States as one of the most
"rigid" constitutions in the world.[25] Rigid constitutions require supermajorities

---

[22] The Tenth Amendment to the constitution makes local governments a matter of state law
rather than federal law, and states are granted wide discretion in determining the powers and
regime features of county and municipal governments. Variations in the formal powers of local
governments are thus a product of state laws. The primacy of state governments over municipal
governments has also been enshrined in what is known as "Dillon's Rule," based on legal
writings in the 1860s and 1870s by a federal judge named John Forrest Dillon. Dillon's Rule
asserts that municipal governments have only the powers that are expressly granted to them
by the state legislature. He described such governments as "mere tenants at the will of their
respective state legislatures" whose powers or existence could be "eliminated by the legislature
with a stroke of the pen." Quoted in David Miller, *The Regional Governing of Metropolitan
America* (New York: Westview Press, 2002), 1–2.

[23] This fiscal situation would change dramatically during the New Deal, as would its transformative effects on southern politics. See Bruce J. Schulman, *From Cotton Belt to Sunbelt: Federal Policy, Economic Development, and the Transformation of the South, 1938–1980* (New
York: Oxford University Press, 1991). See also Bensel, *Sectionalism and American Political
Development*, for an in-depth examination of North–South political economy dynamics of the
period.

[24] Perhaps the most exhaustive examination of post–Civil War Southern sectionalist strategies in
national politics is Bensel's *Sectionalism and American Political Development*.

[25] Arend Lijphart, *Patterns of Democracy: Government Forms and Performance in Thirty-Six
Countries* (New Haven: Yale University Press, 1999).

to be amended. Amending the U.S. Constitution requires both a supermajority of Congress and a supermajority of states (two-thirds of the country's state legislatures must also ratify constitutional amendments). There are thus two potential veto groups blocking change: legislative minorities and territorial minorities. If that were not enough, the United States is also marked by the tradition of judicial review. In such a system, the courts (ultimately a supreme or constitutional court) decide on the constitutionality of laws passed by the national legislature.[26]

This means that any process of territorial regime change in the United States will involve Herculean coalition-building efforts. It will also ultimately involve the courts. Therefore, in addition to its political dimension, any battle to alter federalism will also have an important jurisprudential component.[27]

NATIONAL RIGHTS AND LOCAL POLITICAL REGIMES IN AMERICAN FEDERALISM

> It is quite clear that there is a citizenship of the United States, and a citizenship of a State, which are distinct from each other.
>
> U.S. Supreme Court Justice Samuel Miller,
> Majority Opinion, *The Slaughterhouse Cases*, 1873

> A citizen of a State is ipso facto a citizen of the United States.... The citizen of a State has the same fundamental rights as a citizen of the United States.
>
> U.S. Supreme Court Justice Noah Swayne,
> Dissenting Opinion, *The Slaughterhouse Cases*, 1873

In 1833 the U.S. Supreme Court ruled that the Bill of Rights restrained only the powers of the national government (*Barron v. Baltimore*).[28] State governments were under no legal obligation to provide its protections under their constitutions. At stake in the court case was the answer to this question: Are civil and political rights defined nationally, or is their substantive content to be decided by the states? Put in more general terms, does the central government have the power to define and enforce a uniform standard of citizenship throughout the country? The 1833 Supreme Court decision settled the question unambiguously. Under the U.S. constitution, the power to define the substantive content of local inhabitants' rights in their dealings with state authorities was a power delegated to the individual states.

[26] In countries without judicial review, it is usually the legislature that decides on the constitutionality of its own laws. Federal countries tend to have judicial review, but not always (Switzerland is very federal, but lacks judicial review).

[27] In his analysis of 19th- and 20th-century struggles for black enfranchisement, Valelly thus advances a useful "party-building-jurisprudence-building" model to capture the political process. Valelly, *The Two Reconstructions*, 15–17.

[28] Stanley I. Kutler, *The Supreme Court and the Constitution: Readings in American Constitutional History* (Boston: Houghton Mifflin, 1969).

Thus, under 19th-century U.S. federalism, very few "national" rights existed. This was a key property of the territorial regime's political decentralization. As Richard Vallely has written, "this may seem strange to the contemporary ear because today Americans often have the correct impression that they do enjoy such national rights. But in the nineteenth century... national civil and political rights per se did not exist."[29]

This historical fact reveals a great deal about the relationship between federalism and the development of democracy in the United States. It also sheds light on how territorial regimes and democratization are dynamically intertwined. In their landmark volume on democratization, *Transitions from Authoritarian Rule*, Guillermo O'Donnell and Philippe Schmitter note that the foundational principle of democracy is that of citizenship. The "citizenship principle" is one of political equality, and democratization is the process by which political equality is extended to broader segments of the population.[30] In 19th-century American federalism a basic principle of constitutional law was one of *dual citizenship*: individuals were both citizens of the nation and citizens of the state. National and state authorities, however, could have different concepts of citizenship so that individuals could be subject to two separate standards of citizenship at the same time. The federal government could guarantee a range of citizen rights, but the state could deny those very same rights in its own dealings with people. Establishing a nationally uniform standard of citizenship required, therefore, a radical change in the national territorial regime. A uniform standard would be possible only if the central government were given the power to impose its definition of citizenship on all units of the federation – in other words, via the political centralization of federalism.

19TH-CENTURY TERRITORIAL REGIME PREFERENCES: BOUNDARY OPENERS AND BOUNDARY CLOSERS

Figure 3.2 provides a visual display of Republican and Democratic preferences about the peripheralization of American federalism. Position A captures the status-quo situation leading up to the Civil War – limited national rights and asymmetrical territorial representation in the national senate and Electoral College. Southern Democrats favored this position, although their ideal position incorporated a somewhat higher level of asymmetry in representation. This is captured in position B, which adds partisan overrepresentation of southern Democrats to the territorial overrepresentation of the South captured in position A. This they could achieve via the disenfranchisement of black voters. Blacks would still be counted fully for the purposes of apportionment of seats to the congress, but they would be denied the right to vote. Hence, the full benefits of that apportionment would flow to white Democrats. In

---

[29] Vallely, *The Two Reconstructions*, 104.
[30] Guillermo O'Donnell, Philippe Schmitter, and Laurence Whitehead, *Transitions from Authoritarian Rule* (Baltimore: Johns Hopkins University Press, 1986).

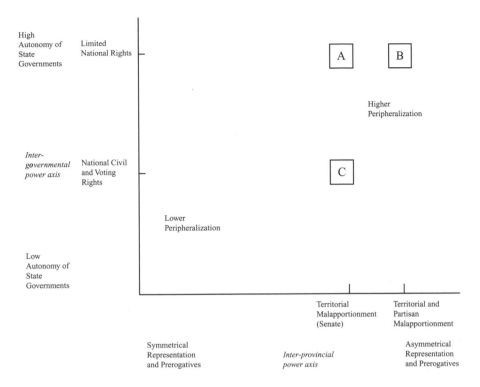

A = 19th Century Federalism
B = Boundary Closers' Ideal Position
C = Boundary Openers' Ideal Position

FIGURE 3.2. National Territorial Regime Preferences: 19th-Century Boundary Openers and Boundary Closers

contrast, Republican boundary openers preferred position C, which, by expanding national rights, produced a centralization of the territorial regime along the intergovernmental power axis. The formal asymmetry of representation would remain unchanged, but the nationalization of political rights would prevent disenfranchisement and the resulting partisan gain in representation sought by southern Democrats.

Reshaping Federalism: Establishing and Enforcing National Rights

The ambitious plans of Republican boundary openers were guided ideologically by a vision of citizenship in a federal system that challenged the most basic principles of U.S. constitutional law. Radical Republicans were proponents of what analysts have labeled "Reconstruction Constitutionalism," which challenged "dual citizenship" notions of 19th-century federalism. According to Vallely, its advocates held that "the constitution was not simply a set of limits on government, but a source of sovereign, positive, regulatory government *able to establish and enforce national rights.*"[31] Foner describes Reconstruction Constitutionalism as driven by a "utopian vision" under which full equality of citizens would be secured by the national state and by a conviction that "federalism and state rights must not obstruct a sweeping national effort to define and protect the rights of citizens."[32]

Yet how was Reconstruction Constitutionalism to be put into practice? To mobilize broad support, Radical Republicans had to find a constitutional basis for their designs on the South. They eventually found it in a clause in the constitution stipulating that the United States "guarantee each state a republican form of government."[33] Originally designed to suppress insurrections and the resurgence of monarchical and aristocratic institutions, the "guarantee clause" lay dormant until the Civil War. Radical Republicans found it useful because it might impart constitutional legitimacy to federal intervention on behalf of citizens' rights. A statement by Massachusetts Senator Charles Sumner captures the Radicals' enthusiastic assessment of this clause's power to advance their transformative vision of federalism. It was, he wrote, "a sleeping giant... never until this recent war awakened, but now it comes forward with a giant's power. There is no clause in the Constitution like it. *There is no other clause which gives to Congress such supreme power over the states.*"[34]

The political opportunity to assert that power came with the series of Republican congressional victories against President Johnson in 1866 and 1867 that put an end to "Presidential Reconstruction." The president's plan to readmit the ex-Confederate states under their prewar leadership had revealed its repressive implications for southern blacks with astonishing speed.[35] By late 1865 southern leaders had used their regained political autonomy to disenfranchise ex-slaves and also to create new arrangements of labor peonage and involuntary servitude. The measures became infamously known as the "Black Codes." After their initial enactment in Mississippi in November 1865, they were copied by legislatures throughout the ex-slave states.

---

[31] Vallely, *The Two Reconstructions*, 95 (emphasis added).

[32] Foner, *Reconstruction: America's Unfinished Revolution*, 231–32.

[33] Article IV, Section IV of the U.S. constitution, entitled "Republican Government," reads as follows: "The United States shall guarantee to every State in this Union a Republican Form of Government, and shall protect each of them against Invasion; and on Application of the Legislature, or of the Executive (when the Legislature cannot be convened) against domestic Violence." For analyses of the clause's impact on Reconstruction politics, see Charles O. Lerche, Jr., "Congressional Interpretations of the Guarantee of a Republican Form of Government during Reconstruction," *Journal of Southern History* 15 (May 1949). See also William Wiecek, *The Guarantee Clause of the U.S. Constitution* (Ithaca: Cornell University Press, 1972).

[34] Quoted in Foner, *Reconstruction: America's Unfinished Revolution*, 232 (emphasis added).

[35] For historical accounts of Presidential Reconstruction under Andrew Johnson, see John Hope Franklin, *Reconstruction after the Civil War* (Chicago: University of Chicago Press, 1961); Dan T. Carter, *When the War Was Over: The Failure of Self-Reconstruction in the South, 1865–1867* (Baton Rouge: Louisiana State University Press, 1985); Eric L. McKitrick, *Andrew Johnson and Reconstruction* (Chicago: Chicago University Press, 1960); and Richard Bensel, *Sectionalism and American Political Development*.

In early 1866 both houses of congress established a Joint Committee on Reconstruction charged with giving congress control over the Reconstruction process. One of the first important statutory measures was the Civil Rights Act of 1866. This bill accomplished several things, including the abolition of the Black Codes. It granted blacks (and all other "citizens") the right to make contracts, engage in lawsuits, bear witness in court, and own private property. Most importantly, the bill marked the first major statutory effort to incorporate the concept of "national rights" into American federalism. It defined all persons born in the United States as national citizens and outlined rights they would enjoy regardless of race. No state "statute, ordinance, regulation, custom, or usage," the act proclaimed, could deprive any "citizen of the United States of any rights, privileges, or immunities secured by the Constitution."

Thus was fired the opening salvo of the battle for territorial regime transformation by boundary openers in the Republican Party. The Civil Rights Act codified the national government's power to define the rights of citizens, regardless of the jurisdiction in which they lived.[36] As Foner writes, "As the first statutory definition of the rights of American citizenship, the Civil Rights Bill embodied a profound change in federal-state relations.... Reflecting the conviction, born of the Civil War, that the federal government possessed the authority to define and protect citizens' rights, the bill represented a striking departure from American jurisprudence."[37]

Invoking federalism, President Johnson vetoed the Civil Rights Act.[38] Congressional Republicans overrode his veto, however, and the bill became law. Power flowed toward the coalition of northern Republicans asserting congressional supremacy in the development of policy toward the South. Among the early measures passed by the national congress assembled in 1867 were several Reconstruction Acts. The first one declared the absence of adequate legal protections for local inhabitants in "rebel states" and converted 10 of the 11 states into five military districts, each ruled by a major general.[39] The center-led transition to democracy in the southern states – carried out at the point of federal bayonets – thus began in earnest. The Reconstruction acts gave the military primary responsibility for registering new voters, ensuring access to the ballot box, disenfranchising individuals for "participating in the rebellion,"

---

[36] It should also be noted that the Civil Rights Act, and subsequent statutory measures protecting voting rights, also caught many state governments in the North and West by surprise. No laws in any states protected the civil and voting rights of blacks. Furthermore, the national civil and voting rights were passed while such states as New York and California were busily enacting measures to disenfranchise black citizens. See John R. Howard, *The Shifting Wind: The Supreme Court and Civil Rights from Reconstruction to Brown* (Albany: State University of New York Press, 1999).

[37] Foner, *Reconstruction: America's Unfinished Revolution*, 244–45.

[38] In his veto message the president also invoked concerns about racial "decorum" and other matters. However, the basis of his challenge was that congress had exceeded the bounds of its constitutional authority over the states. See McKitrick, *Andrew Johnson and Reconstruction*.

[39] Stanley P. Hirshon, *Farewell to the Bloody Shirt* (Bloomington: Indiana University Press, 1962), 21.

and overseeing complex processes of local political and institutional reform. The military districts were to remain in place until the states had drafted new constitutions. These were to be written by delegates elected by the biracial electorates crafted by "Military Reconstruction." Under the supervision of federal troops, therefore, state constitutional conventions were held throughout the South in 1867 and 1868.[40]

Congress also amended the national constitution. In 1866 it passed the 14th Amendment, which was ratified by the states in 1868. The amendment adopted a broad definition of citizenship that granted full citizenship to ex-slaves: "all persons born or naturalized in the United States... are citizens of the United States and of the State wherein they reside." It prohibited the states from abridging the rights guaranteed by the national government. The amendment also gave the national congress the power to enforce its provisions in the states. Ratification of the 14th Amendment by the southern states was then made a condition of their readmission into the union.[41] A subsequent amendment guaranteeing voting rights bolstered national rights of citizenship. In 1870, the 15th Amendment, granting full voting rights to all citizens regardless of "race, color, or previous condition of servitude," was ratified. All southern states that had not yet rejoined the union were compelled to ratify the 15th Amendment as a condition of readmission.

Ratification of the 15th Amendment was a culminating point for the constitutional reform efforts of the Republican coalition. After its ratification the congress moved swiftly to ensure its implementation with a series of Enforcement Acts in 1870 and 1871. These bills responded to terror campaigns in southern states against blacks exercising their new national rights.[42] They established criminal codes that criminalized official and private interference with voting and the exercise of civil rights. They also authorized the use of federal troops to suppress terrorism in the states. Just as significantly, the Enforcement Acts provided yet another statutory affirmation of the supremacy of national rights over states' rights – all U.S. citizens, the text of the 1870 Enforcement Act asserted, were entitled and allowed to vote, "any constitution, law, custom, usage, or regulation of any State or Territory... to the contrary notwithstanding."

In a remarkably short span of years, therefore, a national partisan coalition enacted revolutionary changes in the national territorial regime. However, there was one additional hurdle in the American constitutional order to

---

[40] Michael A. Ross, "Justice Miller's Reconstruction: The Slaughterhouse Cases, Health Codes, and Civil Rights in New Orleans, 1861–1873," *Journal of Southern History* LXIV (November 1998).

[41] This last condition was a direct response to defiance by the states of the amendment. By February 1867 all ex-Confederate states except for Tennessee (all had been readmitted as states under Presidential Reconstruction) had denied their ratification, as had three ex-slave states that were neutral during the war. Vallely, *The Two Reconstructions*, 30.

[42] The 1871 Enforcement Act is also known as the "Ku Klux Klan Act." It targeted the violence campaigns of the Klan throughout the South.

overcome – judicial review. The insertion of the national courts into the political fray, particularly the U.S. Supreme Court, was only a matter of time. As it turned out, judicial review would tear asunder the redesign of American federalism by Republican boundary openers. However, let us first examine the effects of Reconstruction on the democratization of southern politics.

National Action, Local Effects: The Democratic Transition in the Southern States

The center-led transition revealed the enormous consequences of enhanced federal powers for territorial democratization in the United States. It unleashed a wave of enfranchisement, party-building, and rights enforcement throughout the South – the most dramatic case of territorial democratization in history. Under Military Reconstruction more than 700,000 blacks were registered as new voters, as well as more than 600,000 whites.[43] The number of black voters grew steadily in subsequent years, exceeding one million in the early 1870s.[44] However, most of the new voters were registered during the summer of 1867, a period of major political mobilization and enfranchisement labeled by one historian as a "registration summer."[45] Richard Vallely reports that between December 1866 and December 1867 the proportion of blacks eligible to vote in the United States soared from 0.5 percent to 80.5 percent. All of this increase took place in the former Confederate states.[46]

The pace and scope of political mobilization throughout the South in 1867 were dizzying. Historian Eric Foner characterizes it as an "annus mirabilis," in which the demise of local authority "opened the door for political mobilization to sweep across the black belt."[47] National actors – Republican Party agents, soldiers, central government bureaucrats, clergymen, and civic leaders – flooded the states to enfranchise blacks and poor whites, forge cross-sectional associations, build party organizations, and organize biracial cadres of new political leaders and activists. Vallely documents the frantic pace of outside involvement in southern political mobilization and infrastructure-building during this period. In the "registration summer" of 1867, he reports, up to 135 Republican Party organizers toured the southern states seeking to bolster local party-building. Military-appointed registrars, a significant proportion of them black, traveled in every county in ten of the former Confederate states to register voters.[48] The Republican Party also embarked on a crash program to establish Union Leagues throughout the South. The Leagues were Republican-affiliated

---

[43] Franklin, *Reconstruction after the Civil War.*

[44] Michael D. Cobb and Jeffrey A. Jenkins, "Race and the Representation of Blacks' Interests during Reconstruction," *Political Research Quarterly* 54 (March 2001).

[45] Julie Saville, *The Work of Reconstruction: From Slave to Wage Labor in South Carolina* (Cambridge: Cambridge University Press, 1996), 160.

[46] Vallely, *The Two Reconstructions*, 3.

[47] Foner, *Reconstruction: America's Unfinished Revolution*, 282.

[48] Vallely, *The Two Reconstructions*, 41.

clubs developed in the North (and clandestinely in the South) to support the Union cause during the Civil War. They now spread throughout the region as a vehicle for the political organization of ex-slaves. The Freedmen's Bureau, the central government agency charged with providing social assistance to newly freed blacks, ratcheted up its political activities as a vehicle for the identification, training, and organization of black political leaders with the intent of promoting "the rise of an entirely new political class."[49]

The historic outcasts of the southern political order responded in kind. Recent historiography on the Reconstruction period has revealed the extent to which blacks were more than passive objects of outside mobilization. They actively exercised their rights and challenged local authorities. Veterans of black Union Army regiments volunteered as voter registrars and members of armed militias that protected black political activity. Church congregations poured their energies into civic activism and education for illiterate ex-slaves. Civil society organizations saw their memberships swell, and they brought instances of malfeasance by local authorities to the attention of federal officials. Vallely documents that by the summer of 1867 the Union League organizations in the South had two to three hundred thousand members, most of them black, organized into about two to three thousand local chapters.[50] Eric Foner also writes that "by the end of 1867, it seemed, virtually every black voter in the south had enrolled in the Union League or some equivalent political organization."[51] Black office holding at all levels was also a hallmark of the period: at the local level where blacks formed electoral majorities, in state legislatures, and in the national congress.[52]

The center-led transition shattered the parochial confines of southern state politics. The contrasts between the closed and repressive political communities restored by Presidential Reconstruction in 1865 and 1866 and the "hothouse atmosphere of political mobilization" of Radical Reconstruction one year later could not have been starker.[53] Under the federal government's protection, new biracial electorates in state after state elected constitutional conventions, ratified them, and took control of the postconvention political orders. These new constitutions were radical departures from those drafted by local power holders during Presidential Reconstruction. They proclaimed their state

---

[49] Richard Lowe, "The Freedmen's Bureau and Local Black Leadership," *Journal of American History* 80 (December 1993), 990.

[50] Vallely, *The Two Reconstructions*, 39.

[51] Foner, *Reconstruction: America's Unfinished Revolution*, 283.

[52] Twenty blacks were elected to the U.S. House of Representatives between 1869 and 1901, and two to the U.S. Senate (both from Mississippi). In total, it is estimated that 2,000 blacks served in elective offices at the local and national levels. For information on black office holding, see Carol M. Swain, *Black Faces, Black Interests: The Representation of African Americans in Congress* (Cambridge: Harvard University Press, 1993); Eric Foner, *Freedom's Lawmakers* (Baton Rouge: Louisiana State University Press, 1996); and Terry Seip, *The South Returns to Congress* (Baton Rouge: Louisiana State University Press, 1983).

[53] Quotation from Foner, *Freedom's Lawmakers*, 285.

governments' commitment to political equality and full citizenship rights, contained provisions for unrestricted access to the ballot box by registered voters, and mandated the election of judges and local administrators. They also struck down restrictions on office holding and political organization, guaranteed equal access to public services and accommodations, and in many cases also expanded state roles in the provision of social services and workplace regulation.[54]

The center-led transition was also a boon to the Republican Party. As Lawrence Powell has written, it "made Republican politics a live possibility and office holding a thing to be pursued."[55] A leadership cadre of local dissidents (known as "scalawags"), Northern émigrés (known as "carpetbaggers"), and black activists emerged quickly to fill the party's new leadership positions in the states.[56] The electoral base was also biracial. Thus emerged competitive party systems in the southern states dominated by two local parties with national political organizations. One was biracial, the other white.

Strains on the Boundary-Opening Coalition

Democratic opposition to Reconstruction, however, took a major toll on the boundary-opening efforts. Republicans may have controlled most state governments after the war, but local Democrats were anything but passive. They used violence on a massive scale. Several authors have noted that the violence and terror campaigns of the late 1860s and early 1870s had chilling effects on voter turnout and political contestation. They made it impossible in some states for Republicans to run for office and strained Republican Party networks.[57] Fraud was also employed in competitive areas or areas under Democratic control. One historian has labeled the Democratic Party's policy in the South during Reconstruction as a "rule or ruin" policy.[58]

---

54 For information on this period of state constitutional reform, see Jack B. Scroggs, "Carpetbagger Constitutional Reform in the South Atlantic States, 1867–1868," *Journal of Southern History* 27 (November 1961); Richard L. Hume, "Negro Delegates to the State Constitutional conventions of 1867–1869," in *Southern Black Leaders of the Reconstruction Era*, ed. Howard N. Rabinowitz (Urbana: University of Illinois Press, 1982), 129–54; Richard L. Hume, "Carpetbaggers in the Reconstruction South: A Group Portrait of Outside Whites in the 'Black and Tan' Constitutional Conventions,"*Journal of American History* 64 (September 1977); and John Hope Franklin, "Public Welfare in the South during the Reconstruction Era," *Social Service Review* 44 (December 1970).

55 Lawrence Powell, "The Politics of Livelihood: Carpetbaggers in the Deep South," in *Region, Race, and Reconstruction: Essays in Honor of C. Vann Woodward*, eds. J. Morgan Kousser and James M. McPherson (New York: Oxford University Press, 1982), 316.

56 See Foner, *Reconstruction: America's Unfinished Revolution*, 316–20, for a description of the racial composition of support for the Republican Party as well as of the Republican delegations to the constitutional conventions of 1867–68.

57 See, for example, George C. Rable, *But There Was No Peace: The Role of Violence in the Politics of Reconstruction* (Athens: Georgia University Press, 1984); Elizabeth S. Nathans, *Losing the Peace: Georgia Republicans and Reconstruction, 1865–1871* (Baton Rouge: Louisiana University Press, 1968); and Vallely, *The Two Reconstructions*.

58 Powell, "The Politics of Livelihood," 315.

Local Democrats in the states also pursued more legitimate strategies. They exploited local Republican factionalism, appealed to voter racism, and stoked local resentments against national government policies.[59] A plague of national problems in the 1868–76 Grant administration weakened the Republican Party nationally and cost it local electoral support. Having swept the South in the early Reconstruction years, Republicans controlled only the governorships of Florida, South Carolina, and Louisiana by the mid-1870s.[60]

In addition, at the national level the Republican Party's commitment to the Radical Reconstruction program was waning. Even at the height of the Radicals' power, Liberal Republicans expressed concerns about Reconstruction's implications for political stability in the South. They also complained about its precedent-setting potential for governmental activism in other policy realms.[61] Their concerns echoed those of the party's national business supporters, who urged a more conciliatory stand toward the southern political establishment.[62] As the program wore on their concerns intensified. Furthermore, the U.S. Army was stretched thin in the South and was under pressure to deploy troops to the western frontier regions of the country.[63] Republican Liberals thus echoed Democrats' demands for the removal of troops from the South.

And then, of course, there was the issue of race. Civil and voting rights measures passed by congressional Republicans applied to all states of the union. Thus, although motivated by a region-specific democratization agenda, the Republican program made black political empowerment a political issue all over the country. Black populations in the North and West were miniscule at the time, but the cause of local equal rights for blacks was very controversial.[64] In 1867, when the registration summer gave resounding victories to the Republican Party in the South, the same party suffered significant electoral setbacks in the North and West. The Democratic Party, running against Republicans on the race issue, advanced significantly in those regions. Party leaders on both sides of the partisan divide concluded that race had been decisive in the elections' outcomes, a conclusion supported by the

---

[59] See ibid. for a discussion of Southern Republican factional problems.

[60] Hirshson, *Farewell to the Bloody Shirt*, 22.

[61] See Andrew L. Slap, *The Doom of Reconstruction: The Liberal Republicans in the Civil War Era* (New York: Fordham University Press, 2006).

[62] See Hirshson, *Farewell to the Bloody Shirt*, for evidence of business interests lobbying against the continuation of Radical Reconstruction. Bensel, *Yankee Leviathan*, views this as a result of an economic contradiction over national policy between the party's dominant political wing and its economic base. He also writes about the broader effects of social reforms in the South under Radical Reconstruction: "the installation of federally sponsored loyalist groups in the South implied broader policies of wealth distribution that threatened private property rights and had no natural northern constituency." Ibid., 16–17.

[63] See Vincent P. de Santis, "Rutherford Hayes and the Removal of the Troops and the End of Reconstruction," in *Region, Race, and Reconstruction*, 417–50. See also Bensel, *Yankee Leviathan* and Vallely, *The Two Reconstructions*.

[64] Desmond King and Stephen Tuck, "Decentering the South."

defeat of ballot initiatives in favor of black suffrage in Ohio, Minnesota, and Kansas.[65]

The Republican Party was paying a national electoral cost for its aggressive commitment to black rights in the South, and by the early 1870s two different visions for southern democratization competed for influence in the party. One remained committed to the Radical ideal of electoral inclusiveness, biracial Republican leadership, and national enforcement of racial political equality. The other was a restrictive vision of local democratization that contemplated building competitive local Republican parties in which "the Negro will be less prominent for some time to come."[66]

Judicial Review and the Defeat of Reconstruction Constitutionalism

In this context the Supreme Court stepped into the fray with a series of blows to Reconstruction constitutionalism. It started with a court decision that apparently had nothing to do with black enfranchisement or civil rights. In 1873 the Supreme Court ruled on the right of states to regulate sanitary conditions in Louisiana slaughterhouses. However, the decision went to the heart of national enforcement of civil rights under the 14th Amendment to the constitution. In the decision the Court "flatly rejected the idea that the 14th amendment incorporated the Bill of Rights" into state constitutions.[67] It also reaffirmed the concept of "dual citizenship" under federalism. The majority opinion asserted that the 14th Amendment had not expanded "national" rights. To construe the Reconstruction amendments as establishing a wide array of "national" rights, the majority opinion read, would mean "a great departure from the structure and spirit of our institutions." The Court opinion further justified its decision as a defense of federalism, one consistent with its historic role in maintaining, "with a steady and even hand, the *balance between state and federal power* [emphasis added]."[68]

Thus the U.S. Supreme Court, in a defense of 19th-century federalism doctrines, launched its first assault against the remapping of the territorial regime by congressional Republicans. Ultimately, as one author put it, the decision

---

[65] Foner, *Reconstruction: America's Unfinished Revolution*, 315. The Liberal Republican Southern agenda is well documented in James M. McPherson, "Grant or Greeley? The Abolitionist Dilemma in the Election of 1872," *American Historical Review* 71 (October 1965).

[66] Statement by Ohio politician, quoted in Foner, *Reconstruction: America's Unfinished Revolution*, 316. The Liberal agenda was not merely a theoretical proposition. In the national election of 1872 Liberals mounted a major challenge on the "Southern Question" against President Grant's reelection. The Liberals' southern interlocutors were a movement in the Democratic Party known as the "New Departure," which presented itself as a reformed Democratic movement supportive of the Reconstruction constitutional amendments and open to local coalitions between Democrats and conservative Republicans. See James M. McPherson, *The Struggle for Equality: Abolitionists and the Negro in the Civil War and Reconstruction* (Princeton: Princeton University Press, 1964).

[67] Kutler, *The Supreme Court and the Constitution*, 192.

[68] Majority Opinion, U.S. Supreme Court, *The Slaughterhouse Cases*, reprinted in ibid., 235.

had "devastating effects for the freedmen" in the South.[69] However, the extent of the damage was as yet unclear in 1873. If "national" rights were indeed as limited as suggested by the Court, how constrained were federal authorities in protecting the rights of inhabitants of southern states?

Two other cases would settle the question. The first dealt with the federal government's right to prosecute individuals for violating the political rights of citizens. In April 1873 armed whites killed more than 130 blacks over a disputed local election in a Louisiana county (Grant Parish). The state of Louisiana took no action, so a federal court intervened. It tried and convicted a number of the whites involved in the killings. The case was taken to the Supreme Court, and in the 1876 ruling on *The United States v. Cruikshank*, it voided the convictions. Citing the "dual citizenship" principle affirmed in *Slaughterhouse*, the court rejected the imposition of national rights on the states. In addition, in a blow to the 1870 and 1871 Enforcement Acts, it asserted that because the Grant Parish massacre had been committed by individuals, the case did not fall under federal government jurisdiction.

Soon thereafter the Court handed down another decision, this one on voting rights. In *The United States v. Reese* the Court voided the federal conviction of a local Kentucky official for turning a black man away from a voting station for noncompliance with a local tax law (despite the man's efforts to pay the tax). Following on the *Cruikshank* case, the Court ruled that the 15th Amendment did not grant the right to vote. That right could only be granted by the states. According to the Court the 15th Amendment only prohibited state authorities from denying this right on racial grounds. Citing the lack of compelling evidence that the man had been excluded on racial grounds (it was his failure to pay the tax, not his race, apparently), the Court denied federal jurisdiction over the case. In so doing, it crippled the Enforcement Acts, because voting restrictions throughout the South were usually framed in nonracial terms.[70]

Other decisions confirmed these rulings and made continuation of the center-led transition in the South untenable. In the words of historian John Howard,

> The impact of *Cruikshank* and *Reese* was immediate, practical, and devastating.... Along with the defeat of a new enforcement bill in 1875 *Cruikshank* and *Reese* contributed to the demoralization of Southern Republicans. In practical terms the Court had eroded the legal basis for an effective federal presence in the South under circumstances in which state and local authorities could not be expected to protect blacks against Klan and mob terror.... In *Cruikshank* and *Reese* the Supreme Court disarmed one of the sides in the struggle to maintain black access to the ballot.[71]

[69] Stanley I. Kutler, *Judicial Power and Reconstruction Politics* (Chicago: University of Chicago Press 1968), 166.

[70] The following quote in a local newspaper reveals that, in the *Reese* case, the motives were clearly racial: "The city elections passed off quietly.... The negro population largely outnumbers the whites, but a provision of the city charter requiring the payment of a capitation tax as a prerequisite to the right to suffrage disenfranchised about two thirds of the negro vote and left the Democrats an easy victory." Quoted in Howard, *The Shifting Wind*, 106.

[71] Ibid., 109.

In the early 1870s Frederick Douglass had asserted that, for blacks in the southern states, "the Republican Party is the ship and all else is the sea."[72] By the end of the decade, however, southern black voters found themselves increasingly exposed on the region's foreboding political waters. An 1876 deal between northern Republicans and southern Democrats formally ended Reconstruction, and by the early 1890s the national Republican Party conceded the region to the Democratic Party. Absent national regulation of local political and civil rights, most visions of building competitive party systems in the states were chimerical. In addition, national partisan dynamics tempered Republican interest in the South even further. The party scored important electoral victories in the northern and western regions of the country in the 1890s. These successes gave it comfortable control over national political institutions. With electoral successes outside the South, the Republican Party no longer needed the region, or its forlorn black electorate, to be a viable national contender.

II. BOUNDARY CLOSERS SEIZE THE INITIATIVE: PAROCHIALIZATION OF POWER AND THE MAKING OF THE SOLID SOUTH UNDER HOME RULE

> Folkways became stateways.
>
> J. Morgan Kousser[73]

At Reconstruction's end in the late 1870s, the Solid South's architects showed little knowledge of institutional engineering. Although they had rid their bailiwicks of the federal leviathan and stemmed the national Republican Party's local advances, they continued to rely on familiar strategies. Terror campaigns, electoral fraud, and informal political arrangements were the coins of the political realm in the years after Reconstruction's end.[74] The elaborate institutional architecture of boundary control that in later decades gave stability to the Solid South emerged only gradually, as incumbents grasped the potential payoffs of institutional design in a decentralized federal system.

Despite its failings, Reconstruction left significant political and institutional legacies. Southern politics remained contentious and fraught with challenges to Redeemers well after Reconstruction's end. Voter turnout rates in the 1880s remained high for both whites and blacks, and members of both groups voted in large numbers for the opposition. It is for this reason that J. Morgan Kousser,

---

[72] Quoted in James M. McPherson, "Grant or Greeley?," 50.

[73] Kousser, *The Shaping of Southern Politics*, 262.

[74] A local observer in the 1880s described the methods used in a Mississippi election: "Independent candidates were run out of their counties, beaten, or murdered.... Ballot boxes were stuffed, fraudulent returns were made, and thousands of opposition votes were thrown out on technicalities. With mock solemnity, newspapers reported that boxes containing anti-Democratic majorities had been eaten by mules or horses." Quoted in C. Vann Woodward, *Origins of the New South*, 105.

in his landmark study of southern politics, characterized the region in the 1880s as the "Unsolid South."[75]

In this context the primary boundary-control tasks facing Redeemers were to insulate local politics from national competitive trends and construct Democratic Party hegemony without sparking national legislative action. These were daunting tasks, because the making of the Solid South involved destroying living democratic polities. The passing years would reveal how, through trial, error, and interstate partisan collaboration, the early brutality of southern boundary control would give way to higher levels of institutional sophistication.

In a dark sense the southern "Redeemers" and the Democratic Party factions that followed them were pioneers in institutional design – in the design, that is, of authoritarian subnational institutions.[76] Home rule would lead to home-grown authoritarian institutions. Lacking an imported blueprint, southern incumbents created one. Yet it took shape only after a long process of experimentation, adaptation, and discovery.

From Informal Arrangements to the Legalization of Authoritarianism

In the 1880s the Democratic Party lost control of only two states in the South, Tennessee and Virginia. Elsewhere they held onto power. However, their tactics were deficient in key respects. First, they did little to quell political activity. Southern elections were tumultuous affairs, and official violence and fraud only drew national attention. Herein lay the most important deficit in the Redeemer boundary-control strategies: they failed to insulate the states from pressures from the national democratic polity. In fact, they increased the vulnerability of local political systems to outside intervention.

And national Republicans were indignant. Spurred on by media and public outrage in the North about political conditions in the South, congressional Republicans got to work drafting new federal election monitoring bills. Even in the national executive branch, top Republican cabinet officials threatened federal action against the states. After the 1888 elections, when Republicans regained majority control of both houses of congress, the threats acquired new levels of immediacy.

External threats prompted a shift in local strategies and resulted in a new institutional morphology of southern boundary control. Legal measures gradually replaced illegal and informal political arrangements to secure Democratic

---

[75] Kousser, *The Shaping of Southern Politics*, 15.

[76] The "Redeemers" were leaders of Southern Democratic parties that who led the fight against Reconstruction, and controlled Southern state governments at its conclusion. They were mostly conservatives committed to a restoration of the antebellum status quo and white supremacy, and they drew important support from the South's "Black Belt" agricultural aristocracies. In later years, as southern Democratic parties incorporated other political factions, Redeemers often shared power or were displaced by new leadership factions. Their institutional legacy of one-party rule and white supremacy, however, defined local politics until the middle of the 20th century.

Party hegemony. The legal authority of the states would now achieve what was previously done by private individuals or under informal arrangements. Between the late 1880s and the late 1890s an institutional revolution swept the South that codified and consolidated subnational authoritarian rule. "Folkways" indeed became "stateways," and a new legal architecture shielded southern incumbents from the dual threat of Republican partisan incursions and federal regulation of local political regimes.

The logic behind the institutional revolution was simple and powerful. Were the states to make the suppression of democracy legal, their relationship to the national polity would change dramatically. Substituting legal for extralegal methods would alter the meaning of federal monitoring of local electoral processes. U.S. federalism gave states the power to design their political institutions and define the substantive content of political rights. They could thus design disenfranchisement along perfectly legal lines. Under these conditions, federal enforcement of local electoral laws would actually enhance disenfranchisement, not hinder it.

A legal foundation would also give the hegemonic party systems of the South a veneer of national legitimacy. After the brazen abuses of the 1880s, it was clear that the autonomy conferred on states by American federalism was conditioned on political decorum. There were limits on how openly authoritarian a state could be in a nationally democratic country. As one author put it, "any general acceptance of disenfranchisement required a show of democracy."[77] In other words, local authoritarian rule had to be made institutionally compatible with the national democratic polity.

Suppressing the Vote: Institutional Bases of Disenfranchisement

> It eliminates the Negro from politics, and in a perfectly legal way.
>
> Anthony Dickinson Sayre,
> Tennessee State Representative, 1892[78]

In 1894 an Alabama newspaper suggested that reliance on illegal methods of election control had reached a point of exhaustion: "We doubt," the newspaper's editors wrote, "whether there is one more governor and one more legislature in the stuffed ballot box."[79] Alabama was actually a bit behind the times. Most southern states were already in the midst of the institutional revolution that legalized democracy's greatest experience in disenfranchisement. Institutional forms and sequences then varied from state to state. In many states, particularly the early movers, suffrage restriction was primarily a statutory process. State legislatures passed measures that restricted voting rights

---

[77] Valelly, *The Two Reconstructions*, p. 125.

[78] Tennessee state representative Anthony Sayre, commenting on "the Sayre Law," which was passed by the state legislature in 1892. Quoted in Kousser, *The Shaping of Southern Politics*, 134.

[79] *Mobile Daily Register*, November 16, 17, 1892. Quoted in Kouser, *The Shaping of Southern Politics*, 134.

in conformity to the language of existing state constitutions. Between 1888 and 1893, as national Republican regulatory threats loomed large, different states passed a panoply of statutory measures that restricted voting and party competition.

However, all state constitutions in effect at the time had been enacted during Reconstruction. Their democratic guarantees, crafted under northern Republican duress, continued to be problematic to Redeemers. Thus, beginning in 1890, the legal suppression of democracy became a constitutional process in many states. Mississippi began the constitutional reform trend. It held a constitutional convention in 1890 that codified restrictive measures raising the costs and the accessibility of voting. These included poll taxes, literacy requirements, cumbersome registration and residence requirements, clauses requiring proper "understanding" of the constitution, and considerable discretion to local election officials to determine voter eligibility. Known collectively as the "Mississippi Plan," the measures became models for other states as they launched their own constitutional reforms. Between 1890 and 1908 most southern states held constitutional conventions that did away with the Reconstruction era constitutions and enshrined the legal bases for hegemonic party rule.[80] As Robert W. Mickey has written, these state constitutional reforms "constituted foundings of new regimes" throughout the South.[81]

The institutional revolution revealed a very high level of intraregional coordination between state power holders. This coordination would be a hallmark of the Solid South for decades to come. Democratic partisan networks transmitted information about reforms and their effects to officials across the region, thereby facilitating learning and imitation. State officials traveled to other states to learn about the merits of different institutional techniques and returned to apply them in their own states. Successful experiments in one state were thus quickly copied by other states, creating, in a remarkably short period of time, a common and impregnable institutional architecture that varied only in details across subnational political systems.[82]

Two institutional practices proved paramount in the quest for disenfranchisement: the poll tax and literacy requirements. The former imposed an economic cost on voting, and its effects were obviously greatest on low-income voters.[83] However, the poll tax also placed a logistical burden on voters. Some

---

[80] The timing and range of different institutional reforms are well documented in historical literatures. Kousser and Valelly provide particularly useful visual summaries of the types of reforms, their timing, and the states that adopted them. V.O. Key provides a state-by-state description of disenfranchising methods that were in full operation through the middle of the 20th century. See Key, *Southern Politics in State and Nation*.

[81] Robert W. Mickey, *Paths out of Dixie: The Democratization of Authoritarian Enclaves in America's Deep South, 1944–1972* (Princeton: Princeton University Press, 2012).

[82] Valelly notes that the process amounted to a dark version of the "policy diffusion" processes often vaunted by exponents of Federal systems (Valelly, *Two Reconstructions*, 124). Kousser suggests that "the cross-fertilization and coordination between the movements to restrict the suffrage ... amounted to a public conspiracy" (*The Shaping of Southern Politics*, 39).

[83] The amount of the poll tax varied from state to state. However, the usual range was between 75 cents and $2.00. At the turn of the 20th century this was a lot of money. Kousser reports

TABLE 3.1. *Black Voter Turnout in the Southern Ex-Confederate States*

1880	1892 (1st Reform Wave)	1900 (2nd Reform Wave)	1912
61%	36%	17%	1.8%

Note: Averages calculated from Redding and James (2001).

states required payment months in advance of the election. Others required documented proof of payment on Election Day. Election monitors on the ground enjoyed considerable discretion in making final determinations of whether individual voters had adequately fulfilled their poll tax obligations.

Literacy tests were also effective disenfranchisers. In the late 19th century a majority of black residents in the South were illiterate, as were a substantial proportion of whites. This literacy test, combined with laws mandating paper ballots requiring advanced reading skills and prohibiting visual aids or voter assistance by party activists, made voting a daunting task to the region's large illiterate populations.

The effects of legal disenfranchisement on voter turnout were significant. Kousser calculated that voter turnout across the region dropped an average of 37 percent in elections after enactment of the laws, and the average drop in black voter turnout was 62 percent.[84] Matters got worse for black voters as the years went by. A study by Kent Redding and David James reveals that black turnout in Mississippi dropped from 45 percent before the 1890 state constitutional convention to 1 percent in elections held in 1892. In other states black voter suppression was less dramatic in the short term, but over time the numbers disenfranchised measured up to those of Mississippi. In 1880, when voter suppression was pursued largely by illegal means, black voter turnout in the 11 ex-Confederate states averaged 61 percent. By 1912, when the legal architecture of disenfranchisement was well established, black voter turnout in the ex-Confederate states averaged 1.8 percent.[85] It would remain at those levels for decades. Table 3.1 reveals the progression of disenfranchisement as the South's institutional revolution spread over time.

Suppressing Party Competition

If disenfranchisement reduced the size of the electorate, why did a competitive party system in a restricted electorate fail to emerge? After all, an all-white two-party system was a desirable scenario for many Republican leaders. The answer is that a separate set of institutional innovations by southern Democrats targeted electoral contestation. The two most important innovations were

that the bottom 76 percent of the Southern population earned on average $55 to $64 per year (*The Shaping of Southern Politics*, 65). Valelly puts the value in 2001 dollars of a $1 poll tax at $135.00 (*Two Reconstructions*, 124).

[84] Kousser, *The Shaping of Southern Politics*, 240–42.

[85] Kent Redding and David R. James, "Estimating Levels and Modeling Determinants of Black and White Voter Turnout in the South: 1880 to 1912," *Historical Methods* 34 (2001), 141–58.

the malapportionment of seats in state legislatures and the establishment of a whites-only primary system for state Democratic parties.[86]

Democratic incumbents introduced malapportionment into state legislatures in their state constitutional conventions. Subnational malapportionment created a partisan bias in state electoral systems by underrepresenting geographic areas in which opposition parties were likely to prosper.[87] This 19th-century American invention was an institutional counterweight to the geographic determinants of competitive party systems. V. O. Key, who stated that "the existence of a two-party system virtually requires a sectionalism or an urban-rural division of sentiment," noted its function in southern politics and its theoretical importance.[88] In authoritarian provincial contexts, urban jurisdictions provide the demographic basis for the pluralization of party politics. As noted earlier, the province-empowering features of American federalism provided an intergovernmental check on the power of urban municipalities in southern state politics. Subnational legislative malapportionment was the electoral side of that coin. Incumbents drew urban populations off the electoral maps of their states.[89] By neutralizing urban electorates in local politics, malapportionment enhanced Black Belt dominance of state politics and suppressed the development of opposition parties well into the 20th century. As Robert W. Mickey has written, the effects of malapportionment "reverberated through the party state."[90]

Equally damaging to opposition parties was the white primary. By 1915, all states in the Solid South used it. Despite its name, the white primary was not mainly a disenfranchising institution. Disenfranchisement of blacks was achieved by other means. The white primary was an institutional device for limiting party competition by reducing threats from white factionalism to the Democratic Party. Even the "better elements" of a society get into fights. The

---

[86] There were many other measures as well, including high barriers to getting parties on the ballot. It also bears repeating that illegal suppression never lost its place. The Populist Party challenges of the 1890s (which coincided with agrarian Populist revolts in other parts of the country) were crushed by means legal and illegal. In his study of agrarian populist revolts, C. Vann Woodward quotes a lament by a white populist that would have been indistinguishable from any made by black activists: "The feeling of the Democracy toward us is one of murderous hate. I have been shot at many times. Grand juries will not indict our assailants. Courts give us no protection." C. Vann Woodward, *Tom Watson, Agrarian Rebel* (Oxford: Oxford University Press, 1972), 225.

[87] For a discussion of partisan bias in the design of electoral systems, see Ernesto Calvo and Juan Pablo Micozzi, "The Governor's Backyard: A Seat-Vote Model of Electoral Reform for Subnational Multi-Party Races," *Journal of Politics* 67 (November 2005).

[88] Key, *Southern Politics in State and Nation*, 285.

[89] Bruce J. Schulman provides some telling examples of the effects of malapportionment. In Georgia the electoral system awarded rural Chattahoochie County the same electoral weight in the legislature with 132 votes cast as Fulton County, containing the capital city of Atlanta, with 14,092 votes cast. In Alabama and Florida less than one-third of the voting population could elect a majority in the state legislature. See Bruce J. Schulman, *From Cotton-Belt to Sunbelt*, 121.

[90] Mickey, *Paths out of Dixie*.

white primary thus opened the selection of the party's nominees to all white-led political groups. The winner of the primary would go on to certain victory in the general election, backed by a united Democratic Party. The white primary created powerful incentives, therefore, for white dissidents to forego opposition parties and to refrain from appealing to constituencies outside the white Democratic universe. Its main effects were thus felt in the area of contestation – restricting the development of competitive opposition parties. It made the Democratic Party the only game in town.

By the early 1900s the South's internal politics were "solid" indeed. The transition to legal institutional boundary control had effectively insulated local polities from national competitive pressures. As J. Morgan Kousser observed,

This legalized structure far surpassed the informal, customary arrangement in psychological strength. When segregation had been extralegal and ill-defined, Negroes could feel that the state laws and the federal Constitution upheld their right to be treated equally.... A Republican Congress might pass a law guaranteeing fair elections or, as it did twenty-six times from 1880 to 1901, seat Southern Republicans or Populist congressional candidates defeated by fraud. After the revolutionary Southern legal changes, the segregated and disenfranchised retained no hope and no allies.[91]

By the turn of the century the national Republican Party had receded from the local political landscape, as did federal regulatory and legal threats against local political practices.[92] As a result, in the words of one prominent historian, "the region lapsed into a period of political torpor more stultifying than any in its long history."[93]

III. NATIONALIZING INFLUENCE: THE SOLID SOUTH IN AMERICAN POLITICS

The development of the Solid South was tied to active national strategies. At the heart of the territorial architecture of boundary control was the state-level hegemonic party, which was the key institutional linkage between national democratic politics and local authoritarian politics. The authoritarian Solid South was, in Robert Mickey's apt phrase, "doubly embedded in a federal state and a confederal national party."[94]

---

[91] Kousser, *The Shaping of Southern Politics*, 264.

[92] In fact, in many respects they continued to rule in local boundary closers' favor. The U.S. Supreme court continued with rulings favorable to southern political autonomy, including a landmark 1896 decision, *Williams v. Mississippi*, that validated the state's legal social segregation of blacks and whites and opened the way for region-wide adoption of Jim Crow laws that were unchallenged by congressional action.

[93] C. Vann Woodward, *Origins of the New South*, 106.

[94] Robert W. Mickey, *Paths out of Dixie*.

Influence in National Governmental Institutions

Consider the presence of southern legislators in the national congress. The South had a large and influential delegation of legislators in the Senate and the House of Representatives. Hegemonic party control at home ensured that almost all those legislators were Democrats and that they were united in preserving authoritarian rule in the states. Asymmetrical representation in the federal system also enhanced their national influence. The 11 states of the ex-Confederacy held 22 seats in the Senate. In 1906, this constituted nearly one-quarter of all seats in that body. If senators from neighboring or "border" states similarly dominated by Democratic parties were added to the mix, southern Democratic interests by themselves constituted a veto coalition in the Senate. Southern influence in the House of Representatives was also formidable, because conservative southern Democrats were significantly overrepresented in that national body because of the partisan effects of local disenfranchisement.

The institutional hierarchies of the national congress conferred another benefit to the Solid South. The seniority system in both houses determined who controlled congressional committees and other agenda-setting perches.[95] Local hegemonic party rule granted job security to southern legislators, and as a result, they were extremely powerful. In the early 20th century southern Democrats chaired half of all House committees, and in the Senate the proportion was even higher.[96] Southern legislators thus influenced national agenda setting and, through the powers of congressional oversight, also held sway over bureaucratic offices of the national executive branch.

They also influenced agenda setting for the appropriation of federal funds to their states. Fiscal agenda setting would become particularly important during the New Deal period, when central government transfers to the southern states expanded dramatically. It gave incumbents in statehouses and congressional committees the power to limit federal oversight of spending in the states and to temper their potential threats to the local status quo.[97] It also gave state incumbents another tool for asserting supremacy over municipal governments. Southern members of congress, some of whose pork-barrel skills during this period became legendary, were largely loyal to state governors and state legislatures. The state government-congressional nexus gave state authorities the power to ensure that federal aid and investments benefited the interests of state governments and local actors loyal to the dominant factions of the state Democratic Party. The municipal-empowering potential of federal aid

---

[95] On the congressional committee system and its role in the mediation of national sectional conflict, see Bensel, *Sectionalism in American Political Development*.

[96] The Speaker of the House in most years between 1930 to the early 1960s was also a Southerner.

[97] See Bruce J. Schulman, *From Cotton-Belt to Sunbelt*, esp. chapter 5, for discussion of the dilemmas and opportunities posed to southern incumbents by the expansion of federal spending in southern states during the New Deal.

and investment in the South was thus mitigated, further allowing incumbents to postpone the political effects of social transformations wrought by the New Deal.

Black Disenfranchisement: The National Scale of a Local Strategy

Black disenfranchisement played a strategic role in the local and national web of southern boundary control. The racial issue makes the U.S. case unique among those explored in this book. However, in addition to the singular dimensions of racism in American history, there was also a strategic dimension to disenfranchisement that should be of interest to students of territorial politics and democratization. To take an overused but apt term, local black disenfranchisement was the linchpin in an assembly of national and local territorial strategies. Remove it and the assembly no longer held together.

The black electorate occupied a strategic place in local opposition politics in the 1880s. Despised as they may have been by white supremacists of all stripes, southern blacks were nevertheless a reservoir of electoral support for any white-led dissident movement. They were thus key to the logic of political contestation of southern politics. As an Arkansas black newspaper commented at the time, "the greatest danger that threatens Democratic supremacy in the south is that the 'out faction' always gravitates toward the Negro and secures his aid to rout the 'ins.'"[98]

Thus, disenfranchisement had a clear local partisan effect. It also had a stabilizing effect. By removing structural incentives for dissident white electoral challenges to the Democratic Party, it reduced instability in the hegemonic partisan order. Disenfranchisement also helped insulate local politics from national competitive pressures. National Republicans would continue to look south as long as a reservoir of black electoral support made local forays electorally feasible. Black disenfranchisement thus reduced local incumbents' vulnerability to external partisan challenges. Without it, the construction of subnational hegemonic party systems was unthinkable.

Black disenfranchisement also contributed to the nationalization of southern influence. It amplified the overrepresentation of conservative Democratic interests in the national congress and Electoral College and strengthened local leverage over the national Democratic Party. With these advantages, southern incumbents were able to monopolize all economic and political linkages between the states and the national political system. The site of this political action was local, but its scale was truly national. Completing a decidedly non-virtuous cycle of territorial politics, the national effects came back to enhance incumbents' control over local polities (see Figure 3.3). It is thus not surprising that Democrats pursued this particular institution with such determination over the decades.

[98] Quoted in Kousser, *The Shaping of Southern Politics*, 18.

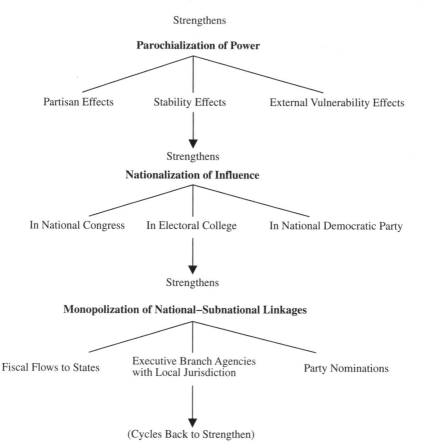

Southern Democrats Disenfranchise Local Black Voters:

Strengthens

Parochialization of Power

Partisan Effects   Stability Effects   External Vulnerability Effects

Strengthens
Nationalization of Influence

In National Congress   In Electoral College   In National Democratic Party

Strengthens

Monopolization of National–Subnational Linkages

Fiscal Flows to States   Executive Branch Agencies   Party Nominations
                           with Local Jurisdiction

(Cycles Back to Strengthen)

Local Boundary Control by Southern Democrats

FIGURE 3.3. The Strategic Value of Black Disenfranchisement: A Local Strategy's National Effects

The Southern Block in Congress: More about Boundary Control than Regional Economic Interests

The southern Democrats' national presence provided a strong shield against external intrusions against their political systems. In fact, this was its most important political function. The southern legislative bloc was far more important for boundary control than it was for the advancement of other southern regional interests.

Two studies reveal the importance of regional unity in the national congress for safeguarding the institutional supports of local authoritarian rule. In his study of roll-call voting in the 1930s and 1940s, V. O. Key found southern legislative cohesion to be extraordinarily high in votes on national civil rights legislation, particularly regarding federal regulation of race relations. Cohesion on these issues was higher than on any other issue (or by any other regional group). "The common element in the critical votes," he wrote, "is objection to Federal intervention."[99] In a 1993 study, Katznelson, Geiger, and Kryder go further. They confirm Key's findings about southern legislative cohesion against national civil rights legislation but also find that during the New Deal years their unity and clout extended to federal action threatening the socioeconomic foundations of local authoritarian rule. In vote after vote, the southern legislative bloc, often in alliance with conservative Republicans, thwarted legislative initiatives on labor rights and social welfare that were integral to the national Democratic Party's New Deal agenda. On all other issues, even those linked to regional economic interests, southern unity was lower and at a level almost indistinguishable from that of other regional groups.[100]

These and other studies reveal the extent to which the much vaunted "southern veto" in the national congress was less a vehicle for the protection of southern regional interests than it was for the protection of southern authoritarianism. Southern legislators could differ with one another on tax policy, they could compete against one another for patronage resources, and they could break ranks with their leadership on a range of other national or regional legislative priorities. However, when it came to federal action affecting the political or socioeconomic bases of local authoritarianism, the South's redoubtable contingent of national legislators closed ranks around boundary control.

Southern Influence in the National Democratic Party

Southern leaders controlled the national Democratic Party from the late 1890s until the early 1930s. They were the party's majority faction during that period. Southern state power brokers could be counted on by the national party to deliver large blocs of votes for the party's presidential candidates and large congressional delegations. These mitigated the effects of the party's fluctuating electoral fortunes elsewhere over the decades. Whereas in other regions the Democratic Party managed to win at best 40 percent of the vote in congressional elections from the late 1890s to the early 1930s, in southern states votes for Democrats never dropped below 86 percent.[101] From 1896 to 1932 southerners comprised two-thirds of the total Democratic delegation in the

---

[99] Key, *Southern Politics in State and Nation*, 352.

[100] Ira Katznelson, Kim Geiger, and Daniel Kryder, "Limiting Liberalism: The Southern Veto in Congress, 1933–1950," *Political Science Quarterly* 108 (1993), 302. The authors also note that the southern veto not only prevented the expansion of New Deal economic rights agendas into the South but also tempered the national Democratic Party's social democratic agenda in the country as a whole. This repeated a pattern visible at the turn of the century: the annulment of federal voting rights statutes at the turn of the century caused setbacks in black voting rights elsewhere, as state authorities in the North and West also had the threat of federal regulation lifted against them.

[101] Ibid., 284.

national congress. After 1932 the Democratic Party expanded its electorates significantly in the North and West, and southern Democrats became a minority faction. However, they continued to wield veto power within the national congressional delegation.[102]

The Electoral College system for the election of presidents in the federal system conferred another source of southern leverage over the Democratic Party. Interestingly, no Southerner ever headed a Democratic presidential ticket. However, up to the 1930s southern Democrats held a veto over the party's presidential nominations. From 1900 to the late 1920s its share of the Democratic Party's total Electoral College vote ranged from a low of around 28 percent in 1912 to more than 90 percent in 1924.[103] In addition, an internal party rule requiring a two-thirds majority of convention delegates to determine the party's presidential nominee (a rule jealously guarded by the party's southern faction) solidified the region's veto influence in Democratic Party presidential politics.

During the heydays of the Solid South, local Democratic incumbents enjoyed the best of all possible worlds in their relationship with the national Democratic Party: they had both local autonomy and national leverage. The party's confederal structure granted state parties the former attribute. State parties ran their own primaries, selected their own delegates to national party bodies, and devised their own internal governance rules. Their leaders also controlled vital national–subnational institutional linkages within the party, including the nomination of candidates for federal positions and national party positions and resource flows between the national and state parties. In return, state party leaders were expected to deliver electoral votes to the national party and help it remain nationally competitive. This they did in abundance, and as a result they reinforced their leverage over the national party. The privilege of local autonomy combined with the luxury of national leverage constituted the twin pillars of the southern relationship with the national Democratic Party.

No period captures this as dramatically as the New Deal era in the 1930s and 1940s. The Democratic Party's sweeping electoral victories made it a truly national party. The southern Democratic faction was now a minority faction. The party's northern wing was committed to an agenda of social and economic reform that was threatening to the political orders of the southern states in many ways. Nevertheless, the Solid South was a vital electoral component of the New Deal coalition. Even as a reactionary core, it was a necessary ingredient of the coalition's national electoral viability. It delivered a solid regional bloc of votes to Franklin Roosevelt in 1932, and throughout his presidency its share of the Democratic Party's Electoral College votes never went below 23 percent.[104] Furthermore, by virtue of their institutional power in the Congress,

---

[102] Ibid., 284.
[103] Calculated from electoral data accessible online at "270 to Win," http://www.270towin.com/.
[104] Ibid.

southern Democrats were critical to the national implementation of New Deal policies.

As a result, southern Democrats played two roles in the New Deal, one enabling and one obstructive. They threw their support behind the federal promotion of economic development, economic relief, and public works, while blocking civil and political rights agendas threatening to their bailiwicks. For southern Democrats there was much to like in the New Deal, and they were well situated institutionally to capture its benefits. They controlled all institutional linkages regulating the flows of patronage to their states and were capable of monitoring the actions of local branches of the federal bureaucracies implementing New Deal programs. Their problems arose when pro-civil rights coalitions in the national party threatened to advance their agendas throughout the country. Lacking majorities in the Congress to prevent civil rights issues from coming to the fore, the southern bloc resorted to its obstructive institutional power. In the words of Katznelson and colleagues, "they dealt with their defensive quandary by controlling the legislative agenda and utilizing the filibuster."[105]

Thus, during this period southern Democrats possessed institutional resources to extract economic benefits from the New Deal *and* to block its challenges to local authoritarian rule. In effect, they held the New Deal hostage to northern Democratic acquiescence to subnational authoritarian rule. President Roosevelt himself acknowledged this situation to a group of black leaders seeking his support for federal anti-lynching legislation in the 1930s. He could not support the legislation, he explained, because southern legislators "are chairmen or occupy strategic places on most of the Senate and House committees. If I come out for the anti-lynching bill now, they will block every bill I ask Congress to pass.... I just can't take that risk."[106]

Over time the New Deal's effects, some of them imperceptible at the time, would undermine the social supports of authoritarianism in the southern states. However, as the New Deal's reformist years came to an end, the South's traditional power structures remained intact. It would take more than two decades of political mobilization and shifting partisan territorial dynamics to bring about a region-wide democratic transition. This one, like the first, would be a center-led transition. That fact stands as the final testament to the power of southern boundary control. For despite the resilience and courage of local civil rights movements in the mid-20th century, they, by themselves, were no match for the institutionally entrenched authoritarian orders. In the words of J. Morgan Kousser, "shackled by a political system that largely prevented even minimal, gradualist responses... the South had to wait for national forces to compel it to begin again the process of social and political reconstruction."[107]

---

[105] Katznelson et al., "Limiting Liberalism," 294.

[106] Quoted in Kari Frederickson, *The Dixiecrat Revolt and the End of the Solid South: 1932–1968* (Chapel Hill University of North Carolina Press), 20.

[107] Kousser, *The Shaping of Southern Politics*, xiii.

CONCLUSION

The Solid South did not emerge: it was built. It was built brutally and chaotically at first, but with increasing institutional sophistication as the years wore on. Its construction required the defeat of a center-led democratic transition of massive proportions and, subsequently, the destruction of living democratic polities. As a case of boundary control it has no historical equal.

What insights does this remarkable case provide as we shift our sights to another hemisphere and another century? At a very general level the case reveals that the political universe of the southern states in the 80 years following the Civil War was decidedly nonlocal. Southern incumbents created closed political regimes that isolated local opponents and kept outsiders at bay. However, they maintained those regimes in place via a seamless tapestry of national and local strategies. The harsh control of local authoritarian political systems was linked to the flexible manipulation of the national democratic order. The Solid South lasted so long largely because local incumbents succeeded in making it institutionally compatible with national democratic politics and politically useful to national democratic actors.

This case study also reveals the intricate connections between federalism and territorial democratization in U.S. political development. One cannot be understood without the other, and the story of the Solid South is as much a story about federalism as it is about democratization. Democratization of the U.S. southern states in the late 19th century was predicated on the political centralization of federalism – namely, granting the national government the power to define the content of rights in the states and to enforce them. The defeat of that centralization project shifted the strategic terrain away from local and national boundary openers and gave southern incumbents institutional cover to consolidate local authoritarian rule.

The national territorial regime also affected the structure of subnational authoritarian control. Under centralized federalism during Reconstruction, southern incumbents relied on informal and illegal tactics. After the restoration of decentralized federalism, their tactics became institutional. U.S. federalism granted states wide-ranging powers to design local institutions and electoral laws, and southern incumbents gradually took advantage of those powers to make the suppression of democracy legal. It was the legalization of authoritarian rule that made it impregnable to national competitive and regulatory pressures, and it was the national territorial regime that made that legalization possible. The asymmetrical representation of states in national politics also aided boundary control's national strategies by bolstering southern leverage in the congress, the Electoral College, and the national Democratic Party. Furthermore, the province-empowering features of U.S. federalism tempered the boundary-opening potential of urban governments and urban electorates, giving state incumbents yet another institutional tool for dominating jurisdictions inside state boundaries.

The Solid South also provides insights into party politics and its relationship to boundary control. Local authoritarianism was buttressed by the construction of subnational hegemonic parties, and V. O. Key's suggestion that such parties were as important to "national affairs" as they were to local control is amply borne out by the evidence. They were important to incumbents' influence across the vertical hierarchies of the territorial system. They provided horizontal networks for coordinated action across state lines. They also gave southern incumbents enormous influence in the national Democratic Party, and the national party remained a steadfast protector of the authoritarian political orders of their states.

A lingering question remains. Could the Solid South have emerged in the absence of the institutional sequences stressed in this chapter? Was the defeat of federalism's centralization necessary for the consolidation of authoritarian rule in the southern states? After all, by Reconstruction's end southern Democrats had reversed many of the boundary openers' advances in the region. Northern exhaustion, shifting Republican territorial interests, and the sheer determination and power of southern Democrats may well have been enough to stem territorial democratization in the region.

We can only speculate about the answer. However, it is more than reasonable to suggest that, in the centralized territorial regime envisaged by Republican boundary openers, the southern political landscape would have looked more like a mosaic of democratic and authoritarian states than the unassailable regional fortress it became. Fluctuating northern political will would have created inconsistent patterns of opposition party-building, but the contentious nature of southern politics would have provided constant temptations for national interventions in the region. The democratic constitutions crafted during Reconstruction and a federal system that formally endowed *national* rights to state inhabitants would have remained in place, depriving southern boundary closers of the benefits of legalized authoritarianism. Party-led transitions would have remained an ongoing possibility in many states, and the outcasts of their political orders would not have been compelled to wait a half-century for a second center-led transition to deliver them from authoritarian rule.

4

Boundary Control in Democratizing Argentina

> A close relationship exists between the constitutional structure and the authoritarian character of the political regime.[1]

In 1983 party competition erupted across Argentina's federal political system unlike any other time in its history. After decades of military governments and restricted democratic regimes, free elections transformed the country's political landscape. Two national parties, the *Unión Cívica Radical* (Radical Party [UCR]) and the *Partido Justicialista* (Peronist Party [PJ]) dominated competition in national and subnational elections. In presidential politics, the Radical Party had unshackled the country from the "iron law" of Argentine elections, which had stipulated the invincibility of the Peronist Party whenever elections were free and fair. Political observers hailed the emergence of a truly competitive two-party system in national politics.

The competitive national wave put pressure on the parochial worlds of provincial politics. Boisterous contests between parties emerged not only in provinces with long histories of political pluralism but also in sleepy oligarchies across the country's periphery. In several of these provinces local Peronist politicians, accustomed for decades to the job security of clan-controlled patronage machines, found their grips on the local polity weakening. Once-hegemonic systems became competitive as an ascendant national Radical Party bolstered local opposition parties.

If observers were hopeful that the democratic wave from national politics would wash away Argentina's long-standing authoritarian subnational enclaves, however, they would be sorely disappointed. Today Argentina's federal political system is as much a mix of democratic and authoritarian provinces

---

[1] Comment on the province of Santiago del Estero in a 2004 federal government report to the Argentine national congress. Gobierno de la Intervención Federal en la Provincia de Santiago del Estero, *Séptimo Informe De La Intervención Federal Al Honorable Congreso De La Nación* (2004), ch 2: 1.

as it was decades ago. This fact has been documented both by scholarly case studies of provinces and by journalistic reporting in Argentina.[2] Most recently it has also been established by comparative quantitative measurements of regime characteristics in Argentine provinces. In two separate studies of post-1983 politics, Augustina Giraudy and Carlos Gervasoni reveal striking variations in the level of democracy across provinces. Giraudy describes 5 provinces, 20 percent of the total, as clearly "undemocratic"; 5 as having attained "high and sustained levels of democracy"; and the remaining 14 existing in varying states of democratic health.[3] Using different methods and measurement criteria, Gervasoni reaches similar conclusions, suggesting that, when it comes to subnational democracy in Argentina, "there is plenty of inter-provincial variance to be explained."[4]

We saw in the preceding chapter on the United States that the mixes of boundary-control strategies – violent and nonviolent, legal and illegal – shifted with features of the national territorial regime. This chapter describes boundary-control conflicts in a federal regime that is peripheralized. Violence and illegality play their parts in Argentine subnational authoritarianism. However, the peripheralized federal regime provides legal means for incumbents to make their regimes impregnable. Hegemonic party systems are very hard to displace. Local constitutions and electoral laws see to that. In addition, a wave of provincial constitutional reforms in several provinces since the 1980s has restricted democracy, as our 19th-century Tennessee legislator would have put it, "in a perfectly legal way."

---

[2] Scholarly case studies include Edward L. Gibson, "Boundary Control: Subnational Authoritarianism in Democratic Countries," *World Politics* 58, no. 1 (2005); Rebecca Bill Chavez, "The Construction of the Rule of Law in Argentina: A Tale of Two Provinces," *Comparative Politics* 35, no. 4 (2003); and Jaqueline Behrend, "The Unevenness of Democracy at the Subnational Level: Provincial Closed Games in Argentina," *Latin American Research Review* 46, no. 1 (2011). Books by journalists include Raúl Dargoltz et al., *Santiago: El Ala Que Brota* (Buenos Aires: Editorial Utopías, 2005); Sergio Carreras, *El Reino De Los Juárez: Medio Siglo De Miseria, Terror, Y Desmesura En Santiago Del Estero* (Buenos Aires: Aguilar, 2004); Alejandra Dandan, Silvina Heguy, and Julio Rodríguez, *Los Juárez: Terror, Corrupción, y Caudillos en la Política Argentina* (Buenos Aires: Grupo Editorial Norma, 2004), 269–72; and Miguel Wiñazki, Daniel Malnati, and Gabriel Michi, *El Adolfo: Crónicas Del Fascismo Mágico* (Buenos Aires: Planeta, 2002).

[3] Agustina Giraudy, "The Politics of Subnational Undemocratic Regime Reproduction in Argentina and Mexico," *Journal of Politics in Latin America* 2 (2010): 58. The five "least democratic" provinces in Giraudy's ranking are San Luis, Santiago del Estero, La Rioja, Santa Cruz, and Formosa. The most democratic are Mendoza, San Juan, the City of Buenos Aires (a Federal District), Chubut, and Entre Rios.

[4] Carlos Gervasoni, "Measuring Variance in Subnational Regimes: Results from an Expert-Based Operationalization of Democracy in the Argentine Provinces," *Journal of Politics in Latin America* 2 (2010), 42. Gervasoni is loath to characterize any province as authoritarian, preferring to analyze those at the low end of his "subnational democracy index" as "hybrid regimes" possessing both authoritarian and democratic attributes. Nevertheless, his ranking of provincial regimes is similar to Giraudy's. For Gervasoni's ranking according to his subnational democracy index, see "A Rentier Theory of Subnational Regimes," *World Politics* 62, no. 2 (2010).

FIGURE 4.1. Argentina: Provinces
Source: Hugo Ahlenius, Nordpil, 2012

Just as these factors affect the way subnational authoritarian regimes are made, they also shape how they are unmade. Transitions from subnational authoritarian rule in Argentina tend to be center-led. The defeat of local hegemonic parties follows an intervention by national governmental authorities that changes the local rules of the game and creates a more level playing field for opposition parties in local electoral contests. We now turn to a brief review of institutional and partisan dimensions of Argentine federalism (Figure 4.1).

I. STRUCTURING THE STRATEGIC TERRAIN: ARGENTINA'S TERRITORIAL REGIME

Argentina's constitutional framers modeled their country's federal system on 19th-century American federalism. Succeeding generations of institutional engineers kept its basic elements in place. As a result, Argentina's federal territorial regime today is highly peripheralized. On one hand it is politically decentralized. The design of provincial constitutions and of electoral laws is the exclusive domain of provincial authorities, and governors have wide discretion over local economic and political life. On the other hand it is asymmetrical in the representation of provinces in national institutions. Low-population provinces are significantly overrepresented in the national legislature, and until a 1994 constitutional reform, they were also overrepresented in an electoral college that elected the country's president. In subnational politics Argentine federalism is province-empowering. The provincial tier of government dominates intergovernmental relations within the province, and governors are the key political brokers in the national territorial system.[5]

Subnational Autonomy and Argentine Federalism

Argentina's national government is composed of a presidential executive and a bicameral legislature consisting of a senate and a lower chamber. Presidents and national legislators from each province are elected according to procedures established in the national constitution and national electoral laws. However, when it comes to the election of subnational officials (for example, governors or provincial legislators), the country's 24 provincial districts (including the Federal District) enjoy complete political autonomy. Each is governed by its own constitution, drafted by local constituent assemblies. The national constitution stipulates that provinces must adhere to a "republican" form of government, but leaves its institutional form to the discretion of local authorities.[6] As a

---

[5] See Constitucion Nacional Argentina, especially Articles 5, 122, and 123. Until the 1994 constitutional reform another province-empowering feature was the election of national senators by provincial legislatures. Provincial authorities (usually governors), rather than electorates in urban hubs, thus had major sway over the composition of senate delegations.

[6] Article 5 of the Argentine constitution states that each province will design its own constitution, with the only proviso being that it be in accordance with the "representative republican system and the guarantees of the national constitution." The same article gives provinces the power

result, Argentina is an assortment of distinctive provincial political systems. The structure, size, and powers of provincial legislative branches vary considerably. In 2010, 8 provinces had bicameral legislatures, whereas the other 16 had unicameral legislatures. Furthermore, each province is responsible for designing the electoral laws and districts that govern the election of representatives to provincial legislatures. Provincial electoral systems thus vary widely and change often. They consist of combinations of proportional representation systems, single-member district systems, and mixed formulas for electing legislators and municipal authorities. Their rules governing the elections of governors and their powers over other branches of government also vary widely.[7]

There is a cloud hanging over this assembly of autonomous provinces, however: the central government's power of "federal intervention." Argentina's constitutional framers adopted a key clause from the U.S. constitution – the guarantee clause that mandates that the central government guarantee a "republican form of government" in all every state. This was the "sleeping giant" in the constitution mobilized by U.S. Republicans to launch Reconstruction after the 1861–65 Civil War. In Argentina this power was to be no sleeping giant.[8] It was awake from the constitution's adoption and has been used by presidents against provincial rivals to this day.[9]

Yet this central government prerogative does not change the peripheralized nature of Argentine federalism. The power of federal intervention is used on an ad hoc basis. The partisan stars have to be properly aligned for the president to muster political support from congress and governors to launch federal

to design their "municipal regime." In the section on provincial political systems, Article 122 puts the design of provincial political regimes well out of the reach of the national government. It states that provinces "create their own institutions and are governed by them. They elect their governors, legislators, and other provincial authorities, *without intervention by the federal government*" (emphasis added).

[7] For in-depth studies of contemporary subnational political systems in Argentina, see Ernesto Calvo and Marcelo Escolar, *La Nueva Política De Partidos En La Argentina: Crisis Política, Realineamientos Partidarios Y Reforma Electoral* (Buenos Aires: Prometeo: Pent, 2005); Edward L. Gibson and Julieta Suarez-Cao, "Federalized Party Systems and Subnational Party Competition: Theory and an Empirical Application to Argentina," *Comparative Politics* 43, no. 1 (2010).

[8] The Argentine guarantee clause is in Article 5. In contrast to the U.S. constitution, the Argentine constitution includes an additional article (Article 6) granting the federal government the power to intervene in the provinces for this purpose.

[9] The scope of central government interventions has varied; sometimes the national government has virtually occupied the province and displaced the occupants of all branches of government. At other times they have only targeted one branch of government or have interrupted local political developments temporarily without altering the local political status quo. Studies have also shown that federal interventions have also tended to have strong partisan objectives. See, for example, Mario Serrafero, "La Intervención Federal En Argentina. Experiencia Y Jurisprudencia" (2009), available online at http://www.forumfed.org/libdocs/Misc/Arg8_Serrafero%20paper%20Esp.pdf]. See also Ana María Mustapic, "Conflictos Institucionales Durante El Primer Gobierno Radical: 1916–1922," *Desarrollo Económico* 24, no. 93 (1984).

interventions. In contrast, the autonomy granted to provinces by the constitution is continuous and systematic. It is interrupted very infrequently by federal interventions, and only after major local missteps or shifts in the territorial interests of national political actors.

Interprovincial Power and Argentine Federalism

Argentina's federal system overrepresents poor and underpopulated territories more than any federal system in the world. In a number of studies the national senate has ranked highest on scales of territorial overrepresentation among the world's upper chambers.[10] In the 1990s the 19 smallest provinces, with 30 percent of the country's population, held 40 of 48 seats in the senate – 83 percent of the total. This overrepresentation extends to the lower chamber, where the 19 smallest provinces, with 30 percent of the population, hold 52 percent of the seats.[11]

Asymmetrical provincial representation in national politics has several implications for boundary control. Coalitions of overrepresented provinces that depend on central transfers to fund their provincial budgets are formidable opponents in negotiations with the central government and the country's richer provinces. Over time they have perpetuated a marked redistributive bias in their favor in formulas for national revenue-sharing.[12] This aspect of Argentine federalism helps perpetuate subnational authoritarianism under which federal transfers are key to the operation of the clientelistic machines of provincial hegemonic parties. By increasing the national leverage of local incumbents, asymmetrical representation makes it costly for national authorities to challenge the local status quo.

The institutional overrepresentation of the periphery has also had consequences for party development. Historically, no winning national electoral or legislative coalition could be put together without support in peripheral provinces. Elections in the urbanized and economically prosperous regions have tended to be competitive affairs. Therefore, victorious national parties tend to be those with institutional ties to regional power brokers capable of delivering the vote in the "interior" regions of the country.[13]

---

[10] Edward L. Gibson, *Federalism and Democracy in Latin America* (Baltimore: Johns Hopkins University Press, 2004); Richard Snyder and David Samuels, "Legislative Malapportionment in Latin America: Historical and Comparative Perspectives," in *Federalism and Democracy in Latin America*, ed. Edward L. Gibson (Baltimore: Johns Hopkins University Press, 2004); 131–72. Alfred Stepan, "Toward a New Comparative Politics of Federalism, Multinationalism, and Democracy: Beyond Rikerian Federalism," in *Federalism and Democracy in Latin America*, ed. Edward L. Gibson (Baltimore: Johns Hopkins University Press, 2004), 29–84.

[11] See Gibson and Calvo, "Federalism and Low-Maintenance Constituencies."

[12] See Larry Sawers, *The Other Argentina: The Interior and National Development* (Boulder: Westview Press, 1996).

[13] After the mid-20th century, the Peronist Party (PJ) was the dominant party in the Argentine periphery. See Manuel Mora y Araujo and Ignacio Llorente, *El Voto Peronista* (Buenos Aires:

Inside Subnational Jurisdictions: Province-Empowering Features of Argentine Federalism

Argentina's territorial regime does not only decentralize power to provinces; it also concentrates power in the hands of governors. In provinces governors have no peer. They tower over mayors and cast their giant shadows over provincial and national legislators. Some of their powers are the product of evolved informal practices. However, they are buttressed by prerogatives granted to governors by the national constitution and by the arrangements of fiscal federalism.

Constitutional Design and Subnational Power: Strong Provinces, Weak Cities

Argentine federalism establishes the constitutional supremacy of provincial governments over municipal governments. Constitutional framers rendered municipal governments virtual administrative dependencies of provincial governments. Article 5 of the national constitution makes provincial constitutions responsible for guaranteeing the autonomy of municipal governments, but remains silent on the definition and attributes of municipal autonomy. As a result, to this day only half of the country's provinces formally recognize municipalities as autonomous governmental entities.[14] Furthermore, where formal recognition exists, it is often tempered by informal practices and sweeping provincial powers over municipal political regimes. Constitutional Article 123 (governing provincial political systems) reaffirms that each provincial constitution will "assure" municipal autonomy, but gives provincial authorities the power to "regulate its reach and content in the institutional, political, administrative, economic, and financial orders." The hegemony of governors over mayors in provincial life has thus been a regular feature of Argentine federalism to this day. As Kent Eaton has written, "throughout the country provinces have trumped municipalities as the key subnational level of government."[15]

Dependent Provinces, Strong Governors: The Paradox of Fiscal Federalism

Fiscal federalism enhances the power of governors and compounds the subordination of municipal governments in significant ways. Argentina's fiscal federal regime is set up as an automatic revenue-sharing program whereby the

---

Editorial Sudamericana, 1980) and Edward L. Gibson, "The Populist Road to Market Reform: Policy and Electoral Coalitions in Mexico and Argentina," *World Politics* 49 (1997).

[14] Tracy Beth Fenwick, "The Institutional Feasibility of National-Local Policy Collaboration: Insights from Brazil and Argentina," *Journal of Politics in Latin America* 2 (2010).

[15] Kent Eaton, *Politics beyond the Capital: The Design of Subnational Institutions in South America* (Stanford: Stanford University Press, 2004), 38. Municipal autonomy has made some headway in the last decade, particularly in more developed and urbanized provinces.

central government has exclusive responsibility for collecting a range of taxes throughout the country and then sharing those proceeds with the provinces according to a preset formula. The system, known as "co-participation," is vital to provincial economies. Many provinces depend on central government transfers to finance their budgets. In the 19 least developed provinces, central government transfers financed 80 percent of their government budgets in the 1990s. In some provinces the proportion exceeded 90 percent.[16] Furthermore, in most of these provinces the public sector is the largest employer. Public employment and the central fiscal transfers that sustain it are the biggest economic game in town.

Co-participation transfers are delivered directly to provincial governors, who have discretion over their local distribution. Furthermore, all transferred funds are unconditional – they are not earmarked for specific purposes by the central government. How the funds are spent locally is the purview of provincial authorities.[17]

Thus, ironically, economic dependence on fiscal transfers does not translate into political dependence of provincial incumbents on the center. Argentine fiscal federalism has the counterintuitive effect of rendering provinces economically dependent on the central government while rendering their rulers politically autonomous. And, where central government transfers are the primary funders of provincial governments and local employment, the system makes governors local economic hegemons.[18]

In authoritarian provinces, cities are the breeding ground of opposition politics. The route to party-led provincial democratization runs through the capital and the main urban hubs: one breaches the province by capturing the city. However, the province-empowering features of Argentine federalism can make the province an impregnable fortress. Constraints on the autonomy and financial independence of cities often reduce mayors to mere supplicants of governors regardless of party affiliation. The city can therefore be a paltry prize for a national party and an ineffective staging ground for an opposition assault on the governor's mansion.

---

[16] See Gibson and Calvo, "Federalism and Low-Maintenance Constituencies." 42. See also Pablo T. Spiller and Mariano Tommasi, *The Institutional Foundations of Public Policy in Argentina* (New York: Cambridge University Press, 2007).

[17] After 2005, the government of President Nestor Kirchner centralized some fiscal and monetary flows between the central government and the provinces (although it did not alter the structure of the co-participation system itself). See Germán Lodola, "Gobierno Nacional, Gobernadores, e Intendentes en el Período Kirchnerista," in Andrés Malamud and Miguel De Luca, Eds., *La Política en los Tiempos de los Kirchner*, Buenos Aires: Eudeba (2011), 215–25. Kent Eaton provides a compelling account of how the provinces have used their collective leverage against the central government to increase their receipt of co-participation revenues over the last century. See Eaton, *Politics beyond the Capital.*

[18] Carlos Gervasoni describes many Argentine provincial economies as "rentier" economies, analogous to those of oil-producing states, where democratic development is stifled by local economic dependence on external revenues that are monopolistically controlled by local incumbents. See Gervasoni, "A Rentier Theory of Subnational Regimes."

II. BOUNDARY CONTROL IN ARGENTINA: A NATIONAL PERSPECTIVE

The Peronist Party today is the most important national party in Argentina's provinces. It is the only party that has a competitive presence in all provinces of the country. It is not hegemonic everywhere, however. In fact, in most provinces it competes against local chapters of the Radical Party or against provincial parties. Nor has it been the only party with hegemonic control of provincial politics. At different times in the 20th century the Radical Party played that role in a number of provinces. In other provinces, provincial parties, led by conservative political families that date back to the pre-mass politics era, held sway over local politics.

Hegemony by purely provincial parties, however, is largely a thing of the past. In contemporary Argentine politics, subnational hegemonic parties are a Peronist phenomenon.[19] Odds are good today that an individual parachuting randomly into an Argentine province will land in one governed by the Peronist Party. Yet if that parachutist lands in an authoritarian province, odds are overwhelming that a Peronist politician will occupy the governor's mansion.

National Democracy and Subnational Party-Led Challenges

Provincial boundary closers confronted a paradoxical bundle of opportunities and challenges from national politics in the 1980s. On the one hand, they were helped in their efforts by a cooperative Radical Party president. On the other hand, an expanding national Radical Party threatened to upset their control of local political systems. The Radical Party and the Radical president, each driven by different territorial interests, worked at cross-purposes in subnational politics.

Many territorial aspects of the national transition aided Peronist subnational politicians. Even though the Radical Party had won the presidency, it controlled a minority of governorships, and the Peronist Party had a firm hold on the national senate.[20] It also largely controlled the realm of provincial politics. The territorial balance between the parties put the central government at a disadvantage in negotiations with the provinces about federal matters. During the 1980s, Peronist-led coalitions of governors extracted important

---

[19] One exception may be the province of Neuquén, governed by the *Movimiento Popular Neuquino*, a provincial party with Peronist origins, since the early 1960s. The province's regime, however, tends to be ranked in the middle range according to general democracy measurements. See, Gervasoni, "Measuring Variance in Subnational Regimes," and Giraudi, "The Politics of Subnational Undemocratic Regime Reproduction."

[20] In 1983, the PJ controlled 45 percent of the provinces (12 of 22), 32 percent were governed by the UCR (7 provinces), and the other 14 percent were in the hands of provincial parties (3 provinces). Peronist control of the senate during this period was enhanced by the fact that national senators were elected by provincial legislatures. Most Peronist governors enjoyed majorities in their provincial legislatures, ensuring that their national senators would be Peronist senators.

fiscal concessions from the central government.[21] This was a fiscal bonanza for all provinces, but less populated provinces particularly benefited from the redistributive bias of the newly renegotiated revenue-sharing system. The new fiscal arrangements produced a golden age for provincial incumbents bent on consolidating local hegemonic rule.

Furthermore, during this period the central government was preoccupied with consolidating the national democratic regime. Human rights, military rebellions, and escalating economic problems absorbed its attention. It needed gubernatorial support for its legislative initiatives and therefore paid little attention to regime dynamics taking place at the subnational level. The central government saw local politics as the business of local bosses. The Radical president's priority was cooperation with provincial Peronist incumbents to achieve national political objectives. During the 1980s therefore the Radical-controlled national government would mount no center-led threat against local incumbents.[22]

Instead the main threat to local incumbents from national politics was party-led. In provinces with pluralistic traditions, the lifting of national authoritarian pressures meant that local politicians had to adjust to the return of competitive politics. Yet in several provinces the national democratic transition threatened something more fundamental: it threatened to change long-standing regime dynamics. Local Radical Parties buttressed by the national party threatened the hegemony of local Peronist Parties and the political families that controlled them. In 1985 the Radical Party scored additional gains in national legislative elections and expanded its presence throughout the provinces.

Responding to Party-Led Challenges: The Subnational Institutional Revolution

Boundary closers in the provinces faced two national electoral threats: (1) the electoral challenge from the Radical Party and (2) factionalism in the national Peronist Party. The Peronist Party was split between two factions: the "renovator" (*renovadores*) and the "orthodox" faction (*ortodoxos*). The national conflict quickly found expression in local conflicts. Protecting the local body politic from the competitive pathologies of the national body politic thus became a top priority for provincial boundary closers. Argentine federalism would provide the opportunity to develop common institutional solutions to their individual political challenges.

Starting in the mid-1980s, Argentina's subnational political landscape experienced an institutional revolution. Incumbents, the vast majority of

---

[21] See Eaton, *Politics beyond the Capital.*

[22] The Radical President, Raúl Alfonsín carried out no federal interventions against provincial governments during his presidency.

them Peronist Party governors, launched sweeping reforms of provincial constitutions and electoral systems. According to one source, between 1983 and 2003, 32 provincial constitutional reforms were carried out (the country has 24 provincial districts). In addition, incumbents enacted at least 44 reforms of provincial electoral systems during that period.[23]

The overarching goals of the reforms were, in the words of Calvo and Micozzi, to "limit the emergence of local challengers" and to "insulate provincial politics from the competitive trends at the national level."[24] The reforms greatly reduced the dangers of local Peronist Party factionalism by modifying local primary systems and election rules. They also strengthened incumbent party control over provincial legislatures via districting arrangements that introduced partisan biases into electoral systems through malapportionment.[25] The reforms restricted the playing field for opposition parties and often enabled incumbent parties to achieve supermajoritarian control over provincial legislatures. The reforms also sought to strengthen the powers of governors and to permit multiple or unlimited reelections of governors. In 1983 no provincial constitutions permitted gubernatorial reelection. By 2003, 17 of 24 provinces had reelection clauses in their constitutions, most permitting multiple successive reelections.[26]

In most provinces the reforms achieved the desired effect: a clear, across the boards, pro-incumbency effect. Calvo and Micozzi estimate that, on average, the reforms gave incumbent reforming parties an 8 percent seat premium in provincial legislatures.[27] The pro-incumbency evolution in subnational elections between 1987 and 2007 is shown in Table 4.1. The frequency distributions for this period compare party dominance in gubernatorial races and provincial legislatures. Gubernatorial races tended to be competitive as a whole, but the trend was one of declining competitiveness after the 1980s. In 1987, the proportion of gubernatorial races in which the winning party obtained a small majority or a plurality was 92 percent. In 2007, that proportion declined to 78 percent. The number of provinces with noncompetitive gubernatorial races also rose considerably. In 1983, only 5 percent of gubernatorial elections resulted in the winning party obtaining more than 60 percent of the vote. By 2007, that figure had risen to 22 percent.

---

[23] Ernesto Calvo and Juan Pablo Micozzi, "The Governor's Backyard: A Seat-Vote Model of Electoral Reform for Subnational Multi-Party Races," *Journal of Politics* 67, no. 4 (2005): 1051.

[24] Ibid., 1052.

[25] I am using Calvo and Miccozzi's (2005) distinction between "majoritarian" bias and "partisan" bias in electoral systems. The latter systematically favors one party, whereas the former applies to any first-place party. Although both are institutional designs that can contribute to hegemonic party building, majoritarian biases can have other legitimate systemic purposes.

[26] Ernesto Calvo and Marcelo Escolar, *La Nueva Política De Partidos En La Argentina : Crisis Política, Realineamientos Partidarios Y Reforma Electoral* (Buenos Aires: Prometeo: Pent, 2005).

[27] Calvo and Micozzi, "The Governor's Backyard," 1068.

TABLE 4.1. *Elections for Governor and Provincial Chambers of Deputies: Votes Won by the Winning Candidate and Seats of the First-Place Party, 1987–2007*

	Winner Governor's Race						Vote Percentage	Control of Provincial Legislatures by Governor's Party (Lower House)					
	1987	1991	1995	1999	2003	2007		1987	1991	1995	1999	2003	2007
	5%	9%	23%	17%	17%	22%	60 and more	20%	24%	27%	29%	33%	37%
	32%	43%	32%	42%	26%	17%	50–59	60%	52%	59%	50%	46%	42%
	50%	39%	45%	17%	39%	35%	40–49	15%	24%	9%	17%	4%	17%
	14%	9%	0%	25%	17%	26%	39 and less	5%	0%	5%	4%	17%	4%
	22	23	22	24	23	24	N (100%)	20	21	22	24	24	24

In provincial legislative elections, the trend toward declining competitiveness was even more striking. The percentage of provinces in which the incumbent party won a supermajority of legislative seats nearly doubled from 20 percent in 1987 to 37 percent in 2007. An interesting feature is that almost the entire shift toward supermajoritarian control by one party occurred in cases where in 1983 the winning party controlled more than 50 percent of the vote. More competitive or fragmented legislatures tended to stay that way.

The subnational institutional revolution was a decentralized strategic response by the Peronist Party to national challenges to its dominant position in provincial politics.[28] Its general effects were to improve the party's performance in local elections and to stabilize provincial electoral politics in a context in which national electoral politics was in flux. This strategy also fortified the party's national position, solidifying its control of the national congress and ensuring that Peronist governors would continue as the country's key national political brokers. Yet in an important subset of provinces, the institutional revolution was an authoritarian response to competitive politics, a legal method of restricting contestation made possible by the institutional architecture of Argentine federalism.

III. LEGAL AUTHORITARIANISM: DESIGNING HEGEMONIC PARTIES IN THE PROVINCES OF SAN LUIS, SANTA CRUZ, AND LA RIOJA

We now peer more deeply into this process with a brief examination of three provincial cases. Each of these provinces – San Luis, Santa Cruz, and La Rioja – faced competitive challenges in the 1980s, but entered the 21st century with well-entrenched hegemonic party systems. Politics in each of these provinces has also made its mark on national politics. Three of the four Peronist presidents to have served during the post-1983 period came from these provinces, each having served as governor before ascending to the presidency.

Rescuing Hegemony: The Peronist Party in the Province of San Luis

Adolfo Rodriguez Saá, the supreme *caudillo* of the western province of San Luis, is often quoted as saying that "to govern a province for forty years one must rely on family and friends."[29] Indeed he has family and friends in abundance. He descends from a long line of provincial party leaders. His ancestors include two provincial governors and several machine bosses stretching into the early days of the 20th century. His father, a conservative before the dominant provincial clans switched their allegiance to Peronism, was the province's chief

---

[28] Not all provincial reforms were led by Peronists. In a small number of provinces, such as Chaco, Córdoba, Neuquén, Río Negro, and San Juan, non-Peronists carried out pro-incumbent reforms as well.

[29] *"Para gobernar cuarenta años una provincia hay que hacerlo con la familia y los amigos."* Quoted in Pablo Rodriguez Leirado, "La Provincia De San Luis. El Eterno Feudo," *Revista Digital Sitio al Margen* (1998).

of police. He also formed a formidable political duo with his younger brother, Alberto Rodriguez Saá. Saá the younger occupied the governor's chair when the older sibling served stints in the national senate, and also served in the senate when the older sibling served his multiple terms as governor. The fraternal tag team's skills at drawing financial resources from the national government to the province are legendary, and as a result they are beloved by the many clients of the provincial government's patronage machine. Adolfo Rodriguez Saá was also president of Argentina during a chaotic seven-day term after the economic crash of 2001.

Yet despite the love of family and friends, control of provincial politics is rooted in a firm institutional foundation that has restricted local electoral contestation to negligible proportions. The San Luis Peronist Party is, by the strictest definition of the term, a subnational hegemonic party. The legal structure that makes it so was created after a brief opening of competitive politics in the early 1980s. The Peronist Party of San Luis was one of the first movers in the subnational wave of institutional reforms, and its success at consolidating its hold over the local polity inspired others to emulate it.

In the early 1980s electoral politics in San Luis was competitive. Adolfo Rodriguez Saá won the governorship by a 3 percent margin, with slightly more than 40 percent of the vote. The party won a big legislative majority because of an electoral system that gave the first-place party two-thirds of the seats in the provincial legislature. However, even the wiring of this majoritarian bias into the electoral system could not protect the party from the national competitive wave of 1985. In fact, it backfired on the party when the local Radical Party won the legislative elections and captured two-thirds of the seats at stake that year. As a result, the provincial legislature became evenly divided, with each party controlling 15 seats in the 30-member legislature. Adding to the governor's woes was internal factionalism within the provincial Peronist Party. The national factional dispute that was tearing at the Peronist Party after its back-to-back national defeats was also threatening to undermine provincial party unity.

In response to the deadlock, the governor called for a reform of the provincial constitution. He proposed a new method for electing members to the constituent assembly that would have vast repercussions for subnational party politics everywhere. Constituents would be elected by a method known as the *ley de lemas* (or "double-simultaneous voting" as it is known in English). Just like the white primary used in the U.S. southern states a century earlier, the *ley de lemas* was a method of primary manipulation to counter party factionalism. Under this system, primaries and the general election are folded into one event. Party factions present candidates as factions (*sublemas*) to the electorate in the general election. Voters vote for the faction they prefer. The party (*lema*) that wins the election is the party whose factions cumulatively gather the most votes.[30]

---

30 The *ley de lemas*, or double-simultaneous voting (DSV) method, works as follows: Each political party is formally labeled a "*lema*," and each *lema* may have several *sublemas* (candidates or lists of candidates) competing in the race. There are no primary elections. Each party faction

By folding primaries and the general election into one event, the *ley de lemas* eliminated the possibility that losing factions in a primary would defect from the party before a general election. Opposition parties were thus deprived of the ability to make alliances with dissidents in general elections. In the 1987 provincial constituent assembly election, the method lived up to its promise. It kept the Peronist Party together and gave it a solid majority of delegates to the constitutional convention.[31]

Adoption of the *ley de lemas* system was a brilliant stroke of political engineering by the incumbent party, and perhaps because of its novelty its effects could not be clearly seen by other parties. It was a relatively obscure method designed abroad in the 19th century and used only for national party systems.[32] It had never been adopted for subnational elections anywhere in the world before its use in San Luis in 1987. Within a few years, however, it would become the method of choice by Peronist incumbents in other provinces for protecting their parties from internal factionalism.

With a comfortable majority in the constituent assembly, Peronist leaders recast the local institutional order. They secured control of the legislative branch through changes in the provincial electoral system. First, the assembly introduced malapportionment in the conversion of votes into seats. The new electoral law stipulated that each district was to be represented by a minimum of two deputies, regardless of population. This created a strong partisan bias, because it overrepresented underpopulated rural areas that were the electoral strongholds of the Peronist Party. In addition to the partisan bias provided by malapportionment, the reforms further introduced a majoritarian bias into the system. Within each district, seats would be allocated between parties by a proportional representation system known as the D'Hont PR system, which mathematically favors first-place parties, especially in districts with few representatives.[33]

---

presents itself as a *sublema* in the main election. The winning party is the party that receives the most votes from the addition of all its *sublemas*, and the winning faction is the *sublema* that got the most votes within the *lema*. In a race for an executive position (say, president or governor), the candidate from the first-place faction of the winning party wins the seat or office. In legislative races, once the winning party is determined, seats are allocated between winning and losing *lemas* according to an agreed-on distribution method.

[31] Peronist and Radical Party leaders also agreed to hold a special plebiscite to elect a national senator under the *ley de lemas*. Under the Argentine constitution, national senators were to be elected by provincial legislators, but the deadlock in the congress made this difficult, and Peronist party splits made it difficult for the party to agree on a candidate. As a result of the plebiscite, the Peronist Party won the senate seat.

[32] The system was first designed by a Belgian scholar, Charles Borelli, in 1870, and first adopted as a national electoral method in 1910 in Uruguay. The system was used often throughout the 20th century in Uruguayan national elections and has also been used briefly in Honduran presidential elections.

[33] For how the mathematical formulas in the D'Hondt PR system favor first-place parties, as well as how this bias is reinforced in small "district magnitude" contexts, see Dieter Nohlen, *Elecciones Y Sistemas Electorales*, 3rd ed. (Caracas: Fundación Friedrich Ebert : Editorial Nueva Sociedad, 1995).

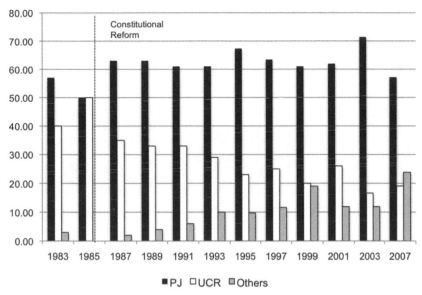

FIGURE 4.2. San Luis: Party Control of Provincial Chamber of Deputies
Source: Data from the Ministry of Interior, Argentina

In Figure 4.2 we see how the new electoral system disadvantaged opposition parties in the provincial chamber of deputies. After the constitutional reform of 1987, the Peronist Party never received fewer than 60 percent of the seats in the chamber. Opposition party representation similarly went into a long-term slide. This situation has persisted despite swings in national electoral politics. In 1999, even though the Radical Party captured the presidency, San Luis legislative politics remained impervious to national competitive pressures.

Peronist reformers were not satisfied with the colonization of the chamber of deputies, however: they also created a provincial senate with powers equal to those of the lower chamber.[34] Incumbents argued before dismayed and powerless opposition parties that an additional chamber was needed to avoid future situations of stalemate. The senatorial districts were designed to dilute the electoral impact of party competition in the capital city and urban areas. Populations in rural districts were overrepresented, and populations in urban districts were underrepresented. Figure 4.3 provides dramatic evidence of the partisan effects of these reforms. The Peronist Party controlled 100 percent of the seats after seven of nine elections between 1987 and 2003. Its "meager" 66 percent share in 1999 and 2001 is tempered somewhat by the fact that the second-place party holding about a quarter of the seats was created by Adolfo

---

[34] Julieta Suarez-Cao, "Arquitectura Institucional Del Legislativo: Los Casos De San Luis Y Tucuman," presented at the XXIII International Congress of the Latin American Studies Association, Washington, DC, 2001.

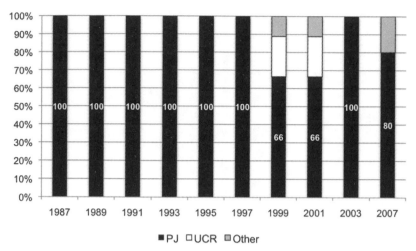

FIGURE 4.3. San Luis: Party Control of Provincial Senate
Source: Data from the Ministry of Interior, Argentina

Rodriguez Saá's younger brother, Alberto, during a brief period of fraternal discord over party matters.[35]

The legislative branch was not the only target of the reformers: expansion of gubernatorial powers also enhanced incumbent power. The 1987 constitutional reform allowed governors to be reelected an unlimited number of times. In San Luis this change stabilized factional competition for the chief executive office around the figure of Adolfo Rodriguez Saá. In addition, the new constitution expanded the executive branch's powers over the legislature.[36]

Adolfo Rodriguez Saá subsequently became Argentina's longest serving governor of the post-1983 democratic period. He would have completed 20 years of continuous service had he not become president for seven days in 2001. He later ran for president in 2003, garnering 14 percent of the national vote. Today he serves as national senator for the province of San Luis. His younger brother, Alberto, reconciled once again with his brother and his party, was elected as governor in 2003 with 90 percent of the popular vote and was reelected in 2007 with 85 percent of the vote.

---

[35] Miguel Wiñazki, Daniel Malnati, and Gabriel Michi. *El Adolfo: Crónicas Del Fascismo Mágico* (Buenos Aires: Planeta, 2002).

[36] The most important of the new prerogatives was the power to designate gubernatorial initiatives introduced to the legislature as "urgent" or "extremely urgent." When a bill is labeled as urgent, each chamber has to enact or reject the proposal within a month. When extremely urgent, the deadline drops to 15 days. If the legislature fails to comply with these deadlines, the bill becomes law. In an impressive display of casuistry, the same Peronist leaders who had added a senate to a unicameral legislature argued that this prerogative was necessary to avoid delays inherent to bicameral legislatures.

Building Hegemony: The Peronist Party in the Province of Santa Cruz

In the years following the 1983 democratic transition in Argentina, the politics of the Patagonian province of Santa Cruz was competitive. A proportional representation electoral system, applied to a single district (the province), generated a very proportional allocation of seats in the provincial legislature.

In 1983 the Peronist Party controlled the governorship and 54 percent of the legislature. Two years later it lost its legislative majority, although it maintained a razor-thin advantage because of the vice governor's power to cast tie-breaking votes in the legislature. Another evenly matched contest between the Radical and Peronist Parties took place in the 1987 provincial elections, in which the Peronist Party won the governorship with a narrow margin of 723 votes. In the legislature the parties remained tied, with each controlling 12 seats.

The Radical Party challenge was not the only problem threatening the governing party's slim hold on the provincial political system. The Peronist Party was being torn apart by internal factional conflict. The national fight between *renovadores* and *ortodoxos* was reproduced with varying ideological manifestations in Santa Cruz. In response, local party leaders borrowed from the strategic playbook of their counterparts in San Luis Province: they adopted the *ley de lemas* system for their party in the 1989 legislative elections. The system kept the party together and helped generate Peronist electoral majorities in the elections of 1989, 1991, and 1993. The party discontinued the *ley de lemas* system in 1995 when it unified internally under the leadership of Néstor Kirchner, who won the provincial governorship in 1991.

In 1994 Governor Kirchner had used his party's legislative majority to enact a constitutional reform that permitted the reelection of the governor for two consecutive terms and introduced new executive powers to invoke plebiscites and referenda. Kirchner subsequently won reelection in 1995, and the Peronist Party held onto its legislative majority. However, a continuing challenge for the Peronist Party was urban politics. The Radical Party won control of the provincial capital city in 1989 and over the years consolidated its electoral strength in other urban municipalities.

Governor Kirchner dealt with these challenges with more reforms. In 1998, as his second term ended, he invoked his new plebiscitary powers to hold a referendum that approved another constitutional amendment. Under the 1999 constitution, which stands unmodified to the time of this writing, the governor is entitled to run for reelection without term limits. The constitution also changed the electoral system for provincial deputies to neutralize urban opposition challenges. The legislature is now elected under a mixed-member electoral system. Ten members are elected in a province-wide single district by a proportional representation formula (as before), and 14 are elected in new single-member districts. This system introduced a marked partisan bias that favored the Peronist Party by overrepresenting rural areas (Peronist bastions)

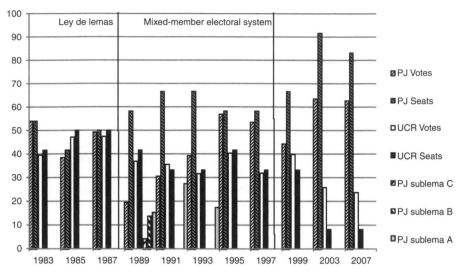

FIGURE 4.4. Legislative elections in Santa Cruz: Votes and Seats, 1983–2007.
Source: Data from the Ministry of Interior, Argentina.

and underrepresenting urban areas (opposition strongholds). As a result, Santa Cruz is today the most malapportioned province in Argentina. Twenty-eight percent of the population elects a majority in the legislature. The partisan effects of the reforms over time are revealed dramatically in Figure 4.4. In 1999 the Peronist Party captured 66 percent of the seats in the legislature with less than 45 percent of the vote. In 2003 it won a spectacular 92 percent of seats with 66 percent of the vote.

Néstor Kirchner was an important player in the network of governors that brokered presidential politics, and in 2003 he won the presidency. As the president-elect prepared to leave the governorship to assume his duties as president, he gave his successor a parting message: "I am not giving you the province; I am lending it to you."[37]

Fattening Hegemony: The Peronist Party in the Province of La Rioja

In the early 1980s La Rioja incumbents could hear the rumblings of the national competitive challenge, but its storms had not yet rolled across the borders of the northwestern province. The Menem brothers, Carlos and Eduardo, controlled the local Peronist Party. They were both long-serving party politicians and were the heart of a political network of friends and acquaintances that dominated the polity and the economy of the province. Carlos had served as governor of the province during the brief and tumultuous national Peronist restoration of 1973–76. In 1983 he was elected governor of the province with 57 percent of the vote. His brother was elected national senator by the Peronist-controlled

---

[37] Carlos March, "La Republica Feudal," *La Nacion*, September 9, 2004.

provincial legislature in that same year. Much like the Rodriguez Saá brothers in San Luis, the Menem brothers formed a gubernatorial-senatorial tag team. From their respective governmental perches the two brothers played important roles in national policy negotiations and in advancing their local interests in national arenas.

Peronist control of the province was buttressed by an electoral system that underrepresented the main urban hubs. This electoral system had been in place since the early 1930s, at the service then of local elites of other partisan colors with similar affinities for party hegemony.[38] In 1983 it delivered overwhelming seat premiums to the Peronist Party in legislative elections: the party captured 84 percent of the legislature that year with 56 percent of the vote. The second-place Radical Party received 16 percent of the seats with 39 percent of the vote. In 1985, a year of national Radical gains, the La Rioja Peronist Party's legislative vote total dropped to 52 percent. However, thanks to the electoral system, the party increased its control of the local legislature to 88 percent.

In 1985, therefore, the Peronist Party possessed a near monopoly of legislative seats and a formidable battery of patronage resources to ensure its control of the governorship in future elections. The incumbents were not satisfied, however, because the provincial constitution prohibited reelection of the governor. Governor Menem therefore prevailed on his party to support a reform of the provincial constitution that would allow the unlimited reelection of the governor. The 1987 constitutional convention, in which Peronists controlled 80 percent of the seats, did just that. Furthermore, for good measure, it biased the electoral system for the legislature even more in favor of the Peronist Party.

The reforms of the electoral system in La Rioja did not have the radical sweep of those in Santa Cruz or San Luis; they merely tightened the screws on opposition parties. The main targets were the urbanized districts (the capital city and the district of Chilecito), where nearly 60 percent of the population lived. The techniques used were the increase of district magnitudes for smaller districts dominated electorally by the Peronist Party and the adoption of a new proportional formula (the D'Hont system) for allocating seats within districts, which in district magnitudes such as that in the capital city systematically favor the first-place party. As a result of the district magnitude changes, the share of seats in the legislature for the two main urbanized districts decreased from 32 percent to 27 percent. Three small districts saw their number of representatives rise from one to two representatives. The remaining 12 rural districts continued with their allocation of one legislator, giving these Peronist strongholds a remarkable overrepresentation that has survived to this day.[39] The assault on the Radical Party's main electoral base was compounded by the adoption of the D'Hont seat distribution formula, which in the larger urban districts (five deputies in the capital and three for Chilecito) managed to pluck

[38] Daniel Cabrera, *Programa De Reforma Política: Informe Final Sobre Las Provincias De Formosa Y La Rioja* (Buenos Aires: UNDP – Argentine Chief of Staff, 2001).
[39] Ibid., 6–7.

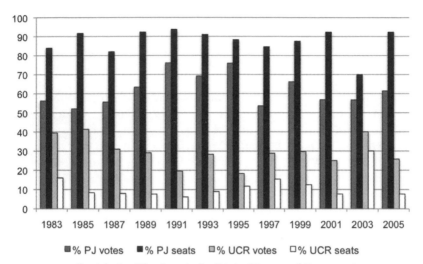

FIGURE 4.5. Legislative Elections in La Rioja: Votes and Seats, 1983–2005.
Source: Data from the Ministry of Interior, Argentina.

yet one more deputy from the Radical nest because of its mathematical bias toward first-place parties.

In 1989 Carlos Menem became president of Argentina. To the president's supporters in La Rioja, the only remaining threat continued to be factionalism within the provincial party. With Menem as president, central government transfers to the province soared.[40] The party patronage trough was a coveted target for local political cliques, and with Menem out of the province factional strife intensified. To solve this problem, party leaders, led by the president himself, borrowed once again from Peronist playbooks in other provinces and pushed for adoption of the *ley de lemas* system for provincial executive and legislative elections. The local Radical Party unanimously opposed the measure, but the Peronist majority enacted it anyway and kept it in place for four years.[41] The Peronist Party held together, and Menem's gubernatorial choices beat back internal challengers. In 1991 and 1995, under the *ley de lemas*, the party won its highest legislative vote percentages in the post-1983 period: 76 percent in each year.

After he left the presidency, Carlos Menem gradually lost control of the La Rioja Peronist Party. The Peronist Party, however, has never lost control of La Rioja. It continues to enjoy electoral majorities and colossal seat premiums in the legislature.

Figure 4.5 suggests how different things might have looked if the electoral system had not been so emphatically rigged in favor of the party. The Peronist Party would probably still have won elections, but politics in La Rioja would

[40] See Gibson and Calvo, "Federalism and Low-Maintenance Constituencies."
[41] Cabrera, *Programa De Reforma Política*, 13–14.

have been closer to a dominant party system than to a hegemonic party system. The Peronist majorities, sometimes quite large, would have been more vulnerable over time to the give and take of coalitional politics as the party's fortunes fluctuated. The institutional "fattening" of a hegemonic party system, therefore, closed off plausible scenarios for the development of party competition in La Rioja.

IV. SUBNATIONAL AUTHORITARIANISM AT THE TURN OF THE CENTURY: STABILITY AND CENTER-LED TRANSITIONS

After the 1980s, subnational authoritarian systems became very stable. Not one province whose political system became hegemonic or started as hegemonic experienced a party-led transition to democracy between 1983 and 2010. The party-led challenges of the 1980s were dispatched by the subnational institutional revolution.

Federalism certainly acted as a shield for the construction and preservation of subnational authoritarianism. It did, however, also provide a sword for boundary openers that brought provincial authoritarian governments down in a small number of cases. Central governments used the power of federal intervention against provincial authorities six times between 1991–2010. All provinces that were "intervened" during this period are among the most undemocratic, according to scholarly rankings.[42] The cumulative effect of the interventions, however, was mixed. As we can see in Table 4.2, federal interventions sometimes democratized the province and other times did not.

In Santiago del Estero in 1991, the goals and effects of the intervention were to stabilize a situation of civil unrest and rescue the local Peronist Party from collapse. Once these goals were achieved, the Peronist president handed the reins back to incumbents loyal to his national party faction. The central government sought no change in the local authoritarian situation, and none was achieved.

The cumulative effect of the interventions in Corrientes in 1992 and 1998 was to broaden a competitive oligarchy. In 1992 the non-Peronist Party cartel that had governed the province continuously since 1983 (and in different incarnations for decades before) broke into factional disputes. Under provincial electoral rules, an electoral college elected governors, and a stalemated outcome brought the province to a political crisis. In response President Menem ordered an intervention of the province. Under the intervention the electoral college was abolished and other institutional changes were made. Afterward an offspring of the previous cartel, which now incorporated local Peronists allied to President Menem, won the governorship. The partisan "family" of local incumbents was broadened to include Peronist factions loyal to their benefactor in the national presidential palace. In 1999 a second round of crisis and civil

---

[42] See Giraudy, "The Politics of Subnational Undemocratic Regime Reproduction in Argentina and Mexico" and Gervasoni, "Measuring Variance in Subnational Regimes."

TABLE 4.2. *Breaching Boundaries: Federal Interventions in Argentina after 1983*

Year	Province	President	Pres-Gov Co-Partisan	Cause	Change of Local Laws	Subnational Democratization
1991	Catamarca	Menem (PJ)	Yes	*Local:* Crisis, opposition mobilization *National:* Factional rivalry between president and governor	Yes: Creation of proportional electoral system	Yes: *Center-led transition;* competitive party system established; stable new competitive pattern
1991	Santiago	Menem (PJ)	Yes	*Local:* Financial crisis, riots *National:* Opportunity to shore up loyal PJ factions	No	No: stabilization, return of incumbents
1992	Corrientes	Menem (PJ)	No	*Local:* Crisis within party cartel; violent mobilizations *National:* Opportunity to shore up loyal factions (PJ and non-PJ).	Yes: Replacement of electoral college for gubernatorial elections with a run-off election formula	Partial: *Center-led transition;* broadening of local party oligarchy
1991	Tucuman	Menem (PJ)	No	*Local:* Stalemate between constitutional convention and provincial government *National:* Opportunity to shore up loyal PJ faction	Yes: Institutional changes negotiated by president and local contenders	No: Partisan intervention, not a democratic transition; intervention altered power balance between Peronist factions
1999	Corrientes	De La Rua (UCR)	No	*Local:* Political crisis and civil unrest *National:* Political opportunity for Radical president to bolster local Radical Party	Yes	Yes: *Center-led transition;* Radical Party wins the governorship; new party added to governing elite
2004	Santiago	Kirchner (PJ)	Yes	*Local:* Crisis, opposition mobilization *National:* Factional tension between president and governor	Yes: Creation of proportional electoral system	Yes: *Center-led transition;* competitive system established

upheavals occurred. This time it was a Radical president who ordered a federal intervention of the province. Unsurprisingly, a Radical Party candidate won the governorship two years later. Federal interventions in this province, therefore, have gradually broadened the spectrum of parties alternating in power in the province.[43]

In Tucumán province President Menem ordered a federal intervention in 1991 to break a stalemate between a constituent assembly charged with drafting a new provincial constitution and the Peronist-controlled provincial government. A local Peronist Party gambit to launch its own provincial constitutional reform backfired when constituent elections gave control of the assembly to a conservative provincial party. The main result of the intervention was not a more democratic Tucumán, but a reshuffling of factional power within the local Peronist Party.[44]

One of the most spectacular experiences of democratization via federal government intervention occurred in the province of Catamarca in 1991. A long-standing family clan, the Saadi family, had controlled local politics for decades and had successfully fought off a party-led transition in the mid-1980s through a constitutional reform that entrenched the hegemony of the Saadi-controlled Peronist Party.[45] The Saadi political order was as violent as it was institutionally innovative, and in 1991 the brutal murder of a woman by members of the political elite sparked mobilizations by local human rights and opposition parties that captured national attention. Long neutralized by the rigged electoral system and the incumbent patronage machine, local oppositions seized on the crisis and lobbied for a federal intervention. Seeing the opportunity to undo a regional rival, President Menem bowed to the national outcry and ordered the federal intervention. During the intervention, the electoral laws in the province were reformed, and a proportional representation system for the legislative elections was adopted.[46] Since then a competitive political system, based on coalitions between Peronists and Radicals, has governed the province. No further attempts have been made to reform the local institutional order.

---

[43] However, as Jaqueline Behrend has noted, this has resulted in the broadening of a political oligarchy rather than democratization on a broad scale. Although the party cartel that dominated the province in the early 1980s has left the scene, the political families that controlled it, notably the Romero Feris family, have continued to be influential in all governing coalitions. Even the election of Radical governors in the first decade of the 2000s has not changed this situation: "the party in power had changed, but yet another family had reached power and was renewing the provincial tradition of family politics, elite settlements and factional disputes." Behrend, "The Unevenness of Democracy at the Subnational Level," 164.

[44] Suarez-Cao, "Arquitectura Institucional Del Legislativo."

[45] For a description of these provincial reforms, see Gibson and Suarez-Cao, "Federalized Party Systems and Subnational Party Competition."

[46] Leandro Carrera, "Procesos De Reforma Electoral En Las Provincias De Catamarca Y Jujuy: 1983–1999," presented at the XXIII International Congress of the Latin American Studies Association, Washington, DC, 2001.

V. SUBNATIONAL POLITICS IN DEPTH: MAKING AND UNMAKING A PROVINCIAL AUTHORITARIAN REGIME IN SANTIAGO DEL ESTERO, 1983–2005

Juarismo sought to keep the province in a state of rigorous isolation . . . until at last the entire country became aware of the need to put an end to its domination.[47]

Two factors should be borne in mind about the authoritarian polity that existed in Santiago del Estero for more than two decades after 1983. First, its politics were contentious. Second, the authoritarian government was very oppressive.[48] These two factors were closely connected. The relative gentility of Rodriguez Saá or Menem family rule in San Luis and La Rioja was not a luxury always available to Carlos Arturo Juárez. His province was larger, more diverse, and fraught with rebellious traditions.[49] During the first decade after the 1983 national democratic transition, he was under siege from factional rivals and opposition party challenges. As a result, the authoritarian regime that he over-saw after 1983 often used violent methods of political control. Surveillance of citizens and opponents by the provincial security services was a dreary, feared, and predictable piece of everyday politics. "Disappearances" or murders of citizens were not unheard of. The government's methods also had shades of totalitarianism. The cult of personality created for the governor and his wife was pervasive and at times surreal. In addition, the power of the government's patronage machine was felt in all corners of provincial economic life. Public employees accepted the monitoring of their political lives as a price of employment. The discretionary allocation of public funds by the governor and his political circle kept ordinary citizens surviving just above the margins of desperation and made and unmade fortunes for small cliques of *Juarista* cronies.

The government also used institutional methods of control. The provincial constitution was arranged to give the Peronist Party hegemonic control, to tame a faction-ridden party, and to ensure the governor's sway over all branches of government. Finally, the provincial order was nurtured by national governments whose favor or indifference Juárez promoted tirelessly as a long-standing but second-tier member of the national political elite. By the late 1990s, Carlos Arturo Juárez had indeed made a fortress of his province. However, it was a fortress built against real dangers to his rule. They pressured from within and they pressured from without, and his boundary-control strategies similarly targeted local and national arenas. The strategies' legal and illegal extremes

---

[47] "La intervención a Santiago del Estero," *La Nación*, April 2, 2004, 20.
[48] A federal government report to the national congress in 2004 characterized provincial politics as follows: "the colonization of justice and the provincial legislature by the executive branch, the infinite extension of clientelistic practices, intimidation and physical coercion against political opponents, and systematic violations of human rights." Gobierno de la Intervención Federal, Provincia de Santiago del Estero: Primer informe del Gobierno de la Intervención Federal al Honorable Congreso de la Nación, 9.
[49] See Dargoltz et al., *Santiago: El Ala Que Brota*.

tell us a great deal about why his reign lasted so long and why his fall was so dramatic.

The beginning of the end seemed inconsequential. On February 6, 2003, in an area of abandoned fields known as "La Dársena," a woman dragging a pull-cart braved the scorching heat to scavenge the fields for cattle bones. She made her living by finding bones and selling them. On that day the seeker of animal bones stumbled on human remains. The bodies of two young women lay partially concealed in the tall grass. Soon thereafter, the murders were linked to prominent members of the Juárez political clique. No prosecutions took place, and compliant local judges let the matter stand.

By themselves the public revelation of the event and the local protests that followed were not particularly threatening to the government. As long as the scale of the conflict remained local, it had little impact. However, in late May 2003 a new president came to power in Argentina, which changed the factional winds of national politics against *Juarismo*. By the end of the year, the joining of national and local politics proved combustible for incumbents. In early April 2004, President Néstor Kirchner invoked the federal government's powers of intervention and ordered the removal from office and arrest of Nina Aragonés de Juárez and Carlos Juárez. He appointed a federal "interventor" to govern the province. The federal interventor announced the dawning of a new democratic age in provincial politics, courtesy of the central government.

Making and Maintaining a Provincial Authoritarian Regime

The Parochialization of Power: Competitive Pressures and the Legal Restriction of Political Competition

National competitive pressures affected local politics in Santiago del Estero in two ways in the 1980s. First, the Radical Party, usually led by politicians co-opted by the Juárez political family, mounted serious electoral challenges. Second, the Peronist Party was ridden by internal factionalism. It took Juárez a decade to neutralize these threats. One of his key boundary-control strategies, not always successful, was institutional design.

Carlos Arturo Juárez was elected governor for the third time in 1983, but he won that race with only 48 percent of the vote against a divided opposition. If he had any concerns about his underwhelming vote total, he could take consolation in his party's capture of legislative seats. Under the local electoral system, legislators were elected in a single district (the province), and the first-place party automatically won two-thirds of the seats. The remaining third was distributed by a proportional representation method between the trailing parties. This was an electoral system crafted by incumbents for incumbents. Peronists had designed it decades earlier, and it served them well in 1983. With only 48 percent of the vote, the party received two-thirds of the seats, giving the governor's party supermajoritarian control of the legislature.

Juárez was quick to act on this supermajority to consolidate power. He had the legislature enact a law mandating a reform of the provincial constitution. He wanted both the right to reelection and an electoral system that gave added advantages to the Peronist Party in legislative elections. Majoritarian bias, in the face of looming party-led challenges from the Radical Party, was not enough to guarantee continued Peronist dominance.

The elections for the constituent assembly were held simultaneously with the 1985 national legislative midterm elections. This proved to be a major miscalculation. The Radical Party won a landslide victory in the national elections, and its coattails ran deep into the Argentine periphery. In Santiago del Estero, the Radical Party won the 1985 constituent assembly elections and, because of the majoritarian bias built into the electoral system, captured 40 of the 60 seats in the assembly. The governor's dreams of reelection would have to be postponed. The Radical-controlled assembly retained the ban on successive gubernatorial reelections. However, in an act of hubris it did not do away with the two-thirds/one-third distribution of seats between first- and second-place parties in the legislature. The majoritarian bias was an attractive feature to an opposition party confident of being the next first-place party in the province.

The Radical Party's optimism was stoked by escalating internal factionalism within the Peronist Party. In 1987 Juárez secured himself a seat in the national senate and placed a loyalist as successor in the governor's office. However, he did so at a high cost, fighting not only against the Radical Party but also against four Peronist candidates who ran under different party labels.

Juárez's chosen successor was not kind to his patron. Once in office he broke with Juárez and formed his own faction. To make matters worse, he began negotiations for an electoral alliance with the charismatic Radical Party mayor of the provincial capital (the one electoral base the Radicals had controlled since 1983) to challenge Juárez in the 1991 gubernatorial election. The national Radical Party prepared to pour resources into the province to support such an alliance.

Classic signs of a subnational party-led transition had appeared: the ruling party had failed to restrict contestation by legal means; factionalism produced a succession crisis within the hegemonic party; an opposition party, supported by its national party, challenged incumbents from its urban base in the capital city; and dissident factions in the ruling party threatened to defect to the opposition.

The national Peronist Party came to the rescue. Concerned about the loss of a provincial bastion, national leaders focused on primary manipulation. They prevailed on Juárez and his party rivals to adopt the *ley de lemas* for the 1991 gubernatorial election. The party went into the election fielding three labels, one of them led by Juárez. The Radical Party, deprived of alliances with dissident Peronists, decided not to adopt the *ley de lemas* and fielded the mayor of the capital as its candidate.[50]

---

[50] For an account of internal Peronist conflicts and events leading up to the 1991 gubernatorial election, see Raúl Dargoltz, Oscar Jeréz, and Horacio Cao, *El Nuevo Santiagueñazo: Cambio Politico Y Regimen Caudillista* (Buenos Aires: Biblos, 2006).

Thanks to the *ley de lemas*, the Peronist Party held together and won the election. It was a bitter defeat for the Radicals. Their candidate received more votes than any Peronist *sublema*, but the aggregation of *sublemas* gave Peronists the victory. The institutional strategy paid off, and the hegemonic party warded off the most serious party-led challenge in its history. Juárez's faction did not win the contest, but the new governor soon allied himself with the old *caudillo*. Juárez loyalists, dominant in the provincial bureaucracy, legislature, and party apparatus, hunkered down to keep a watchful eye on the new occupant of the gubernatorial palace.

Juárez licked his wounds in the national senate. From this strategically valuable perch he sustained his provincial machine, became a steadfast ally of President Menem, and plotted his return to the governorship. His opportunity came in late 1993. The fiscally mismanaged provincial government was unable to pay its employees. Thousands of people dependent on the government trough joined government opponents in a multiday riot known as the *Santiagueñazo*. When the riots had subsided, the gubernatorial palace, the legislature, the provincial judiciary, and the houses of prominent politicians lay burned to the ground.[51] The province was also under central government occupation as President Menem invoked the power of federal intervention to quell the political crisis.[52] The intervention stabilized the Peronist Party and altered its factional balance in favor of Carlos Arturo Juárez. Employing the *ley de lemas*, the party won the 1995 gubernatorial election in a landslide, and Juárez was swept to the governorship as leader of the faction with the most votes.[53] He proclaimed himself a "phoenix' risen from the ashes of the *Santiagueñazo*. President Menem could now count on a stable provincial party to advance his interests in national politics.

The phoenix lost little time in consolidating control over the province. He called for a new reform of the provincial constitution and this time avoided past mistakes. His party gained control of more than 60 percent of the constitutional convention. Within three months, loyalists drafted a new constitution without negotiating with the opposition. Unable to affect the content of the new constitution, opposition parties boycotted the convention.[54]

The new constitution made the Peronist Party hegemonic and *Juarismo* its master. The governor now enjoyed unlimited reelection rights and expanded powers over the judicial and legislative branches. Furthermore, the constitution

---

[51] For an account of the *Santiagueñazo* see Raúl Dargoltz, *El Santiagueñazo: Gestacion Y Cronica De Una Pueblada Argentina* (Buenos Aires: El Despertador Ediciones Sielp 1994). See also Javier Auyero, *Contentious Lives: Two Argentine Women, Two Protests, and the Quest for Recognition*, Latin America Otherwise (Durham: Duke University Press, 2003).

[52] Senator Juárez was one of the most vociferous advocates of the federal intervention.

[53] Juárez himself, as leader of his *lema*, only received about 30 percent of votes cast. He was thus a major beneficiary of the *ley de lemas* system, under which the addition of all the party's factions gave it 65 percent of the popular vote.

[54] Flavio Fuertes, "Ni Mayoritario Ni Proporcional: Nuevos Sistemas Electorales, Los Casos De Santa Cruz, Río Negro Y Santiago Del Estero," presented at the XXIII International Congress of the Latin American Studies Association, Washington, DC, 2001.

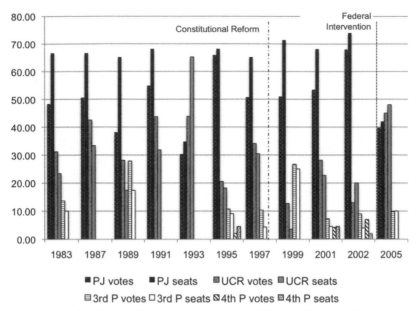

FIGURE 4.6. Legislative Elections in Santiago del Estero: Votes and Seats, 1983–2005.
Source: Ministry of Interior, Argentina.

added a major partisan bias into the electoral system. The reforms redrafted the electoral geography of the province by creating two new districting formulas that greatly underrepresented urban areas. The number of provincial deputies was increased from 45 to 50. Twenty-two of these would continue to be elected in a single provincial district, using the preexisting two-thirds/one-third seat distribution formula for first-place and trailing parties. The majoritarian bias of the old system was thus preserved for this group of seats. However, the other 28 seats would be distributed between six new electoral districts with varying magnitudes. The main urban hub of the province, the twin cities of Santiago–La Banda, was combined into one district with five legislative seats. Five additional rural districts were created with a minimum of four seats each, regardless of population.[55] Rural districts were Peronist Party strongholds: with 30 percent of the population they were allocated 70 percent of the legislature's seats.

Figure 4.6 shows the effects of the reforms on the distribution of power in the legislature. In the 1999 legislative elections, the Peronist Party won 73

55 As if this were not enough, the underrepresentation of urban populations was compounded by the formula for allocating seats in each district. In rural districts dominated by the Peronists, the formula gave 75 percent of the seats to the first-place party. In the urban district where the Radical Party was likely to prevail, 66 percent of the seats were allocated to the first-place party. See Constitución de la Provincia de Santiago del Estero, and Ricardo Gómez Diez, "La Oportunidad De Una Constitución Para El Bienestar Y El Crecimiento," lecture delivered in Santiago del Estero, August 2004), www.gomezdiez.com.ar/files/seminarios/SantiagoEst.pdf (accessed November 15, 2005).

percent of the seats with 51 percent of the vote, and opposition challenges receded thereafter. Carlos Arturo Juárez had at last given a firm legal structure to authoritarian rule. As the federal officials who removed him from power were to note later, the innovative redesign of the provincial electoral system "assured the permanent dominance of an unbeatable incumbent majority and the configuration of a single-party authoritarian system."[56] In 2002 the provincial legislature ordered the Juárez couple's images placed on provincial postage stamps, and a congressional resolution proclaimed them "Illustrious Protectors of the Province."[57]

The Parochialization of Power: Clientelism and Repression in Santiago del Estero

Un regimen de miedo y terror manda en Santiago del Estero.[58]

Traigame un alguito.[59]

The provincial public sector is the driver of economic life in the province of Santiago del Estero. The provincial government budget equals 70 percent of the province's gross domestic product. According to the 2001 national census, 37 percent of the economically active population held public sector jobs, and if public contracts, welfare programs, other transfers, and multiplier effects were also taken into account, the proportion of the population economically dependent on the government was much higher.[60]

In the mid-1990s, central government transfers funded more than 85 percent of the provincial public sector's budget. Nearly all of these funds were transferred directly to the governor, who enjoyed complete discretion over how the

[56] "Séptimo Informe De La Intervención Federal Al Honorable Congreso De La Nación," ch. 2, p. 3.

[57] In 2002, after a devastating national economic and political crisis, Juárez orchestrated the resignation of the governor, the vice-governor, and the entire provincial legislature, and called a special election to replace them. The Peronist Party, firmly controlled by Juarez's faction, won the elections overwhelmingly. For an account of the political maneuvers behind this special election, see Gabriel Vommaro, "La Política Santiagueña en las Postrimerías del Juarismo," in Isidoro Cheresky and Inés Pousadela, Eds. *El Voto Liberado, Elecciones 2003: Perspectiva Histórica y Estudio de Casos*, Buenos Aires: Editorial Biblos (2004), 225–52.

[58] "A Regime of Fear and Terror Rules in Santiago del Estero." Headline of article in Buenos Aires daily *La Nacion*: "Un Régimen De Miedo Y Terror Manda En Santiago Del Estero," *La Nación*, November 28, 2002.

[59] "Bring me a little something." Stated to the author by the Peronist mayor of Colonia Dora (population 2,400), as a condition of future visits. He was openly dismayed by the author's appearance without emoluments, having made the visit recommended by authorities in the governor's mansion. Author interview, June 12, 2004.

[60] For employment data, see Gibson and Calvo, "Federalism and Low-Maintenance Constituencies: Territorial Dimensions of Economic Reform in Argentina." A study by the Catholic University of Santiago del Estero placed the number of employees in the public sector at 50,000, which is close to half of the economically active population. See Ministro de Justicia, *Informe Santiago del Estero*, 12.

money was to be spent and to whom it was to be distributed. Federal government investigators in 2003 noted the generalized "perception of legitimacy that links political militancy with the attainment of a public sector job, and the stability of such employment with the system of loyalties to the governing party."[61]

Control over public patronage was also crucial for disciplining and shaping the provincial economic elite. The economic shadow of the provincial government prevented the growth of an independent local business class. Instead, business opportunities were to be made through lucrative contracts with the provincial government. Juárez made and unmade fortunes for local business elites, playing them off one another and ensuring their political loyalty.[62]

Argentine federalism granted Governor Juárez significant political authority over the province's mayors. Fiscal federalism gave him the economic means to enforce that authority. Municipal governments throughout the province were completely dependent on the governor's discretionary control of their funds. This was particularly important in neutralizing the key structural threat to *Juarista* hegemony: the mayors of the province's urban hubs. Radical politicians may have controlled the mayoralty of the capital city, but the governor controlled the money on which they depended. Before the mid-1990s, when national competitive pressures empowered local Radicals at election time, they managed to mount challenges against Juárez's party. Yet between elections, and especially after Juárez solidified his grip in the late 1990s, Radical mayors were reduced to operating as de facto supporters of the *Juarista* system. As the national newspaper *La Nación* noted in 2002, "the opposition [in Santiago] is almost non-existent due to its fragmentation and cooptation by provincial power-holders."[63]

Where institutional control and clientelism failed to neutralize opponents, outright repression filled the void. The forms of repression that marked the Juárez regime ranged from the bizarre to the horrific. Close to the bizarre end of the spectrum was Nina Aragonés de Juárez's personal political movement, the

---

[61] Ibid., 14.

[62] At the time of Juárez's fall, the provincial economic tycoon with closest ties to the regime was Nestor Ick, who made his fortune in a variety of economic activities tied to his relationship with Governor Juárez. He owned several businesses privatized under Juárez, including the province's largest bank, as well as hotel, construction, gambling, and legal services (he was a lawyer). He also had a monopoly on insurance, credit card, and utility services (water, electricity, cable television) for public employees that were paid by automatic payroll deductions. In addition, he was owner of the province's sole television broadcast station, as well as a radio station and cable TV channel. Before Ick, the favored local tycoon was Victorio Curi, a construction entrepreneur who financed the Juárez couple's 1976–83 exile in Spain and fell out of favor with the couple after 2000.

[63] "Un Régimen De Miedo Y Terror Manda En Santiago Del Estero," 8. Juárez made Radical mayors virtual members of his political family. On the eve of the 2004 federal intervention, some of the most vociferous opponents of the intervention were establishment Radical politicians who justly feared that it might empower more independent rivals in their party.

Rama Femenina, the women's branch of the Peronist Party. Its members were fiercely loyal to her. The *Rama Femenina* regulated access to public employment, and its activists monitored the political behavior of ordinary employees daily.[64] Many of its members were well connected. They included judges and administrators of the clientelistic apparatus. Of the 35 Peronist legislators in the provincial legislature, 18 were members of the *Rama Femenina* in 2002.[65] Sergio Carreras described the duties its members performed regularly for their patron:

When they were judges, they informed her about the details and progress of each case she was interested in; when they were secretaries, they would act as spies and informants about public officials suspected as disloyal; when they became legislators, they were fighters for her projects; when they were teachers they controlled and denounced their superiors and colleagues; when they were maids, they learned how to place themselves within hearing distance of any conversation that mentioned her or her husband; when they were nurses, they accused doctors of harboring opposition loyalties; when they were traffic inspectors they would inform about the amorous adventures of any well placed figure, or would bring to her the hottest gossip about her enemies.[66]

Most sinister and systematic was the provincial intelligence system, which reported directly to Carlos Juárez. The Directorate of Information (known better by locals as "D-2") operated under the direction of the provincial chief of police, Muza Azar. Azar is named in *Nunca Más*, the 1985 report by the National Commission on Disappeared Persons (Conadep), as responsible for the detention, torture, and disappearance of local residents during the 1976–83 military dictatorship. The authors of a report prepared in late 2003 for the national Secretariat of Human Rights referred to the directorate as a "provincial Gestapo." The report noted that, in a province of 800,000 people, the services had created more than 40,000 secret files on the activities of politicians, judges, journalists, clergy, businessmen, and, mostly, ordinary citizens. The Catholic Diocese of Santiago del Estero also documented multiple cases of murder and disappearances, torture, and political persecution between 1999 and 2003.[67]

Monopolizing Local–National Linkages
As leader of the Peronist Party and governor of the province, Juárez enjoyed all the attributes of the provincial party boss. Among the most important was control over local–national institutional linkages. He controlled party nominations for national congressional candidates, operating free from interference by national party leaders in the designation of candidate slates. In fact, the national Peronist Party played a negligible role in provincial party politics in

---

[64] This is addressed extensively in federal government reports on the province. See, for example, Ministerio de Justicia, *Informe Santiago Del Estero*.

[65] "Un Régimen De Miedo Y Terror Manda En Santiago Del Estero."

[66] Carreras, *El Reino De Los Juárez*, 65, 67–8.

[67] *Informe Santiago Del Estero*, 20–21.

general.[68] As head of a provincial hegemonic party, Juárez sent large Peronist delegations to the national congress whose members were loyal to him. As a journalist observed, "he was the puppet-master of the Santiago stage... and the sole intermediary between national leaders and the parochial circles of provincial politics."[69]

As governor, Juárez was the direct recipient of all federal transfers to the province under the national revenue-sharing program. As senator and commander of provincial delegations in the national congress, he influenced congressional decisions about federal public works projects, federal investment promotion initiatives, and discretionary transfers that lay outside the automatic revenue-sharing program. No other local political authority shared access to this vital linkage between the national government and the province.

Juárez's control of local–national linkages also extended to the judicial realm. He was able to neutralize federal judicial oversight over his province. The federal judge appointed to his province in 1984 was a close friend and associate, who shielded the governor and his political family from the intrusive reach of the national judiciary.[70]

The Nationalization of Influence: Santiago in National Politics
Juárez moved frequently in the national sphere and made his influence felt as a visible though second-tier national figure. As a second-tier figure, he harbored no presidential ambitions of his own, nor did he seek positions of leadership in the national party or in gubernatorial organizations. Every national post he aspired to (an occasional national senate seat, for example) was accessible because of his influence in Santiago del Estero. His national influence was based on control of a province, and it was used to enhance that control. The scale of his strategies may thus have been national, but their object was local power.

Juárez was a member of national gubernatorial coalitions that negotiated fiscal concessions from the central government. He threw his support behind the periphery-friendly restructuring of the federal revenue-sharing system in the late 1980s. He delivered votes and legislators to presidents at key political junctures. He placated Radical presidents by supporting national legislative initiatives, ceding the province's main urban centers to the Radical Party, and using key Radical politicians as advocates for the governor with the national government. In the decades after 1983, presidents or national politicians thus

---

[68] Most provinces work with closed list candidate slates (as did Santiago del Estero). The power to put together such slates is an indicator of subnational control over provincial party politics.

[69] Carreras, *El Reino De Los Juárez*, 56.

[70] Several journalistic accounts reported on the close personal and financial ties between the federal judge in the province, Angel Jesús Toledo, and Carlos Juárez, and between the judge and top business leaders tied to the governor in the 20 years he served as federal judge in the province. See, for example, ibid. and Dargoltz et al., *Santiago: El Ala Que Brota*. See also federal government reports on the state of the judiciary in Santiago, most notably *Informe Santiago Del Estero*.

had little interest in attacking the provincial power structure that supported him.

Internal Crisis, External Intervention, and the Fall of the Regime

Not long after the two murdered women were discovered, a local human rights organization named the *Madres del Dolor* (Mothers of Pain) organized a series of silent marches throughout the capital city to call attention to the murders and the state of lawlessness in the province. The protesters received crucial support from the Catholic Church of Santiago del Estero – one of the few local institutions with national linkages not controlled by the *Juarista* government.[71] In 2003, the Bishop of Santiago del Estero provided logistical and moral support to the marches organized by the *Madres del Dolor*, advocated their cause before national church authorities and government officials, and even headed a number of high-profile marches.

The local bishop's high-profile involvement in the anti-Juárez protests drew the national Catholic Church into the conflict. After this happened, events in Santiago became of increasing interest to the national press and to the general national debate. Church involvement also helped make Santiago politics a matter of interest to key members of the national government. One such official was the new Minister of Justice, Gustavo Béliz, who met with the bishop to discuss the provincial situation in mid-2003. Yet Béliz was no ordinary justice minister. As a devout Catholic with very close institutional ties to the Catholic Church, he was receptive to the bishop's appeals, all the more given the bishop's stature in his province.[72]

Complicating matters for the *Juarista* government, the Kirchner administration came to power with a strong commitment to putting human rights at the center of the national political agenda. With this goal in mind, the president created a Secretariat for Human Rights within the Ministry of Justice. The fight against corruption was also a top priority, and the Ministry of Justice became the institutional home for implementing these agendas.

There is little evidence that either the president or his top advisors had *provincial* democratic governance in mind when they created the new Secretariat. In fact, President Kirchner's management of his own province of Santa Cruz would not lead one to assume that combating subnational authoritarian rule was at the top of his priorities. However, to the surprise of many, the Secretariat's leaders soon identified Santiago del Estero as a major site of violations of human rights and rule of law enforcement in the country. With a Minister of Justice in close contact with an oppositionist Catholic Church,

---

[71] This was probably not for lack of trying. The previous bishop of Santiago, an articulate Juárez opponent, died mysteriously in a 1998 car accident on a rural road. The accident's causes were never determined by local authorities, although the federal government reopened the case in 2004.

[72] Carreras, *El Reino De Los Juárez*, 239.

Santiago del Estero suddenly found itself in the cross-hairs of top national governmental figures eager to expand their mandate into new arenas. The new linkages among local civil society organizations, the Catholic Church, and high federal government officials breached the boundaries of *Juarismo's* territorial fiefdom and sparked a bureaucratic response from the center. The Secretariat for Human Rights was instructed to investigate the situation in Santiago del Estero.

Thus, by mid-March 2004, the Juárez political order was under intense pressure from boundary-opening activities between center and province that been building for several months. In late 2003 and early 2004, the federal Secretary for Human Rights made several "fact-finding" visits to the province. During these visits he ordered the inactive federal judge in the province to reactivate pending cases against the Juárez clique, thus partially restoring the reach of the federal judiciary so effectively neutralized by the Juárez regime. He also offered the full support of the federal government to a provincial judge who faced local official pressure against her investigation into the double homicide of the women found in the *La Dársena* fields. Emboldened by this support, she redoubled her investigations and arrests. In addition, federal officials established contacts clearly aimed at opening spaces for opposition political action, meeting with opposition urban municipal leaders and politicians to enlist their cooperation in federal efforts to clean up local politics.[73]

President Kirchner was not fond of Carlos Juárez. Juárez had been a late convert to Kirchner's presidential candidacy and was tarnished in the president's eyes by his long-standing support of Carlos Menem, Kirchner's bitter factional rival. Furthermore, even though Juárez had publicly thrown his support to Kirchner, a majority of the province's voters voted for Menem anyway – in a province Juárez supposedly "owned." In the eyes of close presidential advisors, this constituted at best an act of negligence and, in greater likelihood, an act of betrayal by a provincial party boss expected to deliver the votes to his presidential ally.[74]

In their final stand, the Juárez couple responded to the national assault by closing off provincial avenues for their legal removal from office. Deprived of the use of repression and intimidation by the national spotlight on the province, they worked the local institutional levers at their disposal. They used control of the provincial legislature as a shield against the federal government. With great public celebration, the legislature rejected federal requests to strip the governor of immunity from prosecution. With the legislature closing off all provincial

---

[73] The federal government officials' political agenda of mobilizing action by municipal officials against the governor is clear in the following statements made by the Secretary for Human Rights on his visit to the province: "We believe that the municipalities are the ideal starting point from which to move forward to increase awareness and resolve the problems of human rights.... The current Provincial Government is not supportive of the Human Rights goals being pursued by the national government, and for that reason we are working with civil society, municipal authorities, and some sectors of the legislative branch that are believe in this policy." "Los Malos Pasos En La Interna Del PJ," *El Liberal*, April 1, 2004.

[74] For an interesting discussion of Juárez's missteps in Peronist factional politics, see ibid.

options for the impeachment or removal of the governor, local options to bring an end to the *Juarista* political order were exhausted.

Within the national government, however, debates raged. The president's factional and policy agendas clashed with the Peronist Party's interest in safeguarding its peripheral electoral bastions. As the clamor in the press and the political establishment for central government action grew, key cabinet members, worried about backlash from other governors and the Peronist Party, argued against moving against the provincial *caudillo*.[75] However, the president's policy and partisan agendas trumped those of anti-interventionist forces in his party. On April 1, 2004, President Kirchner ordered a federal government intervention of the province.

A relatively swift but complex series of local and national boundary-opening coalitions among civic, bureaucratic, and partisan actors had crystallized into a center-led transition in Santiago del Estero. Supporting the intervention was a civic coalition of local activists and the national Catholic Church that had linked the local conflict to policy interests of national government bureaucrats and to factional interests of the president. Opposing the intervention was the national Peronist Party and key political operatives in the national government. Local opposition party politicians remained on the sidelines, worried by the uncertainties of the collapse of a system in which they were firmly co-opted and by the partisan intentions of the national intervention (Figure 4.7).[76]

The president appointed Pablo Lanusse, the national government's Secretary of Justice, as federal interventor of Santiago del Estero. Lanusse dissolved all three branches of the provincial government and was given a mandate to reform the province's political and legal system. He initiated criminal investigations of politicians, bureaucrats, judges, and police officers; audits of public finances and provincial administration; and purges within the provincial clientelistic system. Lanusse also launched investigations into the financial relationships between the *Juarista* system and top business interests.

The federal government also leveled the electoral playing field.[77] Federal officials passed a series of reforms that radically changed the local electoral process.

---

[75] The conflict within the government was evidenced when the Minister of the Interior, Aníbal Fernández, went so far as to publicize his opposition to an intervention in an editorial in the influential daily *La Nación*. The editorial was published two weeks before President Kirchner ordered the intervention. See Anibal Fernandez, "En defensa del federalismo," Editorial, *La Nación*, March 16, 2004, 7.

[76] Such key Radical and ex-Radical Party leaders as Rubén Zamora, mayor of the capital city; Hector Chabay Ruíz, ex-mayor of its adjacent urban hub; and José Luís Zavalía, national senator and one-time challenger of Juárez for the governorship, opposed the federal intervention with different levels of intensity.

[77] It first sought to lead a reform of the provincial constitution, but the national Supreme Court blocked the initiative. The court argued that altering provincial constititutions was a prerogative granted exclusively to provincial authorities by Argentine federalism. Key electoral laws in the constitution, particularly those securing legislative malapportionment, would have to stay. Federal reformers were thus limited to altering electoral laws not stipulated in the constitution.

Step 1: Local Activists and Local Catholic Church → Link with National Catholic Church
Step 2: Local-National Activist/Church Alliance → Policy Link with National Executive Branch
Step 3: Local-National Policy Alliance → Partisan Link with President
Step 4: Center-Led Transition

FIGURE 4.7. Nationalizing the Conflict: The Center-Led Transition in Santiago del Estero.

These included new laws governing campaign finance, media coverage of elections, and party primaries. They also included laws establishing election monitoring systems, access to free publicity for parties, the direct election of municipal councils, and the introduction of modernized vote-counting technologies.[78]

The president's men in charge of the province were under clear instructions to make a democratic Santiago del Estero a base for the *Kirchnerista* faction of the Peronist Party.[79] However, their boss in the Presidential Palace, and especially the leadership of the national Peronist Party, would be disappointed. In February 2005, ten months after the start of the federal intervention, elections for a new governor were held. The Radical Party mayor of the capital city of Santiago defeated President Kirchner's chosen Peronist candidate.

Federal government bureaucrats had carried out their policy mandate to democratize the province a little too well. They provided the province its first cleanly held election in generations, and local voters chose to remove the party that had won every gubernatorial election since 1949. National Peronist Party leaders were incensed at the president for losing a long-standing electoral bastion.[80] Their nightmare scenario had come true: democratization led by the central government had actually ended hegemonic-party rule in Santiago del Estero.

After the new governor assumed office, a constitutional convention was held, and a new constitution was promulgated. The new constitution eliminated the worst vestiges of hegemonic party rule. It trimmed gubernatorial powers and limited governors to two terms in office. It explicitly banned the future use of the *ley de lemas*. It eliminated the division of the province into regional electoral districts and abolished the hypermajoritarian system for allocating legislative seats. Henceforth, provincial deputies would be elected in one provincial district, and seats would be allocated by a proportional formula. In 2009 the local Radical Party, now allied nationally to Nestor Kirchner's successor, Cristina Fernandez de Kirchner, won the governorship overwhelmingly. The Peronist

[78] The reforms are detailed in a series of reports to the national congress by intervention officials. See, for example, "Séptimo Informe De La Intervención Federal Al Honorable Congreso De La Nación."

[79] Confirmed in several interviews with intervention officials, including Pablo Fontdevilla, Chief of Staff for the Intervention, Santiago, February 14, 2005.

[80] Party leader Eduardo Duhalde called the intervention "a debacle for the party." "El Gobierno De Kirchner Respondió a Las Críticas De Duhalde," *El Liberal*, March 2 2005. During the election campaign national government leaders campaigned heavily in the province in vain to forestall a Peronist defeat. See "Santiago del Estero se tiñó de Radical," *Página 12*, March 1, 2005, 2.

Party did not field a candidate. However, it remained strong in a now competitive legislature, an ironic beneficiary of electoral reforms that granted minority parties their fair share of seats in the provincial legislature.

CONCLUSION

A national democratic transition in 1983 transformed provincial politics throughout Argentina. A territorial democratization made contests for provincial governments competitive, even in provinces long accustomed to the dreary predictability of authoritarian rule. However, in many provinces these challenges were beaten back. Nearly three decades of national democratic politics have produced an assortment of local regime types in which subnational authoritarianism coexists comfortably and functionally with national democratic politics.

Little was predestined in this turn of events. The 1983 democratic transition had transformed fundamental equations in national politics, and every provincial jurisdiction felt its game-changing power. Provincial authoritarian regimes thus emerged in a radically new national context, and they did so in novel local ways. Their leaders relied on new techniques and institutional forms as old configurations of hegemonic rule crumbled before the powerful tides of national democratic politics in the 1980s.

Just as we saw in the U.S. Solid South, federalism had a major impact on this story. Contemporary Argentine federalism shares key features with U.S. federalism after Reconstruction, and the subset of provinces that became authoritarian in both countries did so in similar ways. Political decentralization, namely the autonomy of provincial governments in local regime design, permitted the creation of local authoritarianism that relied heavily on legal and institutional foundations. Fraud was generally unnecessary and rarely employed as a hegemony-building strategy. The legal rigging of the electoral system in favor of the ruling party often sufficed to give it control over the local polity.

Asymmetrical representation of provinces was important to the nationalization of influence. It enhanced the effectiveness of collective action in negotiations with the federal government, it granted leaders of small provinces powerful national perches from which to advance the interests of their provincial political orders, and it enhanced their clout in the national Peronist Party. Linked to the institutional shields constructed at home, this clout provided a second shield against national incursions against the local status quo.

The manner in which Argentine federalism structured intergovernmental relations within provinces also worked in favor of provincial boundary closers. The constitutional subordination of municipalities to provinces mitigated the democratizing effects of urban politics within the provinces. Fiscal federalism only compounded the situation by adding overwhelming economic resources to the arsenal of municipal-subordinating weapons in governors' hands.

This has also been a story of national party politics. The focus in this chapter has been on the Peronist Party, not because it is the only party of subnational authoritarianism in Argentina, but because it is its most effective practitioner. The focus on Peronism has also revealed another nonlocal feature of provincial boundary control: the interdependencies of local hegemonic party-building and national party politics. As members of a confederal party, local Peronist boundary closers were aided greatly by the horizontal linkages with other provincial parties. The "revolution" of subnational constitutional and electoral reforms that took place in Argentina bore uncanny resemblances to the one carried out a century earlier in the U.S. South. It was a product of coordination and transmission of information between provincial parties, as provinces adopted strategies successfully employed in other provinces. The institutional revolution was only an authoritarian exercise in a subset of provinces. For this group the transmission of information and resources across provinces facilitated local institutional reforms. The national party also facilitated the local adoption of institutional reforms as it came to the aid of electoral bastions in trouble. Horizontal and vertical partisan links across the territorial system thus played a critical role in the making of subnational authoritarian regimes.

The study of Santiago del Estero revealed these processes in all their complexity. The construction of a subnational authoritarian regime was a multilayered and difficult process. The political system owned by Carlos Arturo Juárez did rest heavily on legal and institutional foundations, but these were hard won and took more than a decade to create. Behind the institutional armor of the rigged political system was a supporting cast of violent and illegal practices, coupled with the ruthless use of an overwhelming patronage system made possible by Argentine fiscal federalism. These practices were protected by national strategies that made national actors turn a blind eye to the province's authoritarian system.

In Santiago del Estero, as in the other provinces examined in this chapter, once the legal-institutional armor was in place, party-led challenges receded from the horizon of regime-change scenarios. Center-led transitions thus emerged as the most viable options for subnational regime change. All transitions from provincial authoritarian rule in Argentina after the early 1990s were center-led transitions. In the Santiago case study we examined some mechanisms of this transition type. The key to the opposition's success in nationalizing the local conflict was to link it to the bureaucratic and partisan interests of the highest authorities of the national government.

Notably absent from the center-led transition were political parties. The national Peronist Party was opposed to any move that threatened a provincial electoral bastion, no matter how outrageous its leaders' conduct. Local opposition parties made no appeals to national authorities to intervene in provincial politics. In fact, they opposed the ouster of the *Juarista* system by the national government. It fell to local civic activists to link their protest movements to national actors, first with the national Catholic Church, then with bureaucrats in the executive branch, and finally with a president intrigued by the prospect of removing an untrustworthy co-partisan. Only after the national government intervened and restructured local institutions was a democratic election held and a democratic constitution adopted for the province. It was a happy ending. However, the contingent nature of the process, the mixed motives of its protagonists, and the inheritance of the political system by once co-opted opposition leaders highlight just how difficult the road to democracy remains for boundary openers in Argentina's other provincial authoritarian regimes.

5

Boundary Control in Democratizing Mexico

> Democracy from the provinces: and why not?
>> Vicente Fox Quesada, PAN Governor of the State of Guanajuato, in 1995[1]

> Only God can remove a governor.
>> Ulíses Ruíz Ortíz, PRI Governor of the state of Oaxaca, in 2006[2]

In 2010, a subnational bastion of autocratic rule in Mexico came to an end. In the southern state of Oaxaca, the *Partido Revolucionario Institucional* (PRI) lost a governorship it had held for more than 70 years. The PRI succumbed to a coalition of parties united not by ideology but by the goal of defeating the incumbent party. The local leaders of the right-leaning *Partido Acción Nacional* (PAN) joined local leaders of the left-leaning *Partido de la Revolución Democrática* (PRD) to support an ex-PRI politician in his long-standing quest to become governor of the state. Added to this complicated local picture were the actions of national parties, which, with national objectives in mind, encouraged and empowered the anti-incumbent coalition.

The defeat of the PRI in Oaxaca was a party-led transition from subnational authoritarian rule. Its protagonists were local party activists, civil society organizations, and national party leaders. Bureaucrats from Mexico City kept their distance, and when they did intervene over the years it was usually on behalf of local incumbents. It was a long and hard-fought struggle. The leviathan was weakened gradually by pitched electoral battles in municipal and state arenas, violent confrontations on city streets and rural byways, and national partisan and regulatory pressures.

The state of Oaxaca may have stood out for the resilience and ferocity of its authoritarian politics, but its local regime conflicts reflected a national

---

[1] Quoted in Kathleen Bruhn, "PRD Local Governments in Michoacán: Implications for Mexico's Democratization Process," in *Subnational Politics and Democratization in Mexico*, ed. Wayne A. Cornelius, Todd A. Eisenstadt, and Jane Hindley (La Jolla: University of California Press, 1999), 20.

[2] Quoted in "Dios da y quita el poder-Ulíses," *Reforma*, November, 18, 2006, 1.

pattern. The democratization of the national government in the 1990s was the beginning of a chain of struggles over the democratization of Mexican states (Figure 5.1). Despite the drama surrounding the end of the PRI's control of the national government as the 20th century came to a close, fights over the democratization of Mexican states consumed much of everyday politics in the new century.

There were reasons to be pessimistic in the 1990s about the prospects for territorial democratization in Mexico. The national government was now a source of democratizing pressure on the states, but it had lost many of the instruments that had once kept state leaders in line. Subnational politics thus became both a refuge and staging ground against national democratic trends. Efforts to unseat incumbents via elections slammed hard against the reality of local boundary control. As the 20th century came to a close, one of the most prominent U.S. observers of Mexican politics despaired about the future of democracy in the Mexican states:

During the present phase of the country's evolution the subnational political arena will be the principal source of inertia and resistance to democratization, rather than the prime breeding ground for democratic advances . . . there is reason to doubt that a coherent national-level democratization project can go forward, with an archipelago of deeply entrenched, well-protected subnational authoritarian enclaves still in place, even within a much more competitive electoral system. More vigorous electoral competition per se clearly is not enough to eliminate these enclaves.[3]

By 2010, however, "vigorous electoral competition" had indeed dispatched many members of the authoritarian assembly of Mexican states. Oaxaca fell in 2010, and that year another long-standing authoritarian bastion, the state of Puebla, came tumbling down as well. In earlier years, opposition parties captured several other long-standing PRI-controlled states in dramatic electoral contests. Subnational democratization in Mexico has been messy, sometimes violent, and filled with reversals. Its overall trend, however, has clearly confounded the predictions of pessimists in the early years of national democratization.

The dynamics of subnational authoritarianism in Mexico are very different from those in Argentina or the post-Reconstruction Solid South. In the latter contexts subnational authoritarian regimes were maintained through long periods of dreary institutional stability, and they were brought down only in extraordinary moments of crisis and intervention by national governments. In Mexico subnational authoritarianism is a far more contested and vulnerable affair. State-level hegemonic parties are constantly challenged by local and national adversaries, who stage their attacks from urban hubs

---

[3] Wayne A. Cornelius, "Subnational Politics and Democratization: Tensions between Center and Periphery in the Mexican Political System," in *Subnational Politics and Democratization in Mexico*, ed. Wayne A. Cornelius, Todd A. Eisenstadt, and Jane Hindley (La Jolla: University of California Press, 1999), 11, 13–14.

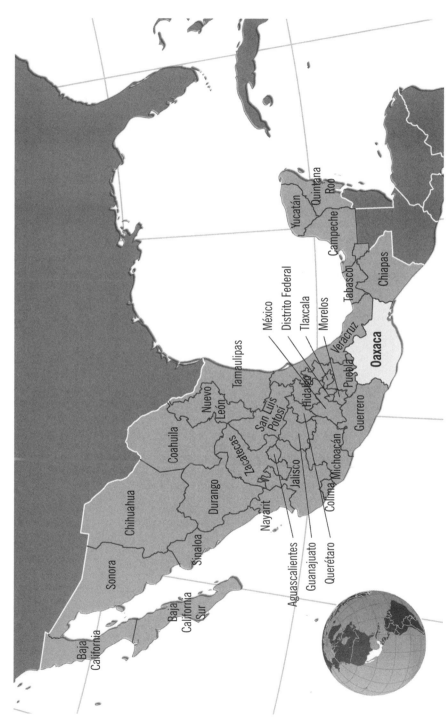

FIGURE 5.1. Mexico: States
Source: Hugo Ahlenius, Nordpil, 2012

and draw support from national parties and electoral monitoring institutions. Every election on the crowded state and municipal electoral calendars is a potential challenge to local incumbents. Boundary closers' chief weapons are not institutional or legal, but informal and illegal. Local coercion, the illicit appropriation of public funds, electoral fraud, and the strategic manipulation of national partisan politics are the pillars of a flexible structure of authoritarian boundary control.

Mexico's patterns of subnational authoritarianism are a result of the political topography of its federal system. The national constitution and national electoral regulation curtail significantly the autonomy of Mexican state political systems. National laws limit the independence of state authorities to design local electoral systems, and national courts and electoral monitoring agencies watch over the administration of local elections. Mexican federalism thus limits the abilities of state incumbents to craft local authoritarianism "in a perfectly legal way." The challenge of crafting a subnational authoritarian regime lies in doing so illegally and informally.

Furthermore, Mexican federalism empowers municipalities. Both the constitution and the arrangements of fiscal federalism grant them autonomy and independent economic resources. Urban hubs are thus an attractive prize for national opposition parties and are often the strategic launching pad for electoral assaults on the state governorship. The key to crafting a state-level authoritarian system lies in neutralizing these municipal-empowering features illegally and informally.

This chapter examines boundary control in a federal system that is nonperipheralized and is municipal-empowering. Its starting point is similar to that in Argentina: a national democratization process that gave rise to a combination of democratic and authoritarian state regimes. The chapter then shows how differently Mexican federalism shaped the evolution of local authoritarianism. The immediate effect of national democratization on territorial politics was a strategic shift between national and local authorities that favored boundary closers. However, there was a counter-effect that was gradual and institutional. National party competition led to the negotiated redesign of federalism in ways that made it harder and harder to sustain authoritarian boundary control in the states.[4] The result has been the submersion of many members of the authoritarian "archipelago" by Mexico's national democratic tide.

---

[4] Andreas Schedler and other scholars label this national process "democratization by elections," whereby oppositions in competitive authoritarian countries use electoral advances to negotiate changes in electoral rules that improve their chances in future elections. This chapter reveals the subnational consequences of these national sequences of elections and negotiations of Mexican electoral federalism. For comparative perspectives of this process, see Andreas Schedler, "The Nested Game of Democratization by Elections," *International Political Science Review* Vol 23, No. 1, (2002):103–22. See also, Staffan I. Lindberg, Ed. *Democratization by Elections: a New Mode of Transition*, Baltimore, MD: The Johns Hopkins University Press (2009).

I. ORIGINS OF THE ARCHIPELAGO: NATIONAL DEMOCRATIZATION
AND CHANGING CENTER–PERIPHERY RELATIONSHIPS

Many of Mexico's contemporary patterns of subnational politics stem from its long history of national authoritarian rule by the *Partido Revolucionario Institucional* (PRI). It is well known that authoritarian Mexico was a complex and highly institutionalized political system whose politics were nevertheless characterized by the informal and discretionary exercise of power by state leaders. This blend of a high degree of institutionalization and informal practices applied to Mexico's territorial system as well. For most of its history, Mexico has had a federal territorial regime. During the decades of PRI rule, federalism organized key hierarchies of government, but its independent effects on daily politics were limited. What governed political life within the federal state was the centralized system of national hegemonic party rule. This system acted as an institutional overlay on federalism that imposed its organizing logic on interactions between local and national arenas.

As a hegemonic party, the PRI held sway over all corners of the national government. Federalism reproduced this national pattern into 32 state hegemonic party systems, where local PRI branches controlled state and municipal governments. Each state operated under its own constitution, held elections according to its own electoral calendars, and was governed by its own chief executive. However, the formal autonomy and prerogatives guaranteed to state and municipal authorities by federalism were rarely visible in the daily management of politics. The partisan hierarchy of the national hegemonic party system trumped the intergovernmental hierarchies of Mexican federalism. Within the hegemonic party, the president held sway over its tightly integrated network of state-level parties.[5]

Challenges to the system came from a number of quarters over the years, but after the 1970s they occurred in a steadily intensifying sequence of subnational electoral confrontations with opposition parties. Between 1976 and 1988, opposition parties won elections in more than 100 municipalities. Most of these were in urban centers and were won by the *Partido Acción Nacional* (PAN).[6] In 1988 the PAN captured its first governorship, in the northern state of Baja California. After 1988 the *Partido de la Revolución Democrática* (PRD) joined the electoral fray in subnational jurisdictions.

---

[5] For studies of the Mexican political system under PRI hegemony, see Wayne Cornelius, *Mexican Politics in Transition: The Breakdown of a One-Party Dominant Regime*, Monograph Series No. 41 (La Jolla: University of California Press, 1996); Jose Luis Reyna and Richard S. Weinert, eds., *Authoritarianism in Mexico* (Philadelphia: Institute for the Study of Human Issues, 1977); and Beatriz Magaloni, *Voting for Autocracy: Hegemonic Party Survival and Its Demise in Mexico* (New York: Cambridge University Press, 2006). See also Andrew D. Selee and Jacqueline Peschard, "Mexico's Democratic Challenges," in *Mexico's Democratic Challenges: Politics, Government, and Society*, eds. Andrew D. Selee and Jacqueline Peschard (Stanford University Press, 2010), 6–7.

[6] As noted in Chapter 2, in Mexican federalism the term "municipality" denotes the tier of government immediately below the "state," regardless of its urban or rural characteristics.

By the year 2000, when the PRI lost the presidency, opposition parties governed almost a one-quarter of the country's municipalities as well as 14 of 32 states.[7]

The opposition challenges shared a key characteristic. They were usually launched from major urban hubs and, when successful, spread toward adjacent areas and statehouses.[8] One observer characterized opposition parties during this period as "asphalt parties."[9] These challenges were urban rebellions against the PRI's national rule fought out in local elections throughout the country.[10] The PRI's overwhelming national electoral machine rendered national opposition challenges quixotic. Similarly, its control over rural electorates in the states made it extremely difficult to dislodge the PRI from governors' mansions. Opposition parties thus focused on those jurisdictions where the PRI was demographically weakest. These were plural spaces where the middle class eluded monolithic party control and where economic development enhanced local economic autonomy – in other words, the cities.

Observers of Mexican politics during this period referred to this process as a democratization "from the periphery to the center" or a "centripetal route to democracy."[11] The idea behind these concepts was that the national government would be the last to fall, as opposition parties captured more and more subnational arenas and spread their democratizing influences from the bottom up. Thus Guanajuato's PAN Governor Vicente Fox, who five years later was elected president of Mexico, could declare in 1995 that he was leading one of Mexico's many "democratizations from the provinces." The facts provided compelling support for his claim. Within two years of his statement, when Mexico City residents elected their mayor for the first time, well over half of the country's population lived in jurisdictions governed by the PAN and the

---

[7] Andrew D. Selee and Jacqueline Pleschard, "Mexico's Democratic Challenges," 13.

[8] Rafael Aranda Vollmer, "Evolución De La Alternancia: De Los Centros Urbanos a Sus Periferias," *Revista Legislativa de Estudios Sociales y de Opinión Pública* 3, no. 5 (2010).

[9] Juan Molinar Horcasitas, *El Tiempo De La Legitimidad: Elecciones, Autoritarismo, Y Democracia En México* (Mexico City: Cal y Arena, 1991).

[10] In his major study of municipal politics between 1988 and 2000, Rafael Aranda Vollmer provides considerable documentation about the urban character of the electoral challenges against the PRI. Interestingly, given the widely noted strength of the PAN in the north of the country and the PRD's strengths in the south, Aranda Vollmer notes that the urban–rural divide was more significant in the transition than any regional divide. Urban challenges to the PRI took place throughout the country, and even in southern states governed by hard-line PRI leaders, the capital cities and major urban hubs of those states were often opposition strongholds. See Rafael Aranda Vollmer, *Poliarquías Urbanas: Competencia Electoral Y Zonas Metropolitanas De México* (Mexico City: Instituto Federal Electoral, 2004). For a discussion of the regional dimensions of the PRI's historic electoral coalitions, see also Edward L. Gibson, "The Populist Road to Market Reform: Policy and Electoral Coalitions in Mexico and Argentina," *World Politics* 49 (1997).

[11] See Yemile Mizrahi, "Pressuring the Center: Opposition Governments and Federalism in Mexico," *Documentos de Trabajo* – CIDE 72 (1997).

PRD.[12] In 1997 the PAN and the PRD wrested majority control of the national chamber of deputies from the PRI. Democratization from the periphery had yielded its first major national prize.

In the mid-1990s, Mexico's democratization conflicts experienced another important transformation. The PRI president, Ernesto Zedillo, announced a new relationship between the presidency and the ruling party. Thenceforth the president would maintain a "healthy distance" between himself and the PRI. In other words, the vast powers and resources of the presidency would no longer be deployed to support the partisan interests of the PRI. The party–state link was thereby severed. The PRI was now left to its own devices in dealing with opposition challenges, and the president was no longer a buttress against a democratic transition whose impetus was now national.

Thus the territorial logic of Mexico's democratic transition was turned on its head. Democratizing pressures, at one time subnational, now emanated from national politics. Local conflicts were being fought out in a dramatically different strategic context. The national arena now threatened, and PRI incumbents were no longer part of a national hierarchy that could sustain or discipline them. Local bosses had lost their mother ship. In this new context of center–periphery relations, subnational authoritarian regimes would have to be organized along new lines.

The New Territorial Politics of the PRI: The Party of the President Becomes the Party of the Governors

National democratization provided both opportunities and challenges to local PRI incumbents. They lost their partisan ties to the center but gained new means for insulating themselves from national competitive trends. First, the removal of the hegemonic party overlay from the federal system empowered subnational levels of government. The partisan logic that had governed the national territorial system was replaced by an intergovernmental logic under which state governors exercised previously dormant powers. Federalism thus initially acted as a shield for local boundary control. In addition, President Zedillo enhanced the formal powers and autonomy of the states with substantial grants of fiscal autonomy and resources to them. His administration's "New Federalism" program was integral to its national political and economic strategies, and although it was a boon to democratic advancement in states with pluralist internal politics, in authoritarian states it gave fiscal muscle to the political autonomy gained by local incumbents.[13]

---

[12] Alonso Lujambio and Horacio Vives Segl, *El Poder Compartido: Un Ensayo Sobre La Democratización Mexicana* (México, D.F.: Océano, 2000), 82.

[13] For a detailed analysis of the economic and political dimensions of the Zedillo administration's New Federalism Program, see Victoria Elizabeth Rodríguez and Peter M. Ward, *Opposition Government in Mexico* (Albuquerque: University of New Mexico Press, 1995). For an analysis of decentralization under the Fox administration, see Emily Edmonds-Poli, "Decentralization

In the new decentered context of Mexican territorial politics, a dramatic redistribution of power occurred within the PRI: the party of the president became the party of the governors. A territorial power structure that had run vertically from presidents to subnational politicians was replaced by a horizontal power structure linking governors across state parties. The powers to decide national party policy and advance politicians' careers flowed to this network of governors. In addition, as the presidency and the congress passed to the opposition, the party's influence on national policy became increasingly a product of gubernatorial collective action.

Control of state governments thus became a survival strategy for the national PRI. This created a nurturing environment for the consolidation of authoritarian state governments. Shoring up state power bases was a rearguard action for advancing key national interests, be they fighting national electoral challenges or maintaining leverage over national politicians. The PRI may have lost the presidency and its congressional majority, but when Vicente Fox was elected president, it controlled most of the governorships. Regardless of the preferences about democracy, national PRI leaders had a strategic interest in preserving the party's authoritarian redoubts in the states.[14]

The territorial dynamics of national democratization thus created powerful incentives for the formation and protection of subnational authoritarian enclaves. The existential imperative to keep hold of state governorships would be a driving force behind the making of subnational authoritarianism. This imperative was captured succinctly by the headline of an article in a prominent Mexican newsweekly magazine shortly after the PAN's Vicente Fox became president: "PRI Governors Become Assertive: From Centralism to Feudalism."[15]

National Patterns of Boundary Control: Checking Center-Led Incursions

Local boundary control was aided by a national strategy: coordinated action by state PRI leaders to check presidential intrusions into local politics. The collective leverage of PRI state governors over the national executive was key to the rise of the archipelago of authoritarian states. It effectively thwarted the immediate threat to the parochialization of power in the early years of national democracy: the center-led intervention.

Judiciaries and electoral national monitoring bodies held little sway over the conduct of local elections at that time. In addition, local PRI machines overwhelmed opposition parties in several states. Thus party-led challenges to PRI

under the Fox Administration: Progress or Stagnation?," *Mexican Studies/Estudios Mexicanos* 22, no. 2 (2006).

[14] As an editorialist put it in 1995, "With a vanishing presidential leadership, the PRI's balkanization shows its first signs and the local barons begin to show their claws. Without a Field Marshall the party . . . has become subject to its regional lords" (Carlos Castillo Peraza, *Reforma*, February 2, 1995).

[15] *Proceso*, September 9, 2000.

incumbents faced daunting odds. However, opposition parties had one important boundary-opening resource: direct appeals to the president to overturn egregious actions by local incumbents. This practice was consistent with a long tradition of PRI presidential control of state politics. President Zedillo's predecessor, Carlos Salinas de Gortari, removed at least 11 governors or governors-elect for various irregularities during his term in office, often ceding the governorship to an opposition party.[16] During Zedillo's presidency, opposition parties appealed repeatedly for presidential interventions to overturn questionable victories by PRI state machines. After the PAN won the presidency, these appeals continued. Ensuring the end of this presidential prerogative was thus a key objective for the new masters of the PRI.

A first test happened early in the president's term, in a violent electoral controversy in the southern state of Tabasco. Roberto Madrazo, the PRI candidate for governor, won the 1994 elections with 56 percent of the vote. However, opposition parties denounced the results as fraudulent. The brazenness of his campaign misconduct embarrassed the national party, and the indifference of state electoral authorities to extensively documented opposition challenges became a national scandal.[17]

With local avenues for redress exhausted, opposition parties externalized their claims. They sought a "political solution" from the president. In early 1995 the president negotiated a solution to the crisis that involved removing Madrazo from office. Reports of the agreement sparked what became known as the "Rebellion of the *PRIistas*," in which the Tabasco state party shut down the state government and launched violent protests to prevent an opposition takeover of the government. Seizing the opportunity, hard-line governors and members of congress compelled the president to end his efforts to remove the rogue governor. The outcome set a precedent for territorial politics. It was the first time since the 1930s that a state governor had defied a PRI president and remained in office.[18] As Todd Eisenstadt has written, it was a successful "demonstration of the maneuverings of a local authoritarian political machine trying to hold on to power, even as the national government was trying to wrest power away."[19]

The center-led incursion failed, and Governor Madrazo completed his term. The incident made him supreme leader of the new cohort of PRI hard-liners

---

[16] For these electoral conflicts see Todd Eisenstadt, *Courting Democracy in Mexico*.

[17] The national scandal intensified when an anonymous release of PRI campaign receipts revealed that Madrazo's gubernatorial campaign had spent more than $75 million dollars (in a state of three million people), an amount that exceeded Bill Clinton's general election campaign expenditures in the 1992 U.S. presidential election. See Eisenstadt, "Electoral Federalism and Presidential Authority in Tabasco," 287.

[18] Cornellius, "Subnational Politics and Democratization," 6.

[19] Todd A. Eisenstadt, "Electoral Federalism or Abdication of Presidential Authority?," in *Subnational Politics and Democratization in Mexico*, ed. Wayne A. Cornelius, Todd A. Eisenstadt, and Jane Hindley (La Jolla: University of California Press, 1999), 270. For an extensive analysis of this and other "PRIista rebellions," see also Eisenstadt, *Courting Democracy in Mexico*.

who shaped party policy from their regional redoubts. He was the presidential standard bearer for anti-reform factions of the party in the presidential elections of 2000, became the party's president in 2002, and was the party's nominee for president in 2006.

This would not be the last act of defiance by PRI state leaders toward the president. In the state of Puebla, Governor Manuel Bartlett, also a man with declared presidential ambitions, strengthened his state political machine through a variety of illegal and irregular tactics.[20] The governor also defied the central government by crafting a state law that diverted federal revenue-sharing funds to the governor's office. Several other PRI governors copied this law, known as "Bartlett's Law." It gave them the power to channel funds from urban municipalities controlled by the opposition to PRI strongholds in rural municipalities. The central government initially challenged the gubernatorial usurpation of federal funds but relented in the face of unified resistance from PRI governors.

Vertical coordination among PRI state parties to thwart presidential action against subnational bastions thus became the most important national boundary-control strategy for the PRI. It remained so during the two PAN presidencies of Vicente Fox and Felipe Calderón. Since 2000, no center-led incursion has been launched against PRI governors, no matter how egregious the offense against local democracy.[21]

II. CHALLENGES TO THE ARCHIPELAGO: THE TRANSFORMATION OF MEXICAN FEDERALISM

Thus the paths to Mexican subnational democratization would be party-led. The transformation of Mexican federalism, a product of continuous negotiations between political parties during Mexico's slow road to national

[20] Bartlett was a prominent national figure. He served as Interior Minister in the 1980s. In that position he managed the controversial election that made Carlos Salinas president in 1988. He also made his mark nationally as a local politician during Zedillo's presidency. Wayne Cornelius described him "as the most consistently effective and politically ingenious challenger of central authority during the Zedillo *sexenio*." Cornelius, Eisenstadt, and Hindley, *Subnational Politics and Democratization in Mexico*, 8. For a discussion of Bartlett's tactics as governor, see Julián Durazo Herrmann, "Social Heterogeneity, Political Mediation, and Subnational Authoritarianism: Comparing Oaxaca and Puebla, Mexico," presented at the conference on "Sub-national Democratization: Latin America, the United States, Russia and India in Comparative Perspective," Buenos Aires, Universidad Torcuato Di Tella, April 15–16, 2010. See also Agustina Giraudy, "The Politics of Subnational Undemocratic Regime Reproduction in Argentina and Mexico," *Journal of Politics in Latin America* 2 (2010).

[21] As Andrew Selee and Jacqueline Pleschard wrote in 2010, "Although it had only a fifth of the congressional seats from 2006 to 2009, [the PRI] remained the only party that could form an alliance with the PAN or the PRD to reach a majority, and its leaders have often availed themselves of this strategic role to protect local politicians affiliated with it as a condition for their support . . . the imperative of short-term alliances has allowed the PRI to protect the most authoritarian elements still within its ranks." See Selee and Peschard, "Mexico's Democratic Challenges," 21.

democratization, would create the institutional framework for these local transitions to take place.

In comparative terms, Mexican federalism imposes significant limits on the powers of state governments to craft their own political institutions and to control municipal governments. It also limits their powers to control fiscal transfers and to wield their influence in the national legislature. These limitations were enhanced considerably with the advent of democratization, but they stem from a long tradition in Mexican federalism. Constitutional framers were loath to grant states the powers granted to their counterparts in other Western Hemisphere federations.[22] As Alberto Diaz-Cayeros has written, a wary view of state power has shaped Mexican federalism:

> Can states in a federation be trusted? The Mexican constitution clearly establishes that they cannot. The Mexican federal pact reflects a deeply embedded distrust of state power.... Federalism is primarily about limiting the power of states.[23]

The 1917 constitution limited the powers of state authorities in several areas. It stipulated that governors, state legislators, and mayors could serve only one term in office, thus depriving local authorities of the power to decide a key element of their political regime. The senate, the national arena for representation of states, was given more limited powers than those granted to the lower house.[24] The constitution also limited the powers of the states in fiscal domains.[25] Mistrust of the states was reflected in its statement that municipalities, not states, are the "basic unit" of the federation. The national constitution guaranteed and spelled out municipal autonomy and its attributes[26] and did not delegate these tasks to states as part of their "internal regime," as in the Unites States and Argentina.

The first major wave of reforms occurred in 1977. The PRI controlled the presidency, all governorships, every seat in the senate, and 83 percent of the

---

[22] For historical perspectives on the evolution of federalism in 19th- and 20th-century federalism in Mexico, see Miguel Carbonell, "El Federalismo En México: Principios Generales Y Distribución De Competencias," *Anuario de derecho constitucional latinoamericano* (2003). See also Alberto Díaz Cayeros, *Federalism, Fiscal Authority, and Centralization in Latin America* (Cambridge: Cambridge University Press, 2006).

[23] Alberto Diaz-Cayeros, "Do Federal Institutions Matter? Rules and Political Practices in Regional Resource Allocation in Mexico," in *Federalism and Democracy in Latin America*, ed. Edward L. Gibson (Baltimore: Johns Hopkins University Press, 2004), 300–1.

[24] In fact, the senate was eliminated outright in the constitution during the 19th century. The 1917 constitution established a senate but limited its authority over the federal budget, giving the chamber of deputies the leading role in crafting and passing budgets. For an analysis of the historical role of the senate in Mexican federal politics, see Ignacio Marván Laborde, "Reflexiones Sobre Federalismo Y Sistema Politico En México," *Política y Gobierno* 4, no. 1 (1997).

[25] For an anatomy of Mexican fiscal federalism as it operated in the late 20th century, see Marcelo Giugale and Steven Benjamin Webb, *Achievements and Challenges of Fiscal Decentralization: Lessons from Mexico* (Washington, DC: World Bank, 2000).

[26] Aranda Vollmer, *Poliarquías Urbanas*, 34.

seats in the national lower house. Nevertheless, its leaders opened spaces for political participation to meet opposition demands and modernize its own electoral machinery. As the opposition victories multiplied over time, so did negotiations over federalism.[27] Opposition parties and the PRI negotiated substantial constitutional and electoral reforms in 1986, 1989, 1993, 1994, and 1996. Together they produced a revolution in the electoral architecture of Mexican federalism whose democratizing effects on state politics would be felt gradually but powerfully.[28]

Reforming Federalism: National Powers over the Design of Local Electoral Systems

Article 116 of the Mexican constitution, which addresses the internal political systems of the states, has been one of the most amended articles in the constitution. Its original version banned the reelection of state governors, legislators, and mayors. Reforms negotiated with the opposition since 1977 have expanded the restrictions on states to craft local political regimes. They mandate that the number of legislators in state legislatures be proportional to the population of each state and that the states adopt a mixed plurality–proportional representation (PR) system for the election of state legislators to facilitate minority party representation.[29] Although the ratio of plurality to PR seats is left to each state, the norm adopted across states hews closely to the 60–40 ratio used in the national congress.[30]

In 1996 Article 116 was amended to require that local laws governing elections to state offices conform to federal electoral legislation. In a clear sign of the strong influence of national law on the design of state regimes, Chapter IV of Article 116 opens with the following phrase: "The constitutions and electoral laws of the states will guarantee that..." It then lists 14 clauses that address the scheduling of campaigns and elections, the distribution of campaign financing, access to local media by political parties, local media coverage of elections, collaboration with federal regulatory bodies, and penalties for specific electoral infractions. Other constitutional provisions address the conduct of local judiciaries in the oversight of state elections. According to Susana Berruecos, "The 1996 electoral reforms in Mexico, somewhat against the grain

---

[27] Andreas Schedler, "From Electoral Authoritarianism to Democratic Consolidation," in *Mexico's Democracy at Work: Political and Economic Dynamics*, eds. Russell Crandal, Guadalupe Paz, and Riordan Roett (Boulder: Lynne Rienner, 2005), 9–37.

[28] See Enrique Ochoa-Reza, "Multiple Arenas of Struggle: Federalism and Mexico's Transition to Democracy," in *Federalism and Democracy in Latin America*, ed. Edward L. Gibson (Baltimore: Johns Hopkins University Press, 2004), 255–96.

[29] The plurality system favors first-place parties, whereas PR systems guarantee minority parties a share of seats.

[30] Ernesto Hernández Norzagaray, "Sistemas Electorales Y Sistemas De Partidos En Los Estados Mexicanos," presented at the VI Congreso de la Asociación Española de Ciencia Política y de la Administración, Barcelona, 2003.

of president Zedillo's 'New Federalism . . . forced the states to bring their own electoral laws into line with federal standards."[31]

Within these nationally mandated restrictions, there is still wiggle room for incumbents to design laws on party registration requirements, district magnitudes for local legislatures, and party financing arrangements. However, the big picture is set by the national constitution. Incumbents can engage in local institutional design at the margins for partisan advantage, but the formal powers to build in outright party hegemony in state party systems are constrained by Mexico's national territorial regime.

Reforming Federalism: National Electoral Monitoring of Subnational Elections

Another significant change in Mexican federalism has been the institutionalization of national monitoring of elections in the states. In 1989 the *Instituto Federal Electoral* (IFE) was created to monitor elections to federal offices in the states. Its autonomy and oversight powers have expanded considerably since it was founded. The IFE's original scope was to ensure the fair conduct of state elections for president and the national congress. In subsequent years, its scope expanded to the review of spending by political parties and campaigns and media coverage of political parties. In 1996 the body was established as an autonomous institution, independent from the national executive branch and political parties.[32]

The creation of the federal electoral institute, and the subsequent expansion of its mandate, was, in comparative terms, a major institutional innovation. It resulted in the institutionalization of independent national electoral monitoring of federal elections held in subnational jurisdictions. There is no comparable institution in any other federal country in the Western Hemisphere.[33]

The 1996 reforms produced another significant breach of state autonomy: they extended national electoral monitoring to elections for *subnational* offices. They required establishment of autonomous administrative and judicial bodies in the states to oversee elections for local offices: state-level IFE-type bodies bearing the name "State Electoral Institute." The reforms also spelled out procedures for appointing members of these bodies locally, mitigating their dependence on state governors or local ruling parties.

---

[31] Susana Berruecos, "Electoral Justice in Mexico: The Role of the Electoral Tribunal under New Federalism," *Journal of Latin American Studies* 35, no. 4 (2003), 801.

[32] Ochoa-Reza, "Multiple Arenas of Struggle," 284.

[33] In Argentina elections for national office are monitored in the provinces by representatives of political parties. In the United States the monitoring of federal elections is a state responsibility and is carried out by state public officials (Secretaries of State) who are elected partisan officials.

The 1996 constitutional amendments also created a national electoral court, the *Tribunal Electoral del Poder Judicial de la Federación* (TEPJF), which functions as the highest electoral judicial authority in the country. The court also has the power to adjudicate disputes over elections for state offices. This revolutionized the world of subnational elections, which were until then the exclusive purview of state authorities. It established federal judicial review of state electoral laws and the conduct of elections for subnational offices by state officials.

The 1996 constitutional reforms thus marked a milestone in the evolution of Mexican federalism. They established detailed national standards for political regimes at all governmental levels and placed the conduct of local elections within the jurisdictional reach of the center. According to Andreas Schedler, the reformers had a prescient understanding of the future challenges of territorial democratization in Mexico: "In a democratizing Mexico, it was understood that taking a laissez-faire attitude toward subnational regimes would have amounted to giving local power cliques a free hand to lock in authoritarian enclaves."[34]

Reforming Federalism: Enhancing Municipal Autonomy and Authority

As noted earlier, the autonomy of municipal levels of government is a core principle of Mexican federalism. The constitution outlines the organizational structure and powers of their governing bodies, stipulating that their leaders are elected directly by local voters and do not have the right to serve more than one consecutive term.[35] The constitutional reform of 1977 went a step further in defining municipal political regimes by mandating that municipalities with populations exceeding 300,000 elect their authorities by proportional representation. A 1983 reform extended this requirement to all municipalities. Thus, state incumbents have been deprived of formal powers to shape the political regimes of municipalities and to isolate those political spaces from local and national partisan competitors.[36]

In matters of fiscal federalism, constitutional provisions and political practice give municipal authorities important powers. A 1983 reform of Article 115 gave them exclusive rights to collect property taxes. It also expanded their scope of authority, outlining specific public services – from street cleaning to

---

[34] Schedler, "From Electoral Authoritarianism to Democratic Consolidation," 30.

[35] Article 115, which addresses the place of municipal governments in the federal structure, makes clear that key attributes of municipal political regimes are to be determined by the national constitution, not by state authorities: "each municipality will be governed by a Council elected by direct popular vote, and will be integrated by a Municipal President and the number of council-members and *síndicos* determined by law. The powers that this Constitution grants the municipal government will be exercised by the Council exclusively, and there will be no intermediate authority of any kind between the Council and the state government." *Constitución Política de los Estados Unidos Mexicanos*, Article 115.

[36] Aranda Vollmer, *Poliarquías Urbanas*, 34–35.

the management of markets and commercial centers – as the exclusive domains of municipal governments.[37] Hegemonic-party control of the states and ambiguities in the laws themselves tempered the actual autonomy granted by these reforms. However, in 1999 opposition parties in the congress, eager to shore up the economic value of urban electoral bases, enhanced the legal taxing and governing powers of mayors. They placed key municipal prerogatives and fiscal rights beyond the reach of state laws (and thus outside the internal regimes of the states).[38]

As in Argentina, Mexican states are heavily dependent on transfers from the central government to finance their budgets. On average, central government transfers account for 85 percent of state budgets.[39] However, unlike Argentina, the Mexican system of federal revenue transfers is a multifaceted arrangement of conditional, unconditional, and discretionary budgetary lines that flow both to the states and to municipalities. It is not one pipeline that flows straight to the governor's office, as in Argentina.[40] Rather it is a complex architecture of financial channels, whose multiple destinations and institutional oversight by the central government hinder its monopolization by state authorities.

Reforming Federalism: Reducing the Territorial Powers of the Mexican Senate

Constitutional reforms pushed by opposition parties also loosened the PRI's hold on the senate and decreased its weight as a territorial chamber. A 1996 reform mandated that one-third of the senate seats representing states be reserved for opposition parties. In the same reform 32 of the 128 seats in the body were reserved for senators elected by proportional representation from a *national* list. These reforms were an important blow both to the PRI and to states in Mexico's federal system. They occurred just as PRI state political machines were gaining autonomy and flexing their muscle in national politics. At the same time, senators were becoming increasingly beholden to their state political machines and were emerging as key allies of governors in the new hierarchy of power in Mexican intergovernmental politics.[41]

---

[37] Proyecto Transparencia, *Reformas al Articulo 115 de la Constitucion Nacional*, http://www .insp.mx/transparencia/XIV/leyes_federales/refcns/pdfsrcs/115.pdf.

[38] In her study of fiscal decentralization in contemporary Mexico, Emily Edmonds-Poli notes that the 1999 reform of Article 115 was driven entirely by opposition parties in the chamber of deputies. The PRI, ever committed to preserving the powers of their state bastions, opposed the constitutional reforms. See Edmonds-Poli, "Decentralization under the Fox Administration," 398.

[39] Ibid., 402–3.

[40] See Steven B. Webb and Christian Y. Gonzalez, *Bargaining for a New Fiscal Pact in Mexico* (Washington, DC: World Bank, 2004).

[41] See Joy Langston, "La Competencia Electoral Y La Descentralización Partidista En México," *Revista Mexicana de Sociología* 70, no. 3 (2008); "Rising from the Ashes?," *Comparative*

In sum, the institutional revolution by opposition parties that expanded their territorial gains produced a federal system that was less peripheralized and more municipal-empowering than it had been under 20th-century Mexican federalism. In time, this remapping of the territorial regime would unleash a powerful force against local authoritarian boundary control: the party-led transition.

III. DISMANTLING SUBNATIONAL HEGEMONIC PARTIES: PARTY-LED TRANSITIONS IN MEXICO, 1997–2010

PRI hegemonic party rule continued to be a fact of political life in Mexican states in early 1997. Twenty-eight states were governed by the party and had been since the Mexican Revolution. Thirteen years later the subnational political landscape had altered considerably: a new trend of subnational democratization had overturned the consolidation of several authoritarian enclaves. Eighteen states governed by the PRI in early 1997 had turned over to an opposition party by 2010. Many more were electorally competitive despite the PRI's continued successes in gubernatorial elections. The primary mechanism for the dismantling or weakening of local hegemonic rule was party competition. Party-led transitions, aided by the new architecture of electoral federalism, spread to all corners of the country.

Table 5.1 displays the magnitude of the party-led transition wave in the Mexican states and reveals a great deal about the national and local dynamics of party-led transitions in Mexico. There were three types of opposition coalitions in party-led transitions: candidacies led by a PRI defector, multiparty opposition candidacies, and solo opposition party candidacies. Of the three, PRI defector candidacies were the most common. The capture of a major urban jurisdiction by opposition parties was also important, as was the role of national monitoring and judicial bodies in overseeing and adjudicating disputes in local elections. Finally, the PRI was able to stage a comeback in several states, indicating that the loss of hegemony did not bring about the death of the party, but an adaptation to a new competitive environment.[42]

Political Studies 36, no. 3 (2003); and Diego Reynoso, "Alianzas Electorales Y Contingentes Legislativos En Los Estados Mexicanos (1988–2006)," *Revista Mexicana de Sociología* 72, no. 1 (2010).

[42] In 2010 the PRI controlled 19 of 32 governorships. The wave of party-led transitions has thus clearly not meant the demise of the PRI as a viable party. Quite to the contrary – it has shown itself to be highly competitive in free and fair elections. Establishing whether the PRI return in particular states signified a resumption of authoritarian politics is beyond the scope of this chapter. However, in all states the comeback occurred in a competitive system governed by other parties, embedded in a framework of national electoral regulation.

TABLE 5.1. *Challenges to PRI Hegemony in Gubernatorial Elections, 1997–2010*

State[a]	Opposition Victory	Opposition Coalition	Prior Opposition Capture Capital or Urban Hub	Prior Office Held by Winning Candidate	Active Role of National Electoral Bodies in Election?	PRI Comeback
Querétaro	Yes: 1997	PAN	Yes: capital (PAN), 1997	President, business association	No	Yes: 2009
Nuevo León	Yes: 1997	PAN	Yes: capital (PAN), 1994	Business leader	No	Yes: 2003
Mexico City	Yes: 1997	PRD	N/A	Presidential candidate, state governor	No	No
Zacatecas	Yes: 1998	PRI defector; PRD candidate	Yes: capital (PRD) 1998	PRI national senator and deputy	No	Yes: 2010 (defection of PRD politician back to PRI)
Aguascalientes	Yes: 1998	PAN	Yes: capital (PAN) 1997	Business leader	No	Yes: 2010
Tlaxcala	Yes: 1999	PRI defector; PRD candidate	No	PRI national deputy	No	Yes: 2010 (2005–11 governor; also PRI defector)
Nayarit	Yes: 1999	PRI defector; PAN-PRD Coalition	No	Mayor, capital	No	Yes: 2005
Baja California Sur	Yes: 1999	PRI defector: PRD candidate	Yes: capital (PAN) 1993	PRI national deputy	No	No

State						
Morelos	Yes: 2000	PAN	Yes: capital (PAN), 1997	Mayor, capital	No	No
Yucatán	Yes: 2001	PAN-led: PAN- PRD	Yes: capital (PAN), 1990	Mayor, capital 1995–98; National senator	Yes: Federal Tribunal rulings critical to 2001 outcome	Yes: 2007
Chiapas	Yes: 2000	PRI Defector: Conv-PAN-PRD	Yes: capital (PAN)	PRI national senator	Yes	No (but 2006 winner a defector)
Michoacán	Yes: 2002	PRD	Yes: capital (PAN and PRD), 1990	National senator and deputy	Yes	No
San Luís Potosí	Yes: 2003	PAN	Yes: capital (PAN) 1992	Mayor, capital	Yes	Yes: 2009
Sonora	Yes: 2009	PAN	Yes: capital (PAN), 1996	National senator	Yes	No
Guerrero	Yes: 2005	PRD	Yes: urban hub (PRD-Acapulco), 1999	Mayor, Acapulco (PRD), national deputy (PRI)	Yes	No
Oaxaca	Yes: 2010	PRI defector; Conv-PAN-PRD	Yes: Capital and urban hub (PAN, Conv., and PRD)	Mayor of capital and national senator	Yes	No
Puebla	Yes: 2010	PRI defector: PAN-led coalition with PRD and Conv.	Yes: capital (PAN), 2002	National senator and deputy	Yes	No

(continued)

TABLE 5.1 (continued)

State[a]	Opposition Victory	Opposition Coalition	Prior Opposition Capture Capital or Urban Hub	Prior Office Held by Winning Candidate	Active Role of National Electoral Bodies in Election?	PRI Comeback
Sinaloa	Yes: 2010	PRI defector: PAN candidate	Yes: capital and urban hub (PAN)	PRI national senator	Yes	No
Campeche	No		Yes: capital (PAN) 1997		N/A	
Coahuila	No		Yes: capital (PAN) 1997		N/A	
Colima	No		Yes: capital (PAN) 2000		N/A	
Durango	No		No		N/A	
Hidalgo	No		Yes: capital (PAN) 1999		N/A	
Mexico State	No		Yes: Ecatepec and Toluca (PAN) 2000		N/A	
Quintana Roo	No		Yes: Cancun (PRD) 2008		N/A	
Tabasco	No		No		Active: Federal Tribunal annulled PRI 2000 victory; PRI won rematch	
Tamaulipas	No		Yes: Reynosa (PAN) 2004		N/A	
Veracruz	No		Yes: Veracruz (PAN)1997		N/A	

[a] By early 1997, the states of Chihuahua, Baja California, and Jalisco had already experienced an opposition party turnover.

In half of the state elections first won by the opposition, the winning candidate was a PRI defector. Factionalism is the gravest threat to local PRI hegemony. It is driven by local politics, but exposure to national party competition is what makes it so damaging. The party's many safeguards against internal factionalism have disappeared over the last 20 years. No longer is there vertical discipline enforced from the president to the lowest municipal authority. There are more places for defectors to go, and the penalties that once made defection unthinkable are no longer what they used to be. Changes in Mexican federalism have opened local electoral arenas to national parties, which often receive PRI defectors with open arms. In addition, local PRI incumbents lack the constitutional powers to redesign local primaries or electoral laws in ways that discourage factional defections. There are no institutional solutions akin to the *ley de lemas* or the white primary available to local incumbents in Mexico's federal system.

The factional route to power makes strategic sense to opposition parties because they often lack local organization networks that can take the PRI head on in an electoral contest. Their local parties are not only weak but are often co-opted by PRI power holders. Luring local PRI dissidents is thus a fast-track alternative to the laborious task of building a party organization from scratch. PRI defectors include top state politicians who run key bureaucratic and partisan institutions. When these leaders defect, they put activists, organizational networks, and patronage resources at the service of the opposition coalition. PRI defectors also bring badly needed name recognition to local opposition parties.

At the heart of the sequential process of party-led transitions is a mechanism that can be labeled "resource capture," in which resources once monopolized by the hegemonic party fall to the opposition in the rough and tumble of party competition. Such resources vary. They include patronage networks, fiscal flows, and taxable jurisdictions. Capture of such resources is an opposition-empowering mechanism that, in the iterative process of party-led transitions, shifts the local power balance against the hegemonic party over time.

In a first illustration of this process, let us examine the factional party-led transition. One advantage of this transition pattern for opposition parties is that it involves considerable resource capture over a short period of time. Figure 5.2 displays the local–national interaction in this process. In Mexico national parties often took the first step in orchestrating the defection of PRI dissidents. This usually involved coercing local affiliates into accepting the defection and the defector-led coalition. In addition to enabling significant resource capture for the opposition, the defection created a template for new coalitions with PRI defectors over time, creating, in effect, a local infrastructure for opposition party challenges. As the local opposition infrastructure expanded over electoral cycles, national parties increased their investments in their local affiliates and empowered them further. Local opposition parties paid a price in autonomy and leverage by entering into these alliances, but their national parties gained a local foothold quickly and a cost-effective acquisition of party organization in the provincial jurisdiction.

Local Hegemonic Party Split → Defection to local opposition (negotiated with national opposition leaders) →

    Resource Capture by local opposition → National parties invest further → Incumbent rule threatened
    (Patronage Resources)
    (Party Organization)
    (Party Leaders and Voters)
    (Name recognition)

FIGURE 5.2. Resource Capture and the Factional Party-Led Transition

The year 2010 was a banner year for defector-led coalitions. Three PRI state bastions – Oaxaca, Puebla, and Sinaloa – fell to the opposition. All of these were defector-led coalitions. The strategy was coordinated nationally. Putting the brakes on the PRI's resurgence before the 2012 presidential elections was a national priority for the national PAN and PRD. National parties were thus on the prowl for potential PRI dissidents in the states. Despite profound ideological differences between the PAN and the PRD, they often coordinated efforts with each another to form multiparty alliances supporting PRI dissidents in many jurisdictions.[43]

"Asphalt" Party-Led Transitions: Urban Politics and Subnational Democratization

In 15 of 18 party-led transitions between 1997 and 2010, opposition parties won the governorship after having held the mayoralty of a major urban hub. In addition, in six of these cases the winning candidate himself had been mayor of a big city. These election results highlight the value of urban political spaces to subnational democratization in Mexico. In any national context, the political and social diversity of cities makes them key breeding grounds for opposition politics. Yet in the context of Mexican federalism, cities are a vital piece of opposition territorial strategies. A mayor can count on independent flows of money from the central government, a modest tax base, and transfers from the state mandated by federal law. He or she may find these resources captured or diverted in a number of ways by an adversarial governor, but mayors have ways of challenging such boundary-closing gambits.

Figure 5.3 portrays the asphalt party-led transition schematically. An initial investment by national parties in local contests empowers local parties and leads to the capture of urban mayoralties. Urban centers yield valuable resources for local party-building, such as governmental experience, credit-claiming, and an autonomous economic base. These resources, at one time monopolized by the hegemon, have now been appropriated by the opposition

---

[43] PAN-PRD coalitions were victorious in two states – Oaxaca and Puebla – in 2010. In Sinaloa, the other state lost by the PRI, an ex-PRI politician won as a candidate for the PAN. The PAN and the PRD formed unsuccessful coalitions in other states as well. See "Alianas Triunfan en Oaxaca y Puebla," Informador.com.mx, August 8, 2011.

Opposition Wins Urban Hub → Local Resource Capture → National-Subnational Linkage Capture →
                       (Patronage resources)   (Fiscal flows)
                       (Policy prerogatives)   (Policy links with national govt.)
                       (Control of state legislators)

National Parties Invest Further → Incumbent control of provincial government threatened

FIGURE 5.3. Resource Capture and the Asphalt Party-Led Transition

party. Controlling urban hubs increases the local party's statewide prospects. This further enhances the party's attractiveness to its national party and encourages additional outside investments in the party. The virtuous cycle sparked by electoral capture of the city now gives the party a credible shot at controlling the province.

IV. CREATING AND DISMANTLING A SUBNATIONAL AUTHORITARIAN REGIME IN MEXICO: THE STATE OF OAXACA, 1998–2010

In February 2004 a charismatically self-confident governor clasped the hand of his designated successor in a victorious salute to local supporters in the southern state of Oaxaca. José Murat, PRI governor for more than five years, had just fulfilled a theoretically anachronistic tradition of Mexican politics. This was the *dedazo*, the unilateral anointing of PRI chief executives by their predecessors – a practice officially dropped by the national PRI in the waning years of the 20th century.

In early 2004, however, the PRI's old rituals were alive and well in Oaxaca. The nomination was accompanied by another time-honored tradition that had theoretically disappeared – *la cargada*, a "stampede" of public displays of support by state unions, municipal presidents, party leaders, and party-affiliated social organizations. In an additional sign of the governor's sway over Oaxacan political life, *la cargada*'s *búfalos* (as the ritual's participants are known) included more than the usual members of the Oaxacan political establishment. Newspaper ads in the days after the unveiling of the candidate featured public displays of support from construction firms, car dealerships, tire dealerships, dry cleaning stores, restaurateurs, pharmacies, and shoe stores.

It was an emblematic moment. The two men on the stage were local incarnations of the hard-line PRI leadership who had risen to power in several states after national democratization. Murat, elected governor in 1998, had taken full advantage of the territorial dynamics of democratization to create one of the most authoritarian states in the country. The national newspaper *La Jornada* dubbed him "a face of the new PRI."[44] Ulíses Ruíz Ortíz, his chosen successor, had been a loyal lieutenant. Now, with the support of the state party's movers and shakers, he was poised to continue his patron's legacy.

---

[44] "Murat, rostro del nuevo PRI," *La Jornada*, April 21, 2002. Internet edition, available at http://www.jornada.unam.mx/.

José Murat and Ulíses Ruíz Ortíz, however, would end up playing very different historical roles. Murat had presided over a notorious subnational authoritarian enclave in the relatively permissive early years of national democratization. Ruíz Ortíz would preside over its turbulent demise under more daunting conditions of national electoral regulation and coordinated opposition challenges from national and local arenas.

Parochialization of Power: Consolidation of Authoritarian Rule under Governor Murat, 1998–2004

The 12 years preceding the election of José Murat as governor of Oaxaca were characterized by a slow pluralization of authoritarian politics in the state. During the gubernatorial term of Heládio Ramirez (1986–92), the Oaxacan PRI responded to growing unrest by co-opting civic opposition and tolerating local electoral victories by opposition parties.[45] Governor Ramirez's successor, Diódoro Carrasco (1992–98), continued his predecessor's approach. During his governorship the left-leaning PRD became the state's second party, and the conservative PAN captured the mayoralty of the capital city of Oaxaca.[46]

José Murat had been a visible player in national and local politics. He worked closely with Governor Ramirez as an interlocutor with local opposition forces. He served stints in the national senate and in the chamber of deputies, during which he also became connected to national networks of influence within the ruling party. By 1998 Murat was a clear contender for the gubernatorial nomination.

There was one problem, however. He was not an insider in Governor Diódoro Carrasco's circles. When Carrasco selected another candidate, Murat went directly to the president. He threatened to defect to the PRD if he was not designated the PRI's gubernatorial nominee in Oaxaca. Given the national competitive pressures on the PRI, Murat's threat was credible. Shortly before Murat had made this threat, Ricardo Monreal, a PRI leader in the state of Zacatecas, had defected to the PRD and went on to win the 1998 gubernatorial election. His defection, known within the party as "el Monrealazo,"

---

[45] For Oaxacan politics under Governor Ramirez, see Richard Snyder, *Politics after Neoliberalism: Reregulation in Mexico* (Cambridge: Cambridge University Press, 2001). For earlier periods see Fausto Díaz Montes, *Los Municipios: La Disputa Por El Poder En Oaxaca* (Oaxaca: Instituto de Investigaciones Sociológicas, 1980); Víctor Raúl Martínez Vázquez, *Movimiento Popular Y Política En Oaxaca, 1968–1986* (Mexico City: Consejo Nacional para la Cultura y las Artes, 1990); Raúl Benitez Zenteno, ed. *Sociedad Y Política En Oaxaca, 1980* (Oaxaca: Instituto de Estudios Sociológicos, 1980); and Colin G. Clarke, *Class, Ethnicity, and Community in Southern Mexico: Oaxaca's Peasantries* (Oxford: Oxford University Press, 2000).

[46] PRI hegemony nevertheless characterized Oaxacan politics. In the municipal elections of 1995, the PRI received 60 percent more votes than its nearest competitor and won the mayoralties of 111 of the 160 municipalities where party elections were held. See Víctor Raúl Martínez Vázquez and Fausto Díaz Montes, eds., *Elecciones Municipales En Oaxaca* (Oaxaca: Instituto de Investigaciones Sociológicas, 2001).

sent shock waves throughout the national PRI. The party was facing defection threats in several other states as well, and in the following year another PRI defector would win the governorship of the state of Zacatecas for the PRD. Rather than risk losing a PRI state bastion to the opposition, President Zedillo relented.[47] He compensated Governor Carrasco with a promotion to the national Interior Ministry. For the next two years Diódoro Carrasco would be a determined adversary of Governor Murat from his powerful perch in the national government.

Murat lost no time in consolidating his control over the Oaxacan polity. The most important threats came from rival PRI factions, namely "Diodoristas," who now had a powerful sponsor in the national government. Neutralizing politicians with ties to that faction was therefore the first order of business. Defying a long-standing norm of respect for *continuidad de equipo* (administrative continuity), Murat purged the state government of officers linked to the Carrasco administration. He also replaced the leadership of the Oaxacan state congress with loyal *Muratistas*.[48] In addition, he isolated the largely Diodorista Oaxacan delegation to the national congress.[49]

The Election of President Fox and the Strengthening of Local Authoritarian Rule

According to one political commentator, "the election of Vicente Fox strengthened Murat's political control."[50] Variations of his statement were made repeatedly in author interviews with politicians and political observers in Oaxaca. The record confirms this prevailing wisdom. The change of government greatly relieved pressures from the center by removing any vestiges of presidential discipline from within the PRI. Second, it relieved Murat of national PRI factional threats. His adversaries in powerful national bureaucracies were no more, and their departure isolated their local allies. An important breach of local boundary control from the governor's own party was now sealed.

The election of a PAN president brought additional bonuses for the governor. Vicente Fox had few partisan tools in the state to constrain the governor's actions. Although the PAN's institutional presence in the state was growing, it was still outstripped by the PRI. The PAN governed the national capital

---

[47] This version was confirmed by ex-Governor Diódoro Carrasco, who asserted that "the designation of José Murat as PRI nominee was a decision by President Zedillo. He would regret it later." Author interview with Diódoro Carrasco, Mexico City, April 4, 2005.

[48] Early on, Murat secured the election of Juan Díaz Pimentel as president of the Oaxacan legislature. Díaz was also co-owner of *El Tiempo*, a local newspaper acquired by Murat and other partners early in his term.

[49] Author interview with Vicente de la Cruz, national congressman for Oaxaca, 1997–2000, Mexico City, February 14, 2004.

[50] Author interview with Vicente de la Cruz, Mexico City, February 14, 2004. Another local observer stated that "this period of party turnover in the national government has greatly favored Murat." Author interview with Víctor Raúl Martínez Vazquez, political scientist, Oaxaca, February 16, 2004.

from 1998 to 2001, as well as a small number of urban municipalities, but these strongholds were dwarfed by the PRI's statewide power in municipal politics.[51] The PAN was most definitely an asphalt party, with a negligible presence in the state's vast and politically vital hinterland. Its influence in legislative politics was even less impressive: it held only 17 percent of the seats in the state legislature, 2 seats in the national chamber of deputies (both proportional representation seats put in by recent constitutional reforms to favor non-PRI parties), and no national senators. The governor thus had little to fear from the local PAN as a presidential instrument for oversight and control of his actions.

Furthermore, the 2000 presidential election brought an inexperienced national government to power in a political context in which the PRI dominated the national legislature and a majority of state governments. Even if the Fox government had known how to use the levers of the national territorial system against its state-based party rivals, it had few incentives to do so. President Fox needed interlocutors in the opposition. PRI governors were major power brokers in the new political context. The president had pressing national agendas to pursue, and challenging authoritarian governors was not one of them. As one Oaxacan politician (then in the opposition) lamented in early 2004, "there is a lack of interest on the part of the federal government in the democratization of the states."[52]

Firmly in control of the Oaxacan PRI, the state legislature, and the state judiciary, Governor Murat turned his attention to municipal politics. In the first five years of his administration, Murat suspended or removed municipal authorities in 140 of Oaxaca's 570 municipalities (nearly 25 percent of the total). The most politically significant interventions took place in urbanized municipalities controlled by the opposition. Of the 140 interventions, 48 were in opposition-controlled municipalities.[53] The governor used a constitutional prerogative available to Mexican governors (the *desaparición de poderes*) that, with the approval of the state legislature, authorizes them to remove municipal authorities in the event of threats to local governability. The governor's control of the state legislature made it quite easy to carry out this prerogative's illegal and blatantly partisan use.

[51] The PAN's control of the capital city was significant, though short-lived. Its 1998 capture of the city placed it in opposition hands for nearly a decade (it passed to *Convergencia* in 2001), and contributed to the gradual weakening of the PRI in state politics. PAN's share of Oaxacan municipalities would grow between 1998 and 2001 from 6 percent to 15 percent. However, this paled in comparison to the PRI's 56 percent share in 2001 and the PRD's 24 percent share. For statistics on party municipal control between 1997 and 2007, see Augustina Giraudy, "Subnational Undemocratic Regime Continuity after Democratization: Argentina and Mexico in Comparative Perspective," Ph.D. dissertation, University of North Carolina, Chapel Hill (2009), 180–82.

[52] Author interview with Juan Manuel Cruz Acevedo, former president of the Oaxacan legislature, Oaxaca, February 17, 2004.

[53] "Murat: retrato de un cacique," *Reforma*, October 19, 2003, 15. Tactics to justify the municipal intervention often included the instigation of violence in municipalities by government loyalists or audits of municipal funds management by the Murat-controlled legislature.

The partisan consequences of these interventions were significant. After the 2001 local elections, the opposition PRD controlled 36 municipalities. By mid-2003 the number they governed declined to 29 – 7 of which had been "intervened" by the governor. Similarly, in 2001 the PAN had won in 29 municipalities. By mid-2003 it controlled only 17. *Convergencia*, a political party/movement of ex-PRI leaders, suffered the largest proportional blow.[54] After the 2001 elections, *Convergencia* controlled six municipalities. By mid-2003 it controlled only one – the capital city of Oaxaca.

The usurpation of municipal governments was a fiscal boon for state authorities. Municipal heads appointed by the governor diverted funds sent to municipalities under the federal revenue-transfer system to the state government. It was also an economic boon for the PRI, transferring economically valuable jurisdictions held by the opposition to its control.[55] In a constitutional context of fiscal and political autonomy for municipalities, it was another boundary-control strategy based on the subversion of national regulations in the jurisdiction.

Control over the state legislature also gave the governor control over the state judiciary, which did not challenge the governor's use of funds, assaults on municipal autonomy, or electoral practices.[56] Press reports of the midterm elections of 2003 document wide-scale electoral manipulation, diversion of federal funds to partisan activities, fraud, clientelistic vote buying, and co-optation and intimidation of the opposition.[57] Grouped collectively under the name *cochinero electoral* (electoral pigpen), these practices solidified *Muratismo's* control over party politics. In 2003 the PRI swept to victory in all of the state's 11 congressional districts.

Monopolizing Local–National Linkages

The Oaxacan state government receives more than 90 percent of its revenues from the federal government.[58] As described earlier, these funds come to the state via a complex system of channels. Some come without conditions and are sent directly to state authorities, some are earmarked for specific uses and monitored by local delegates of the federal government, some are destined directly to municipalities, and others are sent to states but earmarked for distribution to municipalities. The monopolization of national–subnational financial flows is thus not facilitated by Mexican fiscal federalism. It can be achieved only extra-institutionally.

A key factor in monopolizing those flows was Governor Murat's neutralization of the network of federal delegates charged with monitoring federally

---

54 *Convergencia* had become a vehicle of choice in Oaxaca for PRI defectors to run against the PRI, usually in alliance with other parties.
55 See "Murat: retrato de un cacique."
56 In fact, the president of the state supreme court, Raúl Bolaños, was a prominent contender for Murat's nomination as PRI gubernatorial candidate in 2004.
57 "Murat: retrato de un cacique."
58 INEGI, *Finanzas Públicas Estatales y Municipales de México* (Mexico City: Instituto Nacional de Estadística, Geografía, e Informática, 1998).

funded programs in the state. Most of the government's national ministries have appointed delegates in the states for this purpose. The federal delegates are a key linkage between the national government and subnational communities in Mexico's territorial system. In the two years following the election of the Fox government, Murat replaced federally appointed delegates with delegates of his own liking. He did so with virtually no challenges from the federal government.[59] His neutralization of the federal delegate network in Oaxaca gave Murat control over a sizable proportion of federal funds in his state, including funds destined for use by municipalities.[60] This control only tightened the gubernatorial hold over municipal leaders, most notably the opposition mayor of the capital city of Oaxaca, because a sizable share of federal funds was destined to public works projects in that city.

Another national–subnational link was the system for auditing the expenditure of federal funds by the states. Headed by the *Auditoría Superior de la Federación*, it is a cooperative federal–state system whereby federal audits in the states are carried out jointly with state auditing agencies. The personnel of these agencies are accountable or even appointed by state legislatures. The PRI-dominated Oaxacan legislature defanged federal audits of state expenditures and in key cases refused to carry out audits ordered by the federal government. It did so with impunity during Murat's term as governor.[61]

An additional step toward the monopolization of local–national linkages was changing the composition of the state's national congressional delegation. Because of his control over local party nominations, Governor Murat was able to put together a solid bloc of *Muratista* deputies in the national congress by 2001. This enhanced his abilities to extract sizable appropriations from the congress and, of course, to advance the electoral fortunes of the ruling party. Ulíses Ruíz Ortíz was the PRI campaign manager for the Oaxacan federal elections of July 2003. Later that year he remarked happily that "the work carried out by the Oaxacan deputies in the national congress and in the capture

---

[59] As captured by the abject statement by the Federal Secretary for Natural Resources after Murat removed one of his delegates: "We need federal delegates in the states that have a good working relationship with the governors, and this relationship was already very deteriorated." Quoted in "Aclaran Destitución en Oaxaca," *Reforma*, August 22, 2002. Internet edition, available at http://www.reforma.com/.

[60] The main budgetary lines of federal transfers to the states are known as "ramo 33" and "ramo 28." In a colorful display of local political culture, Margarita Ramos, a Murat operative in the city of Juchitan, was known by locals as "Margarita Ramos 33," for her freewheeling distribution of federal funds to party loyalists.

[61] Murat's successor, however, would be constrained by a less permissive national context. In a belated assertion of federal government authority, the National Supreme Court ruled in mid-2006 that the national government possessed the authority to order audits of state use of funds and invalidated the Oaxacan legislature's refusal to carry out such audits. The case was brought to the court not by Oaxacan plaintiffs but by the opposition-controlled national congress. See Suprema Corte de Justicia de la Nacion, Medios y Publicaciones, "La Auditoría Superior de la Federación Sí Tiene Facultades para Fiscalizar Recursos del Ramo 33," August 8, 2006, http://www.scjn.gob.mx/MEDIOSPUB/NOTICIAS/2006/Paginas/Noticia20060808.aspx.

of budgetary appropriations was fundamental to the success of the PRI in Oaxaca.... Murat attracted considerable funding.... This was perceived by the population and it was reflected in its vote."[62]

The Nationalization of Influence: Oaxaca in Mexican Politics

Governor Murat was closely allied to Roberto Madrazo, ex-governor of the State of Tabasco and leader of the hard-line PRI faction that had opposed President Zedillo. In 2001 Madrazo became president of the PRI. Murat projected himself into the national limelight in ways befitting his membership in this hard-line cohort. He was one of the prominent PRI rebels against presidential authority, first against President Zedillo and then against President Fox. In addition to his assaults against federal delegates in his state, he defied national authorities on other issues. When the national government withheld federal funds from the state because of questions about state mismanagement, he organized high-profile sit-ins in the national capital that led to release of the funds. He was a founding member and leader of CONAGO, the National Governor's Confederation created in 2001 to enhance the collective power of governors in national politics. For the PRI leaders who created it, CONAGO was a vehicle for collective action against the PAN-controlled presidency.[63] Murat also played a key role in the election of Madrazo to the presidency of the PRI. As the national newspaper *La Jornada* noted in 2002, "he is considered one of the unquestioned leaders of the *cochinero* [pigpen] that took Roberto Madrazo to the presidency of the PRI."[64]

"Murat's fate is linked to the fate of Madrazo."[65] This statement, made by a Oaxacan political observer in 2004, captures the nonlocal nature of Murat's strategies of territorial control. The national metric of his success as a governor was his electoral usefulness to his national faction, which depended on several actions – delivering votes in primaries, delivering blocs of legislators who supported the faction, and strengthening local electoral machines for future national elections.[66] Thus national party competition provided incentives for the governor to strengthen local authoritarian rule. The more successful at eliminating local PRI rivals and delivering large blocs of votes and legislators to his PRI patron, the more leverage he would have within the national faction to which he was allied.

---

[62] "Murat: retrato de un cacique," *Reforma*, October 19, 2003:, 17.

[63] In a revealing statement about Murat and his allies' view of CONAGO's national objectives, Augustina Giraudy quotes Governor Murat as saying "the CONAGO was created to limit Fox's authority, which it did." Augustina Giraudy, Ph.D. dissertation, 195–96.

[64] "Murat, rostro del nuevo PRI," *La Jornada*, April 21, 2002. Internet edition, available at http://www.jornada.unam.mx/.

[65] Author interview with Víctor Raúl Martínez Vazquez, Oaxaca, February 16, 2004.

[66] Madrazo himself publicly recognized the national stakes in the 2004 gubernatorial contest in Oaxaca: "Oaxaca is strategic because whatever party wants to win the presidency of Mexico has to win the state.... In Oaxaca the next presidential administration is being defined." Quoted in Mica Rosenberg, "Power Politics: Oaxacan Style," *SIPA News* (2004), 23.

The Backlash: Party-Led Efforts to Democratize Oaxacan Politics

Governor Murat's authoritarian rule was largely unchallenged by the local branches of the PRD and PAN. Both had been brought to a low ebb during his governorship. The main local partisan challenge came from PRI factionalism. This was based in Oaxaca City, the sophisticated and politically diverse urban jewel of the state.

In 2001 Gabino Cué Monteagudo, a former PRI Diodorista politician, won the mayoralty of Oaxaca City as a candidate for *Convergencia*. In 2004 he announced his plans to run for governor as a *Convergencia* candidate. The problem for Cué was that he would have to do so as head of a multiparty alliance if he had any hope of taking on the governor's impressive statewide machine. Neither the local PAN nor the local PRD had any interest in forming part of such an alliance. The local parties were weak, starved for resources, and co-opted by the state's governor.[67]

Cué therefore took his case to the national PAN and the PRD, both of which responded positively to his overtures.[68] The parties had different but complementary interests in seeing Murat's candidate defeated. The governor had not turned out to be the "interlocutor" for which Vicente Fox had hoped. Furthermore, his rise as a player in the PRI's national presidential campaign made him a target of the PAN's national leadership. The national PRD was anxious not to lose further ground in the south, and Governor Murat threatened to close off a vital arena in that part of the country.

The unprecedented electoral coalition against the Oaxacan PRI in 2004 was thus a result of intervention by the national PAN and PRD. It was achieved over the opposition of the local branches of both parties. The PAN national leaders brought local PAN leaders to heel. However, Oaxaca's most important PRD leader refused to join the coalition and ran as an independent.[69] This proved devastating to the opposition. Ulíses Ruíz Ortíz won the election by 3 percentage points. The independent PRD candidate garnered 4 percent, arguably siphoning off votes needed to give the opposition a winning margin.

Independent observers, national newspapers, and opposition leaders denounced the election as fraudulent. Large protests took place in the capital and the state's major urban hubs. The compliant Oaxacan state electoral institute quickly certified the validity of the electoral results. Gabino Cué's campaign appealed to local courts, and when they ruled against him, he took his case to the national Federal Electoral Tribunal. The federal court

---

[67] See "El PRD está en bancarrota," *El Imparcial*, February 18, 2004, 3.

[68] Author interview with Jorge Castillo, manager of Gabino Cué Monteaguo's gubernatorial campaign, Mexico City, April 4, 2005.

[69] Sánchez's independent campaign siphoned off 4 percentage points from Cué's campaign. The PRI won by a 3.2 percent margin. The local press reported that Murat financed pro-Sanchez publicity in the local media. See "Renuncia Héctor Sánchez a sus cargos en el PRD," *Noticias de Oaxaca*, February 20, 2004, 15.

acknowledged electoral misconduct but, finding that there was insufficient evidence that it affected the outcome, ruled against the opposition.

PRI opponents called for a federal investigation of the state election to generate that evidence but found no ally in the presidential palace. President Fox praised the conduct of the August 1 state races nationwide and refused to single Oaxaca out as a problematic case even as demonstrations were rocking the capital. With major pieces of national legislation pending, the president was more interested in policy alliances with the Madrazo-dominated PRI than in joining the fight to democratize Oaxacan politics. Indeed, Madrazo and top PRI congressional leaders warned President Fox that the party would refuse to cooperate with him on pending legislation if the Oaxacan election was annulled by national judicial or executive authorities.[70] The policy and governing imperatives of central government authorities were not, at the moment, in harmony with the electoral imperatives of their own party.[71]

The Party-Led Challenge That Worked: Boundary Control and Opposition under Governor Ruíz Ortíz, 2004–10

In mid-2004 the PRI enjoyed overwhelming institutional control over state politics. Although the party-led challenge had made gubernatorial elections competitive for the first time in state history, all other state institutions were firmly in PRI's control. The PRI controlled 62 percent of the seats of the Oaxacan legislature and the lion's share of the state's national congressional delegation.[72] Furthermore, municipal elections held in October 2004, monitored by PRI-controlled state election authorities, yielded a major sweep by the PRI of mayoral races throughout the state. The new governor may have won with little more than a 3 percent margin, but he went on to govern with virtual control over the state legislative branch, with

---

[70] "Pega a ley de ingresos controversia electoral: Advierte el PRI que no aprobará Iniciativas de Fox si no se respetan sus triunfos," *Reforma*, October 29, 2004, p. 1.

[71] A columnist for Mexico's most important national newspaper summed up the opposition's dismay and explained the government's inaction: "It is surprising that, faced with so many evident irregularities the Secretary of the Interior of the Federal Government, Santiago Creel, declared the elections 'exemplary.'... The diligence of the Secretary of the Interior seems guided by an eagerness to compensate the *priistas* for doing the federal government's dirty work. The reform of the Social Security law is still pending, and the Fox government must show its most favorable disposition towards those willing to sink their hands into the mud....It would not be the first time that the federal government and the PAN leadership ignored such electoral plunder." See Humberto Mussacchio, "Oaxaca, un caso de anacronismo," *Reforma* (Mexico City), August 3, 2004.

[72] In the April 2004 elections, the PRI electoral machine delivered victories in 18 of the 25 single-member districts that sent representatives to the provincial legislature. Opposition legislators were from the two main urban regions, the capital city and Juchitán, and the balance were elected by proportional representation. Urban polities and national legislative seats designed for minority parties by the recent reforms of Mexican federalism continued to be the lifeblood of opposition institutional power.

loyal municipal leaders throughout the state, and with a compliant state judiciary.

These were, however, vulnerable times for the local leviathan. Its vulnerabilities were both local and national. Control over local political institutions was countered by a growing loss of control over local civil society and local party oppositions. Both groups had been greatly empowered by the 2004 election and by their growing ties to allies and institutions in national politics. The PRI had also lost control over the territorial scale of debates about Oaxacan politics after the contentious 2004 elections. Oaxacan state politics became a staple of national (and international) press coverage, and local opposition forces, facing a daunting and increasingly repressive local hegemon, worked the national scene relentlessly to ensure that their conflicts with local incumbents stayed in the national limelight.

The state PRI was also facing more coordinated national partisan threats. Gabino Cué Monteagudo won a national senate seat in 2006. The governor's key partisan rival could now pursue his local designs from a perch in the national senate.[73] In addition, the national PAN adopted a strategy of co-opting high-visibility defectors from the national PRI and running them as PAN candidates in the states for national congressional seats. Although the Oaxacan PAN opposed the defector candidates in its own state, it was overruled by a national party bent on increasing its local stock of politicians skilled in the national and local practices of Oaxacan power struggles. One of these candidates was Diódoro Carrasco, the ex-PRI governor, ex-Minister of the Interior, and determined adversary of the Murat-Ulíses Ruíz faction of the state party. He went on to serve as a member of congress for the PAN, filling a proportional representation seat from the state.[74]

In this challenging context Governor Ruíz Ortíz turned increasingly to local repression. In his first years in office the governor unleashed several high-visibility persecutions of his opponents. He shut down the main independent newspaper, *Noticias*, in 2004 and 2005.[75] He also ordered the incarceration of his 2004 election opponent, Gabino Cué Monteagudo, on questionable charges of financial misconduct during his term as mayor of the capital. The governor also presided over a wave of kidnappings, murders, and attacks against opposition groups committed by PRI operatives in the fields and urban alleys of the state. The dire human rights situation caught the attention of the U.S. Department of State, which in 2005 issued a report on human rights violations in

---

[73] Gabino Cué's senate seat was the one of three seats reserved for a candidate from a minority party by the 1996 constitutional reform – yet another piece of evidence of the boundary-opening effects for subnational politics of the transformation of Mexico's national territorial regime. Without that reform, the national senate would have been closed to all opposition party leaders from the state.

[74] For an account of the PAN strategy (and the resistance of the local PAN chapter), see "Postula PAN a ex-priistas para Diputados," *Reforma*, April 26, 2006, p. 6.

[75] The governor's attacks on the newspaper made the international press, most notably an article in the *New York Times*. See *New York Times*, July 18, 2005, 4.

the state. The Catholic Church, in another breach of the PRI's local boundary control, took up the human rights cause in early 2005 by organizing protests against the authoritarianism of the state government.[76]

Local tensions exploded in an urban uprising in the capital city of Oaxaca in mid-2006. Violent police suppression of a teachers' demonstration (led, ironically, by the local branch of the pro-PRI national teachers union) sparked a broad uprising of student groups, unions, and civic organizations against the governor's authoritarian rule. Demonstrators took control of the city center and paralyzed activity in the city for several weeks.

The conflict transfixed the national public. Congressional leaders called on the national government to remove the governor and dismantle the authoritarian structure sustaining PRI rule – in effect, to carry out a center-led transition.[77] Debates about such an intervention raged in national circles during the conflict.[78]

The governor fled the state. Squeezed between a local popular uprising and national outrage, the beleaguered incumbent turned to the national PRI for protection. The party had circled its wagons around the Oaxacan governor two years earlier, after the controversial 2004 election. It did so again now.

The national PRI saved the Oaxacan PRI, and it did so thanks to a fortuitous national deadlock in presidential politics. In the July 2006 presidential elections, the PAN and the PRD ended in a virtual tie. The PAN candidate, Felipe Calderón, squeezed out a 0.58-percent margin of victory. The PRD candidate, Andrés Manuel Lopez Obrador, refused to recognize the PAN's victory. This sparked a vitriolic conflict between the parties that lasted for most of Calderón's presidential term. The deadlock was a godsend to the Oaxaca governor. His patron, Roberto Madrazo, had come in a distant third in the election, but was in a strategic position to extract concessions from the PAN.

In the climate of national crisis, the PAN was ready to negotiate. In exchange for PRI recognition of its victory, it promised cooperation on several issues, including the fate of the Oaxacan PRI. A senate fact-finding commission, dominated by the PAN and the PRI, recommended against a federal intervention against the governor. And in the waning months of his presidency, Vicente Fox, the founding president of Mexico's new democracy, came to the aid of a

---

[76] The president of the Commission of Justice and Peace for the Archbishop of Oaxaca acknowledged the importance of outside monitoring of local human rights abuses in the state. Citing the State Department report, he stated that local groups had long denounced human rights abuses, but it was necessary "to say it in English for people to listen." See "Preocupa a la Iglesia Represión en Oaxaca," *Reforma*, March 2, 2005, 24.

[77] Such an action by the federal government could be constitutionally undertaken by invoking a *desaparicion de poderes* clause that granted the national government powers of intervention in the event of civil conflict or threats to political stability in the states.

[78] For press reports on the debate, see "Piden la Desaparición de Poderes en Oaxaca," *El Universal* (Mexico City), June 17, 2006, http://www.eluniversal.com.mx/estados/61574.html; "Piden a Presidente Resuelva Conflicto; Valora AN en Senado Desaparecer Poderes," *Reforma*, September 27, 2006, 14; "Como Salir de la Trampa en Oaxaca," *Reforma*, October 9, 2006, 6.

subnational authoritarian government. He ordered a 4,000-strong invasion force of federal police to crush the civic uprising. Order was restored to Oaxaca, and Governor Ulíses Ruíz Ortíz returned to the governor's palace.[79]

The National Context Shifts: Electoral Federalism and Party Strategies

Despite the political boundary-closing deals between national democratic politicians, Mexican electoral federalism was deepening its penetration of Oaxacan politics. The Federal Electoral Institute (IFE), which had played a passive role before 2004, became a significant player in local federal elections thereafter. It more than tripled its network of local election monitors in the state, and by the federal elections of 2006 and 2009, its officials were monitoring voting and gathering data on local violations in the state's most important municipalities.

The IFE's national governing body also ruled that in 2009 and 2010 the sitting governor had violated national electoral law by using public funds for campaign purposes. It sanctioned the PRI gubernatorial candidate in 2010 for similar violations, as well as dozens of local media outlets and campaign officials for infractions during electoral campaigns in those years.[80] Three months before the July 2010 gubernatorial election, the IFE dealt local electoral officials a blow by invalidating the entire organizational structure set up by the Oaxacan Electoral Institute for running the election. Citing a range of irregularities and "subjective" criteria in appointing electoral officials, the national body ordered the institute to redesign the plan and replace the electoral officials it had selected to coordinate Election Day activities.[81]

National partisan politics also shifted against the Oaxacan PRI in 2010. The PRI had won a string of victories in state gubernatorial elections between 2006 and 2009 and became a favorite for the presidential sweepstakes of 2012. The PRI's ascendance sparked new strategies by the PAN and PRD national party organizations. PAN party leaders decided on a nationally coordinated strategy of subnational coalition-building with the PRD to prevent another PRI sweep in the 2010 gubernatorial elections. Oaxaca was a key piece in this strategy. Defeating the PRI in one of its most infamous bastions would be a major victory against the resurgent party.

The key to the strategy was to gain the cooperation of the PRD in a string of "contra-natura" coalitions against the PRI. Fortunately for the PAN, the

---

[79] For an account of the civic uprising see Victor Raúl Martínez Vázquez, *Autoritarismo, movimiento popular y crisis política: Oaxaca 2006* (Oaxaca, Mexico: Universidad Autonoma Benito Juarez [UABJO], 2007).

[80] See, for example, "Dan 24 horas a Gobernador para retirar propaganda," *Reforma*, June 13, 2009, 8; *Clarín Veracruzano*, "Prevé IFE Amonestar a Candidato de PRI en Oaxaca," May 12, 2010, http://www.clarinveracruzano.com/preve-ife-amonestar-a-candidato-de-pri-en-oaxaca; *Reflexión Informativa Oaxaca*, "Multa IFE a Radio Cumunitaria de Oaxaca," September 29, 2010, http://www.rioaxaca.com/v1/general/11851–1122-multa-ife-a-radio-comunitaria-de-oaxaca.html.

[81] "Tira TRIFE en Oaxaca Estructura Electoral," *Reforma*, March 18, 2010, 10.

PRD's national party chairman, Jesús Ortega, shared its strategic vision. He broke with his party's de facto leader, Andrés Manuel López Obrador, and negotiated anti-PRI coalitions with the PAN in five states. The PRD's motives were straightforward – to counter a precipitous national decline by expanding the party's hold of key state offices. Oaxaca was a particularly attractive base to consolidate. During the 2006 uprisings, the local teachers union broke its historic ties to the PRI and threw its support to the PRD, giving the party a powerful statewide organization that it was eager not to lose.[82]

The national parties turned once again to the ex-PRI politician Gabino Cué Monteagudo, who enjoyed a broad base of local support after engaging in long and painstaking party-building efforts as an opposition mayor, gubernatorial candidate, and, now, national senator. He coordinated the alliance with the national PAN and PRD from his perch in the national senate. He announced his candidacy for governor in 2009. This time the local branches of the parties joined him as coalition partners.[83]

Under the watchful eyes of national electoral monitoring bodies and the federal judiciary, and in a campaign whose every twist and turn were covered by the national press, the opposition defeated the PRI gubernatorial candidate. The PRI was removed from power in Oaxaca not by the hand of God or the central government. Its demise was the product of repeated electoral challenges that gradually empowered an electoral opposition through local and national coalition-building. It was also the product of a national infrastructure of electoral monitoring and regulation that penetrated the boundaries of one of Mexico's most sanctioned authoritarian states and helped bring about its political transformation.

CONCLUSION

National democratization at first enabled subnational authoritarianism in Mexico. Operating through the territorial hierarchies of party and intergovernmental politics, it empowered state-based hard-liners and gave political cover to local authoritarians bent on resisting the competitive pressures of national politics. National democratization, however, unleashed other national processes that over time reversed those trends and empowered boundary-opening actors in local and national arenas. The political and electoral centralization of federalism, a product of the give and take of national interparty negotiations, reshaped the strategic terrain on which subnational democratization conflicts took place. Over time it created a national democratic infrastructure of laws, electoral monitoring, and judicial oversight that penetrated subnational jurisdictions and wove them into its web. The result was a remarkable wave of party-led transitions in the first decade of the 21st century

---

[82] Julián Durazo Herrmann, "Neo-Patrimonialism and Subnational Authoritarianism in Mexico: The Case of Oaxaca," *Journal of Politics in Latin America* 2 (2010).

[83] See "Avalan en Oaxaca la Alianza Opositora," *Reforma*, February 8, 2010, 4.

that ended hegemonic party rule in some of the most tenacious authoritarian bastions.

However, local authoritarian rule is still a reality in many parts of the country. Its resilience is a testament to the strategic, economic, and political tools available to local boundary closers, as well as to the national partisan networks that organize and protect them. Yet subnational authoritarianism in Mexico, despite its ferocious exercise by incumbents, is a more vulnerable and unstable affair than in contemporary Argentina or the U.S. Solid South. Mexican federalism does not provide incumbents with the constitutional powers to make their authoritarian regimes institutionally impregnable. There is nothing "perfectly legal" about an authoritarian state regime in Mexico. It is maintained by illegal and informal strategies locally and by the exercise of national leverage through partisan collective action.

The authoritarian boundaries of Mexican subnational politics are also highly porous. Opposition parties are active, usually occupy key municipal power bases, and are protected by the legal and administrative institutions of Mexican electoral federalism. Furthermore, even in states where the PRI's electoral machine overwhelms all contenders, it is highly vulnerable to the bane of subnational hegemonic parties everywhere: factional stress. The local polity's integration into a national competitive party system gives PRI politicians ample exit opportunities when they lose internal battles, and opposition parties, national and local, wait with open arms to embrace the defectors as converts to the cause of local democratization. Under these conditions, party competition is the driving force of regime change in Mexican state politics. For leaders of hegemonic state parties, it constitutes a daily challenge.

The study of Oaxaca revealed these dynamics in full detail. It also provided a state-level view of the sequential effects of national democratization on Mexican territorial politics. During the 1990s, as the territorial effects of democratization shifted the strategic advantage to local boundary closers, Governor José Murat reversed a long process of political liberalization and built one of the most authoritarian state systems in the country. His commanding control of the state legislature and of local judges allowed him to subordinate municipal authorities and neutralize opponents inside and outside of the ruling party. Electoral fraud, campaign finance abuses, and political intimidation were the electoral coins of his realm. He defied two presidents by hijacking federal revenue transfers and the local programs they supported. This manipulation of local democratic institutions was protected from national intervention by a national party of governor-kings that deployed its national leverage against democratic presidents in defense of local boundary control.

During Murat's term Mexico's democratic architecture of electoral federalism had a limited influence on the parochial confines of the governor's fiefdom. Even a contested and fraudulent election in 2004 withstood the pressures of national electoral monitoring. This, however, would change significantly in the years thereafter. The 2010 gubernatorial elections were held under conditions of intense scrutiny by national electoral monitoring bodies and national electoral courts. The menu of illegal and informal manipulation of elections narrowed considerably for incumbents, and control of the scope of local conflict escaped from their hands.

Oaxaca's party-led transition was also an iterative process. In the 12 years between Governor Murat's assumption of power and the PRI's 2010 defeat, the local opposition was strengthened by repeated electoral challenges, local governing experience, and national coalition-building. PRI factionalism gave the opposition a game-transforming potential throughout this process. It also made national parties more willing to invest resources in local contests. Through a long painstaking process of coalition building, resource capture, and conflict nationalization, opposition party politics gathered strength in Oaxaca and overturned the hegemonic state party system.

Party-led transitions, therefore, are not merely processes by which provincial authoritarian regimes are brought down. They are also processes by which viable opposition parties are built, developed, and sustained over time. When the curtain falls on a gubernatorial election and the opposition stands victorious, it usually does so after years of experience in party-building and local government. This creates powerful local defenses against authoritarian regressions, regardless of whether the ex-hegemon returns to power in future contests. It is too early to say whether the Oaxacan 2010 election will deliver on its promise of good government and real democracy for Oaxaca's inhabitants. Yet if the party-led transition model continues its march across the country, it augurs well for the possibility that party alternation will indeed mean genuine regime change for the rights-deprived inhabitants of Mexico's remaining archipelago of provincial authoritarian regimes.

6

Boundary Control

Comparisons and Conclusions

Only connect!

E. M. Forster

In territorial politics there are few truly local conflicts. All territorial arenas – whether they be the province, the town, or the national government – are entangled in systematic ways. Certain parties to a conflict will strive to keep the fight localized. Others will not, and in the interdependent structure of a territorial system, national actors will often have an interest in what takes place in the local conflict. Understanding processes of local change, therefore, requires careful analysis of how the locality in question is enmeshed in a larger system of territorial governance.

In applying these insights to subnational authoritarianism in democratic countries, this book has addressed a number of issues. First, it has examined the political situation: the coexistence of a national democratic government with authoritarian subnational governments (in these cases, provincial governments). I have labeled this a situation of "regime juxtaposition," in which the rules and norms governing the behavior of leaders and the rights of citizens at the provincial level are at odds with those at the national level. Far from being an anomalous event in democratic countries, regime juxtaposition is a recurring phenomenon that is linked sequentially and dynamically to national democratization. It also constitutes one of the most important challenges to the spread of democracy within a country's borders once the national government has come under the control of democratically elected leaders.

Another issue explored in this book is the basic conflict pattern in situations of regime juxtaposition. I have labeled this conflict pattern "boundary control." Boundary-control conflicts are struggles between incumbents and oppositions to control the scope of local conflict. Authoritarian incumbents prevail when the scope of conflict is kept local and oppositions are denied access to outside allies and resources. These incumbents are threatened when local conflict becomes nationalized and outside actors enter the local fray. Provincial democratization is a thus a result of the nationalization of subnational conflict.

"Boundary openers" and "boundary closers" pursue both local and national strategies. Each seeks to build power locally, to extend influence into national political arenas, and to control channels of influence and resources linking national and subnational arenas. The prize of a subnational jurisdiction, therefore, is one pursued in multiple battlefields across a territorial system.

The national institutional context in which struggles over boundary control unfold has also been a focus of this book. Characteristics of "territorial regimes," which govern the territorial organization of the national state, have systematic effects on subnational authoritarianism. Territorial regimes can be federal or unitary, but more important than the federal–unitary dichotomy are the specific powers and prerogatives granted to national and subnational governments. Our three country cases, the United States in the 19th century and Argentina and Mexico at the turn of the 21st century, were federal countries. However, there were considerable differences in the powers and prerogatives granted to different tiers of government by federalism in each country. These variations had marked effects on the morphology and dynamics of subnational authoritarian regimes.

The three national democracies analyzed in this book were separated by time, geography, and political trajectory. Yet each experienced subnational authoritarianism as a salient feature of its political history. Furthermore, each experienced similar dynamics of boundary control, suggesting that fundamental patterns of political action are reproduced across time and context when regime juxtaposition occurs. In the next section I address the following commonalities: the fact of regime juxtaposition, the relationship between subnational authoritarianism and national party politics, and the centrality of subnational hegemonic parties to provincial boundary control. Subsequent sections discuss contrasts across the three countries, and their theoretical implications.

I. BOUNDARY CONTROL IN THE UNITED STATES, ARGENTINA, AND MEXICO: BIG-PICTURE SIMILARITIES

Regime Juxtaposition: The Fact and the Significance

We start with the obvious similarity between our cases: regime juxtaposition. The United States in the late 19th century had possessed a national democratic government for some time. Argentina and Mexico in the late 20th century were new democracies, and their national governments, in fits and starts, had achieved significant levels of democratic consolidation. Yet in each country the national democratic scene contrasted with the subnational picture. Incumbents in many provinces defied national democratic trends and crafted, preserved, or strengthened subnational authoritarian governments.

We thus saw that subnational authoritarianism can find fertile soils in both established and new democracies. Furthermore, it can last indefinitely and ebbs and flows with the movements of national politics. In all our cases subnational authoritarianism became part and parcel of normal politics, a key part of strategic relations between actors across the federal system.

The emergence of authoritarian "archipelagos" occurred despite powerful democratic pressures from national politics. The regional bloc of authoritarian states in the U.S. South emerged after a titanic national effort to impose inclusive democratic regimes in the region. Argentina's more diffuse assembly of authoritarian provinces was put together after the 1983 national democratization shook provincial political systems across the country. In Mexico local PRI incumbents in the 1990s preserved party-based authoritarianism at the local level despite the growing competitiveness of national politics.

These cases suggest that subnational authoritarianism in democratic countries is more a crafted phenomenon than one that arises naturally from local conditions. Certain local conditions obviously increase the probabilities of local resistance to national democratic pressures, but in the interconnectedness of a territorial system, fending off such pressures is an active process. In the United States, Argentina, and Mexico national pressures had created local competitive situations that incumbents then suffocated. Depriving nascent local democracies of oxygen required concerted action to isolate the local polity. An unavoidable conclusion that emerges from this study is that, wherever a provincial authoritarian government exists in a nationally democratic country, boundary control is taking place.

National Party Politics and Subnational Authoritarianism

In each of our countries subnational authoritarianism shaped the national balance of power between political parties. The battle over the democratization of U.S. southern states after the Civil War was critical to the Democratic and Republican Parties' national strategies. The clear victory of Democratic boundary closers in that battle gave the national party a reliable territorial base for its national struggles against the Republican Party. In bad times the Solid South ensured that the Democratic Party had veto power in national political institutions. In good times it was a regional buttress for national governing coalitions.

In Argentina, shoring up provincial authoritarian fiefdoms is an integral part of the Peronist Party's national electoral strategy. Argentine party politics is a complex affair, and in competitive provinces its protean quality defies generalization. However, one long-standing feature of the national partisan order has been the Peronist provincial bastion. The national party's dominance during the post-1983 democratic period, owed, just as it did in the middle of the 20th century, a major political debt to the provincial authoritarian regime.

According to one of Argentina's most prominent political analysts, in Peronist Party politics, "hegemony is incubated from below."[1]

In Mexico, shoring up state-level authoritarian governments became a party survival strategy when the PRI lost control over the national government at the end of the 20th century. The loss of its national hegemonic position only strengthened its commitment to preserving state hegemonic parties. Control of state governorships provided leverage over non-PRI presidents. Hegemonic party systems under their control gave PRI leaders large blocs of national legislators to compensate for shrinking numbers of legislators from competitive states. And, during the long winter of retreat, the PRI state bastions offered a vast organizational network on which to organize a national comeback. Conflicts over the democratization of Mexican states thus acquired critical significance for the balance of power between the PRI and its national opponents.

This brings us to the nonlocal nature of boundary control. In earlier chapters I referred repeatedly to three broad strategies of territorial control: the parochialization of power, the nationalization of influence, and the monopolization of national–subnational linkages. The parochialization of power refers to local strategies of political control – actions whose site is limited to the subnational jurisdiction. The nationalization of influence refers to strategies that secure national power to influence decisions about the local jurisdiction. The monopolization of national–subnational linkages refers to the struggle to control economic or political channels that connect national and subnational politics. In practice the three strategies are overlapping and mutually reinforcing. They are also linked causally. Action in one arena influences what happens in another arena. We can see this in the most basic local authoritarian practice: suppressing electoral oppositions.

Parochializing Power: The Nonlocal Dimensions of Suppressing Local Oppositions

In the American southern states, boundary closers restricted democracy primarily through voter disenfranchisement. The main target for disenfranchisement in the United States was the large population of new black voters. This strategy of disenfranchisement had clear local goals because blacks voted as an opposition bloc against the local Democratic Party. However, this electoral strategy had additional layers of complexity. Black disenfranchisement occupied a pivotal place in the local and national web of southern boundary control. It prevented white opponents from building biracial opposition parties and linking up with the national Republican Party. This had national partisan repercussions: shaping the national strategy of the Republican Party and dissuading it from investing resources and manpower in southern states. The success of the strategy strengthened the Democratic Party's monopoly over

[1] Natalio Botana, "El Cenit del Poder," *La Nación*, May 4, 2006.

the local polity. In turn this local monopoly expanded the party's representational clout in the national congress, which strengthened its ability to block national policies threatening the continued local disenfranchisement of black citizens.

In Argentina and Mexico incumbents focused not on participation, but on contestation – restricting the development of opposition parties.[2] In Argentina the reform of provincial constitutions in many provinces spearheaded by local Peronist incumbents restricted the local viability of opposition parties. The expansion of gubernatorial powers and the systematic legislative underrepresentation of urban electorates made it difficult for local opponents to mount effective challenges. As a result, national opposition parties adjusted their national strategies and deployed their resources to more competitive provinces. National Peronist leaders, who may not have shared the authoritarian proclivities of their local co-partisans, nevertheless had a partisan interest in their local electoral success. This shaped the party's national strategy. It also bolstered local incumbents' hold over provincial politics, giving them clout within the national party's inner circles and in national governmental institutions.

In Mexico the suppression of local opposition parties through fraud, coercion, and clientelism kept local PRI leaders in power. It also gave the national PRI strategic control of a large number of governorships. In a party that had gone from being "the party of the president" to the "party of governors," controlling governorships was the centerpiece of its strategy for national influence in the new democratic era. Governors who delivered solid blocs of votes and legislators to the party's national patrons saw their career prospects in national politics improve dramatically. The national gubernatorial coalitions and legislative blocs fortified by local authoritarian practices also acted as effective checks against non-PRI presidents contemplating action against local PRI redoubts.

Figure 6.1 shows this reinforcing process schematically.

Authoritarian Provinces, Plural Cities: Asserting Provincial Government Supremacy as a Boundary-Control Strategy

The city is the hotbed of competitive politics and the key to the development of competitive party systems. V. O. Key noted this in his work on the Solid South,

---

[2] See Robert Dahl, *Polyarchy; Participation and Opposition* (New Haven: Yale University Press, 1971). The difference between the U.S. and Latin American cases may be a function of the times. By the late 20th century the legitimacy of universal suffrage was so widely accepted that even the most authoritarian regimes relied on it for legitimization purposes. In the late 19th century, however, suffrage restriction was more widely accepted. However, this has bequeathed legacies to contemporary times. In the United States today, disenfranchisement continues to be the method of choice in the states for restricting or controlling democratic processes. The United States continues to be, albeit to a much lesser degree than a century ago, the world's largest disenfranchising democracy. In the rest of the world, the preferred method for mitigating the uncertainty of electoral outcomes is the restriction of contestation.

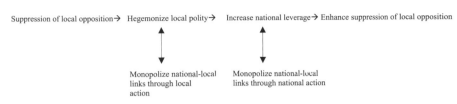

Parochialization of Power: *Nationalization of Influence:*

Suppression of local opposition→ Hegemonize local polity→   Increase national leverage→ Enhance suppression of local opposition

Monopolize national-local   Monopolize national-local
links through local   links through national action
action

FIGURE 6.1. The Nonlocal Cycle of Suppressing Local Oppositions

and we saw it as well in contemporary Latin America. For boundary closers, therefore, dealing with urban areas is critical. The stability of a provincial authoritarian regime requires that the provincial government reign supreme over the province's local governments and that the province be the dominant subnational jurisdiction in the federal system.

These imperatives gave rise to a common boundary-closing strategy in all our cases: reducing the electoral weight of urban areas in provincial politics. One way to do this was to exploit province-wide incumbent party machines. Authoritarian governors controlled provinces because their parties controlled the rural vote. The combination of state patronage resources and the wide geographic extension of party networks usually meant that rural districts "belonged" to the ruling provincial party. By overawing opposition votes in contested urban areas with massive ruling party vote totals in uncontested rural areas, incumbents prevailed in province-wide contests.

Where provincial incumbents had the power to design local electoral laws, they subverted the city through a more effective strategy: introducing a partisan bias to the electoral system by overrepresenting rural districts in provincial legislatures. Southern incumbents introduced malapportionment into every state legislature as part of the wave of late-19th-century constitutional reforms. Argentine provincial leaders similarly made malapportionment a core strategy in their subnational institutional revolution in the late 20th century. In provincial electoral politics, with the right menu of strategies, one could lose the city and still control the province.

In addition to electoral strategies, incumbents also employed an intergovernmental strategy: neutralizing the municipality as an autonomous level of government. This required subordinating mayors to governors and undermining their ability to forge linkages with national governmental or partisan actors. Writing about the democratization implications of subnational intergovernmental politics, Tracy Beck Fenwick has stated that "a successful strategy of boundary control will require that the core federal units capture municipalities within their territory."[3]

---

[3] Tracy Beck Fenwick, "Scaling Down further the Subnational Comparative Method: Insights from Brazil and Argentina," paper presented at panel on "Subnational Authoritarianism in Comparative Perspective," Latin American Studies Association International Congress, Rio de Janeiro, June 12, 2009.

Fenwick's observation was confirmed by our case studies. Where provincial incumbents' ability to "capture" municipalities was weakest, their vulnerability to opposition electoral challenges was greatest. In Mexico, governors were far less successful than U.S. or Argentine governors in capturing urban municipalities within their state borders. Mayoralties were thus valuable electoral prizes for opposition parties. PRI governors were under challenge from opposition "asphalt parties," who waged frequent campaigns to capture mayoralties of urban hubs. In Argentina and the U.S. Solid South, by contrast, national constitutional powers made the political subordination of municipalities to provincial governments considerably easier, and their value as a governmental prize for opposition parties considerably smaller.

Monopolizing fiscal transfers from the national government, as we saw in Argentina, was also key to capturing municipal governments. It severed financial ties between mayors and national governments. It also enhanced the power of governors throughout the provincial polity. Under such conditions, mayors often became supplicants of governors, and the city an administrative appendage of the provincial government.

Figure 6.2 displays the role of municipal capture in the national–local cycles of authoritarian boundary control. The local effects are electoral and intergovernmental. They reduce urban electorates' representation in legislatures, and mayors have fewer legislators beholden to them. In effect, they delink urban electorates and their leaders from province-wide institutions. In addition, these local effects stifle local opposition party development. National effects include enhanced clout for governors in national politics, reduced incentives for national parties to invest resources in local urban contests, and the closing of avenues for intergovernmental alliances between national and municipal authorities.

The Subnational Hegemonic Party in Democratic Countries: Institutional Expression of Provincial Authoritarianism

The designers of the U.S. Solid South invented subnational hegemonic parties. As the world's first experiment in federal democracy, the United States was also the pioneer of subnational authoritarianism and its most important institutional manifestation, the subnational hegemonic party.

Subnational authoritarianism in nationally democratic countries is an institutionally constrained affair. Local authoritarianism must be rendered institutionally compatible with national democratic politics. The requisite compatibility is functional (the local polity must interact institutionally with the national polity) and symbolic (local trappings of democracy are required to legitimize authoritarian rule). In a democratic country, subnational authoritarianism must therefore be organized by political parties. Forced to live with democratic institutions, local authoritarians have little choice but to manipulate them. Because of the obvious imperative to win "by design," by definition the hegemonic party is the only institutional option available to local boundary closers.

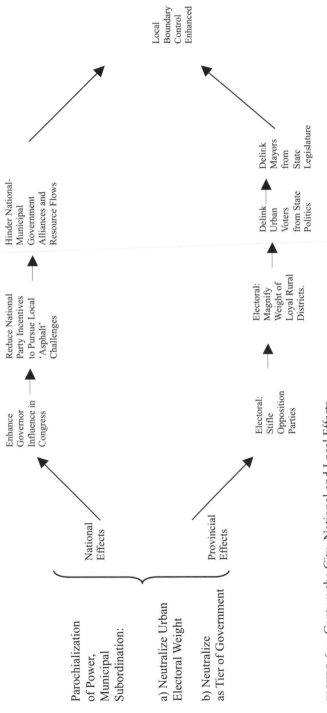

FIGURE 6.2. Capture the City: National and Local Effects

Parochialization
of Power,
Municipal
Subordination:

a) Neutralize Urban
Electoral Weight

b) Neutralize
as Tier of Government

National
Effects

Provincial
Effects

Enhance
Governor
Influence in
Congress

Reduce National
Party Incentives
to Pursue Local
'Asphalt'
Challenges

Hinder National-
Municipal
Government
Alliances and
Resource Flows

Electoral:
Stifle
Opposition
Parties

Electoral:
Magnify
Weight of
Loyal Rural
Districts.

Delink
Urban
Voters
from State
Politics

Delink
Mayors
from
State
Legislature

Local
Boundary
Control
Enhanced

A subnational hegemonic party differs from its national counterpart in two fundamental ways. First, it is embedded in a larger party system. Second, that system is a *competitive* party system. This endows the party with characteristics and dynamics unique to its status as a subnational party. Our cases revealed the following.

Subnational Hegemonic Parties Were Linked Horizontally to a Network of Co-Partisan State Parties

Not all members of the "co-partisan" network were hegemonic parties. In fact, most were not. The bloc of southern states was a minority in a national coalition of state Democratic Parties from competitive state-party systems. Peronist hegemonic provincial parties were similarly minority members of a chain of provincial parties dominated by parties from large competitive provincial party systems. And as the 21st century wore on, authoritarian PRI state parties were a shrinking piece of the national federation of PRI parties competing in increasingly competitive jurisdictions.

Membership in this horizontal network of hegemonic and competitive subnational parties was advantageous to local boundary control. As minority members of a web of mostly democratic parties, local hegemonic parties benefited from the reflected legitimacy of their national coalition. The confederal structure of the national party segmented the exercise of power by jurisdiction. It thus allowed the authoritarian nature of local hegemonic parties to dissolve into the larger web of competitive parties visible from national points of observation.

The horizontal network also enhanced collective action in national arenas. Blocs of provincial parties protected their members by acting in unison against national threats to boundary control. Whether these were cohesive regional blocs like the U.S. Solid South or more geographically diffuse assemblies as in Argentina and Mexico, unity of authoritarian state parties in support of boundary control was the norm.

These networks also facilitated the diffusion of information among state hegemonic parties. A sinister process of information diffusion drove the "subnational institutional revolutions" in U.S. southern states and in Argentina a century later. Successful experiments in one province or state were adopted in others. Over time a remarkable uniformity in the institutional foundations of party hegemony emerged. Coordination and information sharing between PRI state party machines were also the norm for gubernatorial elections. The construction and maintenance of a provincial hegemonic party were thus never lonely experiences. Isolation of local politics from national competitive pressures was a collective effort, tied inexorably to the party's integration into the national co-partisan network.

Subnational Hegemonic Parties' Internal Factionalism Was Fueled by Their Vertical Integration with the National Party System

The subnational hegemonic party may be a redoubtable local leviathan, but it is a porous leviathan. Its location in a multitiered competitive system makes it vulnerable to outsider exploitation. Its dissidents have many exit options. And these options are very attractive, given the resources that a rival national party can offer. The national territorial system also provides channels for dissident interaction with political adversaries beyond the reach of local incumbents. Small wonder, then, that a top boundary-control priority for incumbents was to craft institutions to protect them from factionalism.

The subnational hegemonic party is connected to national party politics through two conduits. The first is intraparty ties with its mother ship, the national party. In the United States, Argentina, and Mexico, local incumbents' vertical links to the national party offered protection. National leaders had a strong partisan interest in shielding authoritarian political systems that bolstered the party's national electoral performance. Yet links to the mother ship also created factional threats for the hegemonic party. Factional conflicts within the national party often reverberated throughout its subnational affiliates. They shaped electoral conflict in Oaxaca from the beginnings of national democratization until the fall of the local PRI more than a decade later. Similarly, in Argentina, national Peronist leaders intervened often in Santiago politics to reshape local factional conflicts, sometimes in favor of Governor Juárez and sometimes against him.

The party's interactions with national opposition parties also affect factionalism in subnational hegemonic parties. Party-led transitions often succeed when national opposition parties co-opt local dissidents. In the U.S. southern states during Reconstruction, the Republican Party relied heavily on wooing white dissidents from the Democratic Party. After Reconstruction, factionalism instigated by national Republicans remained a threat to southern Democrats. In Mexico, a majority of party-led transitions after the late 1990s resulted from the defection of dissident PRI leaders who had recently lost a fight within the state ruling party. National opposition parties of all stripes capitalized on PRI factional stress as a key boundary-opening strategy.

Reliance on the exploitation of hegemonic party factionalism by opposition parties is a testament to the power asymmetries in authoritarian jurisdictions. The hegemonic party systematically suffocates opposition party development. Local opposition leaders often lack the recognition, experience, and resources required to mount solo challenges against incumbents. This creates a nonhegemon's dilemma for local oppositions. They can pursue the expeditious route to power by recruiting incumbent party dissidents and sacrifice control to ex-members of the ruling party. On the other hand, they can forego the factional route and accept years or decades of hard party-building and delayed gratification (and risk remaining a permanent minority and opposition fig leaf for incumbents). It is not surprising that the expeditious route to power was the alternative of choice in so many instances. It is also not surprising that developing institutional safeguards against local factionalism is a key local strategy for boundary closers where they have the powers to do so.

Figure 6.3 provides a schematic representation of local and national sources of hegemonic party factional stress. Direct pressures come from the national party, whose internal conflicts are transmitted to the subnational party. They

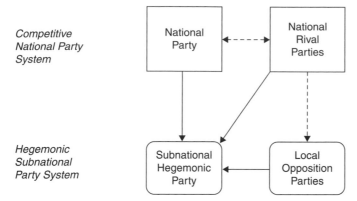

FIGURE 6.3. Besieged: National Party System Aggravators of Factional Stress in Subnational Hegemonic Parties

also come from local and national rival parties, depending on which of the two takes the lead in co-opting potential defectors. Indirect pressures (signified by the dashed arrows) come from interactions between the national party and its competitors in the national party system. They also come from interactions between national opposition parties and their local branches, which affect the latter's ability to draw support from their national party and thus attract local defectors.

So much for similarities among our cases. In the next sections of this chapter we examine how contrasting national institutional contexts produce different processes of continuity and change in subnational authoritarianism. A comparative examination of territorial regimes in the United States, Argentina, and Mexico is thus now in order.

II. THREE COUNTRIES, FOUR TERRITORIAL REGIMES

The analysis of territorial regimes asked three questions. For the first two questions, the basic subnational unit was the province. We examined how the territorial regime structures power between the national government and provincial governments. Is the system centralized or decentralized? We also asked how the territorial regime structures relations between provinces. Is the system asymmetrical or symmetrical in the national representation of provinces? The first question relates to powers between levels of government, the second to power between provincial jurisdictions. Combinations of these attributes determine the degree of "peripheralization" of the territorial regime. The more decentralized and asymmetrical the system, the more peripheralized. Whether a system is peripheralized or nonperipheralized has strategic implications for conflicts over subnational democratization.

We then peered into the province itself. We asked how the national territorial regime structures power relations *within* provinces; specifically, between provincial governments and municipal governments. Is the territorial regime municipal-empowering or province-empowering? That is, does it recognize

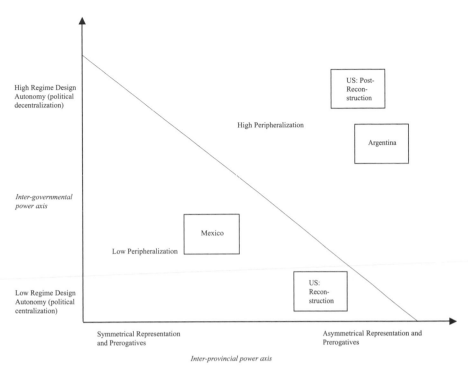

FIGURE 6.4. Peripheralization of Federal Territorial Regimes: The United States, Argentina, and Mexico

municipalities as autonomous governmental units, or does it render them dependencies of the provincial government? Whether a territorial regime is municipal-empowering or province-empowering is important for the ability of state government incumbents to insulate the province from national competitive pressures.

The Province in Federal Systems: Peripheralization and Nonperipheralization in the United States, Argentina, and Mexico

Our comparison of 19th-century United States with 20th-century Argentina and Mexico provided a pairing of territorial regime types. Two territorial regimes were peripheralized federal systems, and two were nonperipheralized. The United States had a nonperipheralized federal system during Reconstruction and a highly peripheralized one after Reconstruction. Late-20th and early-21st-century Mexico possessed a nonperipheralized territorial regime, similar in key dimensions to the United States during Reconstruction. Argentina during the same period possessed a highly peripheralized federal regime, similar in key dimensions to the United States after Reconstruction.

Figure 6.4 provides a visual comparison of the territorial regimes along the two dimensions of peripheralization. The United States during Reconstruction and contemporary Mexico are in the low-peripheralization space of the diagram. In Reconstruction-era United States, state authorities had limited power to design local political regimes. National rights were established by statute and constitutional amendment, and all states, including southern states, were compelled to incorporate these rights into their own political regimes. State constitutions during this period were designed under the clear guidance of national authorities, which ensured that they were in harmony with national standards. Furthermore, electoral federalism was centralized. National electoral regulation and monitoring of state elections were widespread.

Mexico's location in the nonperipheralized space reflects the reforms made to the country's federal system through 1996. The national constitution places significant restraints on local authorities in the design of electoral systems and local political regimes. Furthermore, in the early 2000s national electoral monitoring and regulation of subnational elections expanded dramatically. Mexican federalism is also less asymmetrical than the other cases in regard to the powers of its national senate and the representation of states in the senate and national lower house.

In the high-peripheralization space of Figure 6.4 are the United States after Reconstruction and Argentina in the late 20th century. With the defeat of Reconstruction, U.S. federalism became highly peripheralized, primarily because of its political re-decentralization. National rights were limited once again. States enjoyed almost complete autonomy to design local constitutions and electoral laws. National regulation of subnational elections was virtually nonexistent.

Argentina in the late 20th and early 21st centuries was highly decentralized and asymmetrical in the representation of provinces in national institutions. It is slightly lower than 19th-century United States on the centralization–decentralization axis because national rights are more clearly established and the national government has greater recourse to powers of federal intervention against provincial governments. However, the provinces are unconstrained in their powers to design subnational political regimes. National regulation and monitoring of subnational elections are virtually nonexistent.

On the interprovincial power axis, Argentina is also the most asymmetrical of this group of federal systems. It has one of the most malapportioned senates in the world. In addition, significant malapportionment exists in the lower chamber of the national congress.

Power within the Provinces: Municipal-Empowering versus Province-Empowering Federalism

We now compare our federal systems according to how they structure relations between provincial and municipal governments. Mexico possessed the one federal system that was municipal-empowering. The United States and Argentina possessed province-empowering federal systems. Table 6.1 summarizes these features.

TABLE 6.1. *Provinces vs. Municipalities: Municipal-Empowering Features of Federal Systems*

Municipal-Empowering Attributions	Argentina, Late 20th and 21st Centuries	United States up to mid-20th Century	Mexico
Autonomy of municipal tier guaranteed and stipulated in national constitution	No	No	Yes
Municipal political regimes designed nationally or municipally (not by provincial authorities)	No	No	Yes (mostly nationally)
Fiscal federalism: Central government transfers funds directly to municipalities or earmarks funds for municipal use	No	Yes, but negligible flows until 1930s and effective control of flows by governors and allied national legislators	Yes
Fiscal federalism: Municipalities enjoy local tax-raising powers	No	Limited	Yes (tax-raising powers stipulated in national constitution)
	(Less)	Municipal Empowering	(More)

←——————————————————————————————————————→

III. THE DIFFERENCE A TERRITORIAL REGIME MAKES: CONSTRUCTION AND MAINTENANCE OF SUBNATIONAL AUTHORITARIANISM

Variations in centralization, representational asymmetry, and empowerment of subnational tiers of government shaped strategic options available to boundary closers. These variations produced different patterns in the structure and durability of provincial authoritarianism.

Centralization

The most important of the three dimensions was centralization. In this book we settled on one criterion to distinguish between centralization and decentralization: the autonomy of provincial authorities to design and administer provincial political regimes. Variations in this attribute determined the most important difference across cases: whether subnational authoritarianism would rely on legal and institutional foundations or on informal and illegal practices for its maintenance and reproduction.

Decentralized Federalism: "Perfectly Legal" Subnational Authoritarianism

Where provincial authorities enjoyed high levels of regime autonomy, subnational authoritarianism was an institutionalized and legally sanctioned affair. We saw this in Argentina and in the United States after Reconstruction. In both cases incumbents crafted provincial constitutions and electoral systems that made their jurisdictions virtually unbreachable by party challenges. These were exemplary cases of Sartori's "win by design" condition for defining hegemonic parties. The "design" lay largely in the formal rules governing political and electoral life in the provinces. Repression, clientelism, fraud, and informal arrangements played their roles in these cases, but these were usually supporting roles, especially as the new institutional orders became stable. The long torpor that took hold of the Solid South at the turn of the 20th century and the torpor that characterizes daily life in many Argentine provinces were products of the anesthetizing effects of legal authoritarianism.[4]

In the United States and Argentina, we also observed an interesting sequential phenomenon. After a period of electoral ferment threatened local incumbent rule, a subsequent subnational institutional revolution put an end to the competitive challenges. However, there were important differences in the content of the authoritarian institutional reforms. In the United States, as noted earlier, the emphasis was on disenfranchisement, whereas in Argentina it was on the restriction of contestation. In addition, almost all Argentine reformers expanded gubernatorial powers and reelection rights, whereas few southern reformers did. Yet beyond these important differences there were two common features: legislative malapportionment and manipulation of primaries.

Legislative malapportionment: Malapportionment within provinces served two key functions. It secured hegemonic party control over provincial legislatures by underrepresenting urban areas in provincial electoral systems. It also reduced the influence of municipal governments in provincial politics, particularly by mitigating their leverage over legislatures. Legislators tended to be elected in districts dominated by the ruling party, and they were loyal to governors, not to mayors.

---

[4] In Levitsky and Way's theory of "competitive authoritarianism," the manipulation of formal democratic institutions in national politics is largely a product of informal or illegal practices. This study suggests that attention must also be paid to the legal subversion of democratic rights through the design of formal democratic institutions in competitive authoritarian situations, regardless of whether the unit of analysis is national or subnational. See Levitsky and Way, *Competitive Authoritarianism*, esp. pp. 7–11.

Manipulation of primaries to manage factional tensions: The white primary in the Solid South had its Argentine counterpart in the *ley de lemas*. Both strategies organized local primaries in ways that countered the centrifugal effects of factional conflicts in the hegemonic parties. Primary manipulation in a hegemonic party system was thus a significant inhibitor of competitive party system development. Its mechanisms obviously varied by the local context; for example, the white primary was attuned to the political realities of disenfranchisement and white supremacy. However, by effectively fusing the primary and the general election, each system had the effect of reducing incentives for local dissidents to defect from the party after being defeated in intraparty contests. Given the combined national and local factional pressures bearing on subnational hegemonic parties, primary manipulation proved to be a crucial strategy for holding them together.

Centralized Federalism: Informal and Illegal Subnational Authoritarianism

Where provincial authorities possessed limited constitutional powers to design local regimes or manage local elections, subnational authoritarianism relied on illegal and informal arrangements. We saw this in Mexico and in the American South under Reconstruction. Under the constraints of regime and electoral centralization, "folkways" could not become "stateways," and local authoritarianism relied on a flexible menu of extralegal strategies to survive.

The "design" built into the victories of local hegemonic parties was created by political operatives, not constitutional scholars. Its illegality and informality made it particularly vulnerable to national legal challenges. After Reconstruction, southern incumbents' greatest continuing national threat was federal electoral regulation. In Mexico, particularly as national electoral regulatory bodies expanded their territorial reach, long-standing PRI practices of domination came under serious scrutiny and threat.

In these cases incumbents relied on national leverage to shield them from legal, regulatory, and competitive pressures from without. National leverage was important to boundary control in all cases, but in cases of centralized federalism it was a matter of life or death for authoritarian incumbents. Lacking the local armor of institutional design, incumbents built their shields in national arenas. The success of PRI governors in warding off threats from opposing party presidents through national collective action was critical to authoritarian boundary control. In the United States, incumbents relied on their clout in the national Democratic Party and the congress to shield their illegal political redoubts from the full force and fury of federal law prior to the late-19th-century institutional revolution.

Centralized territorial regimes, therefore, generated boundary-control strategies that were illegal and informal locally, but were highly vulnerable to national legal or regulatory challenges. Incumbents in decentralized federal regimes, in contrast, enjoyed the protections of provincial legal architectures that neutralized most national legal challenges ex ante. Their influence in

Decentralized Parochialization of Power: Nationalization of Influence:
Federalism   **Legal and Institutional** + **National Leverage** → Insulated
                     (Shield 1)   (Shield 2)   Authoritarian Regime

Centralized   Parochialization of Power: Nationalization of Influence:
Federalism   **Illegal and Informal**   + **National Leverage** → Insulated
              (Vulnerable to national legal challenges)   (Shield 1)   Authoritarian Regime

FIGURE 6.5. The Double Shield: Decentralization and Authoritarian Boundary Control

national institutions added another layer of protection against national adversaries. They had, by far, the more secure arrangement. Figure 6.5 displays these contrasting patterns of local authoritarian regime maintenance.

Asymmetry of Representation between Provinces

Authoritarian incumbents in Argentina and the United States, whose provinces were overrepresented in national institutions, had more resources for building national power in the service of boundary control than did their Mexican counterparts. Argentine and American boundary closers held sway over powerful senates. They guaranteed the party unshakable minority blocs and quite often were instrumental to the party's majority control. The electoral college system also gave them considerable say over the selection of presidents and presidential candidates.[5] Because of this influence in their national parties, authoritarian incumbents shaped national decisions affecting the security of their authoritarian enclaves.

In Mexico's more symmetrical federal system, the senate's limited powers reduced its value as a national arena for boundary control. It was a cruel irony for PRI boundary closers, given their strength in the senate and dependent as they were on national leverage, that federal reforms in the late 1990s weakened that body as a forum for state interests. They were thus unable to control it from their state redoubts in the ways managed by U.S. and Argentine governors. The shifting electoral balance among the three national parties permitted the PRI to use its legislative clout on behalf of boundary control in several important occasions, but this, again, was a less stable institutional arrangement.

Empowering Provinces or Municipalities

It was relatively easy for U.S. and Argentine provincial boundary closers to "capture" cities politically and to reduce their weight in provincial politics. These objectives could be achieved by the legal suppression of municipal governments' economic and political autonomy (and through malapportionment).

---

[5] The Electoral College in Argentina was more proportional to provincial populations in its allocation of electors than the U.S. system. However, the system was nevertheless biased toward low-population provinces.

Mexican boundary closers, however, faced a more difficult task. Urban politics was a major headache for authoritarian governors. They had limited legal powers over the design of municipal regimes, and they could not draw urban hubs off the electoral map through malapportionment.[6] Municipal politics, especially urban municipal politics, was the most important territorial source of volatility for the Mexican state hegemonic party.

As a result, capturing municipalities required a creative array of strategies by governors. Control of *rural* municipalities was a vital and usually successful strategy. PRI rural municipal strongholds continued to buttress local electoral majorities, and the governor's party networks did their jobs diligently on behalf of their patrons. Controlling rural areas was normally the "quieter" side of municipal boundary control in Mexico.[7] Capturing cities, however, required more direct action that usually pushed or exceeded legal bounds. The most important case in point in our Mexico study was the abuse by the Oaxaca governor of his power to "intervene" in municipalities facing threats of violence or government wrongdoing. In the late 1990s and early 2000s, Governor Murat removed dozens of municipal governments controlled by opposition parties and replaced them with loyal authorities. His veto-proof control of the state legislature expedited these actions, and control over state judges forestalled legal challenges against their dubious legality. This was, however, the misuse of a local constitutional power, one that required control of other subnational institutions and evasive action against national legal challenges.

The national arrangements of fiscal federalism were quite helpful to boundary closers in the United States and Argentina. In Argentina boundary closers were aided by the province-empowering organization of fiscal federalism. Virtually all central transfers go to provincial authorities, most are unconditional transfers, and governors have almost complete discretion over their internal distribution. Governors thus held sway economically over the province's mayors. In the United States during the heyday of the Solid South, the situation was more complex. Federal flows to the states went through a variety of channels, but before the New Deal the amounts were negligible. As central government funding and investment increased after the 1930s, governors exercised control over financial flows through their influence on congressional legislators and presidents, ensuring that monies were deployed to loyalists and state incumbents.[8] These were not necessarily illegal maneuvers. They were part of the chain of

---

[6] They could, however, exploit majoritarian bias in the electoral system in rural single-member districts. Yet this was a less effective boundary-control option.

[7] "Quieter" only in the sense that it is not heard far outside the locality. As we saw in our study in Oaxaca, municipal violence in the state is widespread, much of it linked to fights over local partisan control. Only in the larger urbanized jurisdictions was the noise of repression and coercion detected by audiences outside the state.

[8] This was all the more so before 1911, when state legislatures, generally controlled by governors, elected national senators. A similar situation in which senators were also elected by provincial legislatures existed in Argentina until 1995.

connections between state Democratic Parties and national institutions that made national legislators agents for state governments.[9]

In Mexico fiscal federalism gives municipalities an important measure of economic autonomy. State incumbent monopolization of fiscal flows is an informal and fluid affair, one that exists at or beyond the margins of legality. As a result, far fewer major urban hubs in Mexican states live in states of captivity than in our other cases. They are valuable prizes for opposition parties and are breeding grounds for the development of competitive party systems. They are also focal points for policy coalitions between the national government and municipal mayors.

In the only theoretically driven statistical study to date exploring links between fiscal federalism and subnational authoritarianism, Carlos Gervasoni looks at Argentina and develops a "rentier theory" of subnational regimes.[10] He concludes that, where provincial governments depend on central government transfers for the lion's share of their budget, fiscal federalism has a "rentier effect," stifling local democracy through local effects similar to those found in oil-dependent countries. Gervasoni's findings are compelling for the Argentine case, where all provinces operate under one national fiscal regime. However, the cases examined in this book, which have the benefit of variation in national fiscal systems, suggest a modified interpretation. It is not dependence of provinces on central government transfers per se, but the structure of the flows and channels to the province that determines the local regime effects of fiscal federalism. Argentine governors receive the bulk of transfers unconditionally and have discretion over their local distribution. Fiscal federalism thus has negative effects on local political competition. Mexican states are almost as dependent on federal transfers as Argentine provinces. Yet the channels, conditionality, and local recipients of federal transfers are more complex. Fiscal federalism has thus a more stimulating effect on local political competition. The more varied the channels and the local recipients of federal revenue transfers, the more pluralizing the effects of fiscal federalism on local regime dynamics, regardless of the overall dependence of state economies on such transfers.

IV. THE DIFFERENCE A TERRITORIAL REGIME MAKES: DEMOCRATIZING SUBNATIONAL AUTHORITARIAN REGIMES

Just as the territorial regime shaped how subnational authoritarianism was made, it also shaped how it was unmade. Chapter 2 presented two types of transition from authoritarian rule: the center-led transition and the party-led

---

[9] The uses of federal revenue transfers were also monitored locally by federal officials. Hence, it was doubly important to ensure that the national crafting of federal flows to localities was designed in state incumbents' interests so that their "proper" use could be sanctioned by local federal monitors.

[10] Carlos Gervasoni, "A Rentier Theory of Subnational Regimes," *World Politics* 62, no. 2 (2010).

transition. The odds of one transition type emerging in a specific jurisdiction are determined by characteristics of the national territorial regime. Our cases confirmed that territorial regime decentralization produced local authoritarian regimes built on legal and institutional foundations. In these cases, the center-led transition was the likely transition scenario. In contrast, territorial regime centralization produced local authoritarian regimes built on informal and illegal arrangements. In these cases, the party-led transition was the likely transition scenario.

Why is this the case? The answer lies in how local power asymmetries shape the political calculus for opposition forces. Where federalism gives incumbents the legal power to rig local political orders in their favor, challenging them electorally under the existing rules of the game will often be futile. Oppositions will thus nationalize the local political conflict by appealing to the national government to bring incumbents down through extra-electoral means and to change the local rules of the game to give oppositions a shot at winning local elections.

In centralized systems incumbents are more vulnerable to competitive pressures because their boundary control lacks a legal shield. They may also be constrained by the regulation and scrutiny of national election centralization. Under these conditions, opposition parties will have more incentives to pursue local party-building strategies and to challenge incumbents electorally, despite daunting short-term odds. As we see later, party-led transitions are often iterative processes.

Our case studies revealed this in vivid detail. Under 19th-century federalism in the Unites States, only a central government intervention of massive proportions stood any chance of bringing competitive political systems to the southern states. Local laws made it nearly impossible for oppositions to compete electorally against incumbents. In late-20th-century Argentine federalism, local party oppositions faced daunting prospects in provinces where incumbents had the power to monopolize the executive branch and wipe opposition territorial strongholds off the electoral map. Appealing to the central government to use its powers of federal intervention to revamp local electoral laws was the only politically viable strategy for initiating local transitions from authoritarian rule. The center-led transition was the only transition type observed after the subnational institutional revolutions of the late 1980s.

In centralized federal systems the situation was very different. At the peak of U.S. Reconstruction, state after state in the American South faced party-led challenges to local incumbent rule. The scale of violence, local elite reaction, and electoral effects of white supremacy were often effective in warding off such challenges. However, challenges continued well after Reconstruction's end. The subnational institutional revolutions of the late 19th century put an end to local party-led challenges until the middle of the 20th century, when another center-led transition tore asunder the legal structure of the Solid South.

In the course of three decades the political centralization of federalism made party-led transitions a regular feature of Mexican electoral politics. The flow

TABLE 6.2. *Party-Led Transitions, Center-Led Transitions, and Federalism in the United States, Argentina, and Mexico*

Territorial Regime	Cases	Dominant Authoritarian Boundary Control	Likely Transition Type
Centralized	U.S. under Reconstruction; Mexico post-1990s	Informal and illegal	Party-led transition
Decentralized	U.S. before and after Reconstruction; Argentina post-1980s	Legal and institutional	Center-led transition

of party-led transitions turned into a veritable cascade. More than half of the states governed by hegemonic party systems in the 1990s became competitive in the early 2000s. Successful collective action by PRI state parties against center-led incursions by PAN presidents thus offered little solace to Mexican boundary closers. While their Argentine counterparts could bask in the comfortable insulation of provincial constitutional reforms, Mexican federalism brought national democratic pressures crashing against their states' borders.

We can now summarize the different transitional patterns according to territorial regime features of our cases (see Table 6.2).

Center-Led and Party-Led Transitions: Dynamics of Change

The Center-Led Transition
Despite its drama, the center-led transition is quite straightforward in its mechanisms. The center intervenes and alters the local rules governing elections. However, the process is complicated by the multiplicity of actors who constitute the "center," their conflicting territorial interests, and the unpredictable partisan patterns that emerge from their interactions. Presidents are often leading actors in these dramas, but our cases revealed that they seldom operated alone and, in fact, often acted at cross-purposes with other branches in the national government. All the federal interventions we observed in Argentina were led by presidents. The national congress sometimes played a supporting role, the national judicial branch was seldom visible, and the national party of the president sometimes supported the intervention and sometimes opposed it.

Center-led transitions in the United States involved all branches of government at different times and often put the government leaders and their national parties out of tune with one another. It was the national congress and the Republican Party that directed the center-led transition of the late 1860s. They

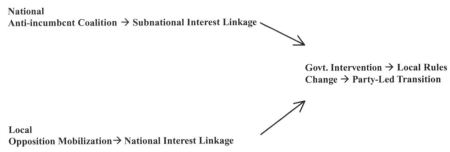

National
Anti-incumbent Coalition → Subnational Interest Linkage

Govt. Intervention → Local Rules
Change → Party-Led Transition

Local
Opposition Mobilization→ National Interest Linkage

FIGURE 6.6. The Center-Led Transition: Sequences and Protagonists

did so in intense conflict with the president. The federal judiciary remained on the sidelines of the center-led transition until scuttling it in the 1870s. Shifting territorial interests in the national Republican Party also propelled Reconstruction in its initial phases and undermined it later.

These examples underscore the difficulty of predicting the likely actors and sequences of a center-led transition. The local–national channels through which the nationalization of conflict will take place can be partisan, bureaucratic, judicial, or any combination thereof. It is also useful analytically to disaggregate the behaviors of national institutional actors who are often conflated in comparative literatures, such as leaders of national parties and leaders of national governments, even when their partisan affiliations coincide. Each has interests that are unique to them. Sometimes these interests can overlap, and at other times these leaders can work at cross-purposes. Predicting the likelihood and nature of their intervention in subnational politics thus requires an empirical knowledge of how national party and government leaders are connected to other actors in the territorial system.

There is also a sequential pattern. A center-led transition is only a first step in the process of subnational regime change. It first involves action by the central government to reshape the local playing field and, second, action by political parties to defeat the incumbent party. Ideally, center-led transitions are followed by party-led transitions. Figure 6.6 lays out these processes and their local or national origins schematically.

The Party-Led Transition

The basic mechanism that shifts the local power balance in the party-led transition is electoral competition. Opposition parties build strength as a result of electoral contests against the local leviathan. The uneven playing field between them shifts with the electoral balance of power. In sum, political parties alter the local balance of power autonomously.

Key to this process is the empowerment of local opposition parties by national parties. Initial successes by local opposition parties can strengthen their ability to nationalize local conflict and entice national parties to invest resources in the local contest. Alternatively, pressing national territorial interests can lead national parties to jump into the local fray without invitation from local branches. Either way, intervention by national actors strengthens local opposition parties' institutional and material capabilities to challenge local incumbents.

Just as important for practical and theoretical purposes is that party-led transitions are rarely one-shot deals. In the center-led transition we have a virtual "big-bang" event of regime change. The central government has in one shot altered local power relations and placed the province's partisan control in the balance. The defeat of incumbents in a party-led transition, by contrast, is often the final step of a gradual process of power change in the authoritarian polity. The party-led transition tends to be an iterative process, where oppositions build power over repeated challenges that are used as starting points for the next challenge (Figure 6.7).

In our Mexican cases the defeat of the ruling party was usually the culminating point of a sequence of opposition party takeovers of territorial bases within the province (urban hubs, for example) that spurred party-building over time. National actors increased their involvement incrementally, calibrating it to local accumulations of power before making investments in pursuit of bigger prizes.

This study of successful transitions from subnational authoritarian rule ended when power was transferred from incumbent parties to opposition parties. It therefore provides little empirical evidence about the long-term consequences for provincial democratization of center-led or party-led transitions. However, it does suggest certain trade-offs in the transition types for opposition parties and subnational political regimes after party turnover.

Party-led transitions have the potential for fostering party-building and competitive party systems before the incumbent regime is defeated. They can also foster links between parties and civil society, forged in the fires of repeated struggles against authoritarianism, which can strengthen the underpinnings of democratic governance after party alternation. Yet opposition parties must operate in a provincial institutional landscape that is manipulated by far stronger opponents throughout this process. They must endure years if not decades of defeat, intimidation, and multiple indignities that the manipulators of democratic institutions inflict on their opponents. Twenty years of playing by the rules in contexts where those rules are unfairly designed or unfairly manipulated is a tall order for any opposition activist, regardless of the intellectual elegance of arguments about iterative political processes.

Center-led transitions offer oppositions the benefits of short-term capture of the pinnacle of provincial power. Local intervention by a national democratic government levels the electoral playing field and does not consign local oppositions or provincial inhabitants to endure the indefinite deprivation of rights enjoyed by fellow citizens living in other provinces. It brings local laws and practices into line with national democracy, an imperative that is as much moral as it may be political. However, oppositions in these situations usually wrest power from local hegemons not after a long labor of party-building,

Local	Opposition	National	Local	New Local
Electoral Challenge →	Captures Offices → (Resource Capture) (Party Building)	Parties Invest →	Power Shift →	Electoral Challenge

FIGURE 6.7 The Party-Led Transition as an Iterative Process

but thanks to external intervention. They often suffer from a lack of political organization, independent governing experience, and links to civil society. In Oaxaca the opposition in 2010 had long experience in local government, party-building, and the strategic utilization of national arenas and laws for local purposes. This experience provided a solid foundation for a competitive political system after party alternation. In Santiago del Estero, the victorious opposition in 2005 had months earlier been firmly co-opted by the authoritarian power structure. The long labors of building a local infrastructure of democratic governance had only begun with party alternation.

CONCLUSION

It's enough of America to be America to me.[11]

As we come to the closing paragraphs of this exploration into subnational authoritarianism, it may be worth asking what it says about the national democracies that harbor and nurture it. The book has stressed, over and over again, the nonlocal and interdependent nature of the forces that make subnational authoritarianism such an enduring presence throughout democratic history. The focus has been analytical and empirical, viewing subnational authoritarianism as a problem of national democracies rather than something that defines them or alters their status as democracies. The term "national" has served conveniently as a jurisdictional marker, one that signifies a level of government in political systems with multiple territorial levels of government. It has thus allowed not only the analytical separation of the national from the subnational, but also the normative separation of the two. The Solid South was "authoritarian." The national government was "democratic," and its democratic status was not impugned by the authoritarian nature of state governments within its territory. This was a definitional distinction, but it had normative implications. It was, in effect, an act of normative boundary control.

If, however, we assume interdependence as a constituent part of authoritarian boundary control in the analytical realm, why not assume the same in the normative realm? Does not the intermixing of the democratic and authoritarian realities of American, Argentine, or Mexican democracy say as much about their national governments as it does about their authoritarian enclaves? And

---

[11] Hip-hop artist Mos Def on the television show "Real Time with Bill Maher." The subject was Louisiana's harsh 2007 prosecution of black youths after a fight with white youths (the "Jena 6" case). Mos Def was responding to Bill Maher's assertion "that's Louisiana, that's not America." Home Box Office Productions, "Real Time with Bill Maher," September 7, 2007.

does it not raise "what is to be done" questions about the continuing scourge of subnational authoritarianism in democratic countries? If this book has any value beyond satisfying the analytical curiosities of political scientists, it should be able to give answers to these questions.

One message that this book provides to political actors is that, if you are concerned about subnational authoritarianism in your countries, look to your territorial regime. Since its modern appearance in the United States, federalism has been the most important determinant of the diffusion of democracy across a country's territorial jurisdictions. Its status as a form of organization of the state has obscured its intimate relationship to the evolution of the political regime. However, to political contenders its importance to democratization has been well known. Republican legislators after the American Civil War knew that expanding democracy to the southern states required a far-reaching transformation of federalism. Their opponents in the South and in national politics also understood the enormous significance for democratization of the battle over federalism. And in the decades following the consolidation of the Solid South, it is not accidental that the invocation of "states' rights," ostensibly a cry in defense of federalism, was primarily a shield for state authoritarianism. Similarly, a century later in Mexico, opposition party activists understood that the transformation of Mexican federalism was a key step toward the pluralization of Mexican states. Their success in removing the impediments to national standards for the definition and enforcement of democratic practices in the states created a national legal architecture supportive of subnational democratization.

It is bad enough when impediments to democratization are local. Yet when impediments to the spread of democratic rights across jurisdictions are woven into the national constitution through the territorial regime, the national democracy cannot escape an intimate association with subnational authoritarianism. It does not only coexist with it. It empowers it and absorbs it into its legal and normative framework. Federalism and democracy can live in happy coexistence only when their union guarantees the provision of democratic rights to all citizens, regardless of the jurisdiction in which circumstance has placed them.

Bibliography

Abrucio, Fernando Luiz. *Os Baroes Da Federacao: O Poder Dos Governadores No Brasil Pós-Autoritário*. Sao Paulo: Editora Hucitec/Universidade de Sao Paulo, 1998.

Alexander, Thomas B. "Persistent Whiggery in the Confederate South, 1860–1877." *Journal of Southern History* 27, no. 3 (1961): 305–29.

Alter, Karen J. *Establishing the Supremacy of European Law: The Making of an International Rule of Law in Europe*. Oxford Studies in European Law. Oxford: Oxford University Press, 2001.

Anderson, Jeffrey J. *The Territorial Imperative: Pluralism, Corporatism, and Economic Crisis*. Cambridge: Cambridge University Press, 1992.

Aranda Vollmer, Rafael. *Poliarquías Urbanas: Competencia Electoral y Zonas Metropolitanas De México*. Mexico City: Instituto Federal Electoral, 2004.

———. "Evolución de la Alternancia: De Los Centros Urbanos a Sus Periferias." *Revista Legislativa de Estudios Sociales y de Opinión Pública* 3, no. 5 (2010).

Auyero, Javier. *Contentious Lives: Two Argentine Women, Two Protests, and the Quest for Recognition*. Latin America Otherwise. Durham: Duke University Press, 2003.

Behrend, Jaqueline "The Unevenness of Democracy at the Subnational Level: Provincial Closed Games in Argentina." *Latin American Research Review* 46, no. 1 (2011): 150–76.

Bensel, Richard Franklin. *Sectionalism and American Political Development, 1880–1980*. Madison: University of Wisconsin Press, 1984.

———. *Yankee Leviathan: The Origins of Central State Authority in America, 1859–1877*. Cambridge: Cambridge University Press, 1990.

Benton, Allyson Lucinda. "Bottom-Up Challenges to National Democracy: Mexico's (Legal) Subnational Authoritarian Enclaves." *Comparative Politics* 44, no. 3 (2012): 253–71.

Berruecos, Susana. "Electoral Justice in Mexico: The Role of the Electoral Tribunal under New Federalism." *Journal of Latin American Studies* 35, no. 4 (2003).

Boone, Catherine. *Political Topographies of the African State: Territorial Authority and Institutional Choice*. Cambridge Studies in Comparative Politics. Cambridge: Cambridge University Press, 2003.

Bruhn, Kathleen. "PRD Local Governments in Michoacán: Implications for Mexico's Democratization Process." In *Subnational Politics and Democratization in Mexico,* edited by Wayne A. Cornelius, Todd A. Eisenstadt, and Jane Hindley. La Jolla: University of California Press, 1999: 19–48.

Burnham, Walter Dean. "The Changing Shape of the American Political Universe." *American Political Science Review* 59, no. 1 (1965): 7–28.

Cabrera, Daniel. *Programa De Reforma Política: Informe Final Sobre Las Provincias De Formosa Y La Rioja*. Buenos Aires: UNDP – Argentine Chief of Staff, 2001.

Calvo, Ernesto, and Marcelo Escolar. *La Nueva Política De Partidos En La Argentina: Crisis Política, Realineamientos Partidarios Y Reforma Electoral*. Colección Democracia, Partidos Y Elecciones. Buenos Aires: Prometeo: Pent, 2005.

Calvo, Ernesto, and Juan Pablo Micozzi. "The Governor's Backyard: A Seat-Vote Model of Electoral Reform for Subnational Multi-Party Races." *Journal of Politics* 67, no. 4 (2005): 1050–74.

Caramani, Daniele. *The Nationalization of Politics: The Formation of National Electorates and Party Systems in Western Europe*. Cambridge: Cambridge University Press, 2004.

Carbonell, Miguel "El Federalismo En México: Principios Generales Y Distribución De Competencias." *Anuario de derecho constitucional latinoamericano* (2003): 379–96.

Carrera, Leandro. "Procesos De Reforma Electoral En Las Provincias De Catamarca Y Jujuy: 1983–1999." Presented at the XXIII International Congress of the Latin American Studies Association, Washington, DC, September 6–8, 2001.

Carreras, Sergio. *El Reino De Los Juárez: Medio Siglo De Miseria, Terror, Y Desmesura En Santiago Del Estero*. Buenos Aires: Aguilar, 2004.

Carter, Dan T. *When the War Was Over: The Failure of Self-Reconstruction in the South, 1865–1867*. Baton Rouge: Louisiana State University Press, 1985.

Chavez, Rebecca Bill. "The Construction of the Rule of Law in Argentina: A Tale of Two Provinces." *Comparative Politics* 35, no. 4 (2003): 417–37.

———. *The Rule of Law in Nascent Democracies: Judicial Politics in Argentina*. Stanford: Stanford University Press, 2004.

Clarke, Colin G. *Class, Ethnicity, and Community in Southern Mexico: Oaxaca's Peasantries*. Oxford Geographical and Environmental Studies. Oxford: Oxford University Press, 2000.

Cobb, Michael D., and Jeffrey A. Jenkins. "Race and the Representation of Blacks' Interests during Reconstruction." *Political Research Quarterly* 54, no. 1 (2001): 181–204.

Cornelius, Wayne A. *Mexican Politics in Transition: The Breakdown of a One-Party Dominant Regime* Monograph Series no. 41. San Diego: University of California Press, 1996.

———. "Subnational Politics and Democratization: Tensions between Center and Periphery in the Mexican Political System." In *Subnational Politics and Democratization in Mexico*, edited by Wayne A. Cornelius, Todd A. Eisenstadt, and Jane Hindley. La Jolla: University of California Press, 1999: 3–16.

Cornelius, Wayne A., Todd A. Eisenstadt, and Jane Hindley, eds. *Subnational Politics and Democratization in Mexico*. U.S.-Mexico Contemporary Perspectives Series 13. La Jolla: University of California Press, 1999.

Dahl, Robert Alan. *Polyarchy; Participation and Opposition*. New Haven: Yale University Press, 1971.

Dargoltz, Raúl. *El Santiagueñazo: Gestación Y Cronica De Una Pueblada Argentina*. Buenos Aires: El Despertador Ediciones Sielp, 1994.

Dargoltz, Raúl, Oscar Jeréz, and Horacio Cao. *El Nuevo Santiagueñazo: Cambio Politico Y Regimen Caudillista*. Buenos Aires: Biblos, 2006.

Dargoltz, Raúl, Oscar Jeréz, Horacio Cao, and Josefina Vaca. *Santiago: El Ala Que Brota*. Buenos Aires: Editorial Utopías, 2005.

de Santis, Vincent P. "Rutherford Hayes and the Removal of the Troops and the End of Reconstruction." In *Region, Race, and Reconstruction: Essays in Honor of C. Vann Woodward*, edited by J. Morgan Kousser and James M. McPherson. New York: Oxford University Press, 1982: 417–50.

Diaz-Cayeros, Alberto. "Do Federal Institutions Matter? Rules and Political Practices in Regional Resource Allocation in Mexico." In *Federalism and Democracy in Latin America*, edited by Edward L. Gibson. Baltimore: Johns Hopkins University Press, 2004: 297–322.

———. *Federalism, Fiscal Authority, and Centralization in Latin America*, Cambridge Studies in Comparative Politics. Cambridge: Cambridge University Press, 2006.

Díaz Montes, Fausto *Los Municipios: La Disputa Por El Poder En Oaxaca*. Oaxaca: Instituto de Investigaciones Sociológicas, 1980.

Durazo Herrmann, Julián. "Neo-Patrimonialism and Subnational Authoritarianism in Mexico: The Case of Oaxaca." *Journal of Politics in Latin America* 2 (2010): 85–113.

———. "Social Heterogeneity, Political Mediation, and Subnational Authoritarianism: Comparing Oaxaca and Puebla, Mexico," Paper delivered at the conference on Subnational Democratization: Latin America, the United States, Russia and India in Comparative Perspective, Buenos Aires, Universidad Torcuato Di Tella, April 15–16, 2010.

Easton, David. *A Framework for Political Analysis*. London: Prentice-Hall, 1965.

Eaton, Kent. *Politics beyond the Capital: The Design of Subnational Institutions in South America*. Stanford, CA: Stanford University Press, 2004.

Edmonds-Poli, Emily. "Decentralization under the Fox Administration: Progress or Stagnation?" *Mexican Studies/Estudios Mexicanos* 22, no. 2 (2006): 387–416.

Eisenstadt, Todd A. *Courting Democracy in Mexico: Party Strategies and Electoral Institutions*. Cambridge: Cambridge University Press, 2004.

———. "Electoral Federalism or Abdication of Presidential Authority?" In *Subnational Politics and Democratization in Mexico*, edited by Wayne A. Cornelius, Todd A. Eisenstadt, and Jane Hindley. La Jolla: University of California Press, 1999: 269–93.

"El Gobierno De Kirchner Respondió a Las Críticas De Duhalde." *El Liberal*, March 2 2005.

Falleti, Tulia. "A Sequential Theory of Decentralization: Latin American Cases in Comparative Perspective " *American Political Science Review* 99, no. 3 (2005): 315–27.

———. *Decentralization and Subnational Politics in Latin America*. New York: Cambridge University Press, 2010.

Fenwick, Tracy Beth. "Scaling Down further the Subnational Comparative Method: Insights from Brazil and Argentina." Paper prepared for panel on "Subnational Authoritarianism in Comparative Perspective," Latin American Studies Association International Congress, Rio de Janeiro. June 12, 2009.

———. "The Institutional Feasibility of National-Local Policy Collaboration: Insights from Brazil and Argentina." *Journal of Politics in Latin America* 2 (2010): 155–83.

Fernàndez, Anibal. "En defensa del federalismo." Editorial. *La Nación* (Buenos Aires), March 16, 2004: p. 17.

Foner, Eric. *Reconstruction: America's Unfinished Revolution, 1863–1877*. New American Nation Series. New York: Harper & Row, 1988.

———. *Freedom's Lawmakers: A Directory of Black Officeholders During Reconstruction*, rev. ed. Baton Rouge: Louisiana State University Press, 1996.

Fox, Jonathan. "Latin America's Emerging Local Politics." *Journal of Democracy* 5, no. 2 (1994): 105–16.

Franklin, John Hope. *Reconstruction: After the Civil War*. Chicago History of American Civilization. Chicago: University of Chicago Press, 1961.

———. "Public Welfare in the South during the Reconstruction Era." *Social Service Review* 44, December (1970).

Frederickson, Kari A. *The Dixiecrat Revolt and the End of the Solid South, 1932–1968*. Chapel Hill: University of North Carolina Press, 2001.

Fuertes, Flavio. "Ni Mayoritario Ni Proporcional: Nuevos Sistemas Electorales, Los Casos De Santa Cruz, Río Negro Y Santiago Del Estero." Paper presented at XXIII International Congress of the Latin American Studies Association. Washington, DC, 2001.

Gelman, Vladimir, and Cameron Ross, eds. *The Politics of Sub-National Authoritarianism in Russia*. London: Ashgrove Press, 2010.

Gervasoni, Carlos. "Measuring Variance in Subnational Regimes: Results from an Expert-Based Operationalization of Democracy in the Argentine Provinces." *Journal of Politics in Latin America* 2 (2010): 13–52.

———. "A Rentier Theory of Subnational Regimes." *World Politics* 62, no. 2 (2010): 39.

Gibson, Edward L. *Class and Conservative Parties: Argentina in Comparative Perspective*. Baltimore: Johns Hopkins University Press, 1996.

———. "The Populist Road to Market Reform: Policy and Electoral Coalitions in Mexico and Argentina." *World Politics* 49 (1997): 339–70.

———. *Federalism and Democracy in Latin America*. Baltimore: Johns Hopkins University Press, 2004.

———. "Boundary Control: Subnational Authoritarianism in Democratic Countries." *World Politics* 58, no. 1 (2005): 101–32.

Gibson, Edward L., and Ernesto Calvo. "Federalism and Low-Maintenance Constituencies: Territorial Dimensions of Economic Reform in Argentina." *Studies in Comparative International Development* 35, no. 3 (2001): 32–55.

Gibson, Edward L., and Tulia Falleti. "Unity by the Stick: Regional Conflict and the Origins of Federalism." In *Federalism and Democracy in Latin America*, edited by Edward L. Gibson. Baltimore: Johns Hopkins University Press, 2004: 226–54.

Gibson, Edward L., and Julieta Suarez-Cao. "Federalized Party Systems and Subnational Party Competition: Theory and an Empirical Application to Argentina." *Comparative Politics* 43, no. 1 (2010): 21–39.

Giraudy, Augustina. "Subnational Undemocratic Regime Continuity after Democratization: Argentina and Mexico in Comparative Perspective." Ph.D. Dissertation, University of North Carolina, Chapel Hill, 2009.

———. "The Politics of Subnational Undemocratic Regime Reproduction in Argentina and Mexico." *Journal of Politics in Latin America* 2 (2010): 53–84.

Giugale, Marcelo, and Steven Benjamin Webb. *Achievements and Challenges of Fiscal Decentralization: Lessons from Mexico*. Washington, DC: World Bank, 2000.

Gobierno de la Intervención Federal en la Provincia de Santiago del Estero. "Séptimo Informe De La Intervención Federal Al Honorable Congreso De La Nación." Intervención Federal, Santiago del Estero, 2004.

Gómez Diez, Ricardo. "La Oportunidad De Una Constitución Para El Bienestar Y El Crecimiento." Santiago del Estero, 2004.

Greene, Brian. *The Fabric of the Cosmos: Space, Time, and the Texture of Reality*. New York: Alfred E. Knopf, 2004.

Hagopian, Frances. *Traditional Politics and Regime Change in Brazil*. Cambridge Studies in Comparative Politics. Cambridge: Cambridge University Press, 1996.

Herbst, Jeffrey Ira. *States and Power in Africa: Comparative Lessons in Authority and Control*. Princeton Studies in International History and Politics. Princeton, NJ: Princeton University Press, 2000.

Hernández Norzagaray, Ernesto. "Sistemas Electorales Y Sistemas De Partidos En Los Estados Mexicanos." Paper presented at the VI Congreso de la Asociación Española de Ciencia Política y de la Administración, Barcelona, 2003.

Hirshson, Stanley P. *Farewell to the Bloody Shirt*. Bloomington: Indiana University Press, 1962.

Howard, John R. *The Shifting Wind: The Supreme Court and Civil Rights from Reconstruction to Brown*. SUNY Series in Afro-American Studies. Albany: State University of New York Press, 1999.

Hume, Richard L. "Carpetbaggers in the Reconstruction South: A Group Portrait of Outside Whites in the 'Black and Tan' Constitutional Conventions." *Journal of American History* 64, September (1977).

———. "Negro Delegates to the State Constitutional Conventions of 1867–1869." In *Southern Black Leaders of the Reconstruction Era*, edited by Howard N. Rabinowitz. Urbana: University of Illinois Press, 1982: 129–53.

Huntington, Samuel. "Will More Countries Become Democratic?" *Political Science Quarterly* 99, no. 2 (1984): 193–218.

Jervis, Robert. *System Effects: Complexity in Political and Social Life*. Princeton, NJ: Princeton University Press, 1997.

Katznelson, Ira, Kim Geiger, and Daniel Kryder. "Limiting Liberalism: The Southern Veto in Congress, 1933–1950." *Political Science Quarterly* 108, no. 2 (1993): 283–306.

Keck, Margaret E., and Kathryn Sikkink. *Activists beyond Borders: Advocacy Networks in International Politics*. Ithaca, NY: Cornell University Press, 1998.

Key, V. O. *Southern Politics in State and Nation*. New York: A. A. Knopf, 1949.

King, Desmond, Robert C. Lieberman, Gretchen Ritter, and Laurence Whitehead, eds. *Democratization in America: A Comparative Historical Analysis*. Baltimore: Johns Hopkins University Press, 2000.

King, Desmond, and Stephen Tuck. "De-Centering the South: America's Nationwide White Supremacists Order after Reconstruction." *Past & Present* 194, no. 1 (2007): 41.

Kopstein, Jeffrey S., and David A. Reilly. "Geographic Diffusion and the Transformation of the Postcommunist World." *World Politics* 53, no. 1 (2000): 37.

Kousser, J. Morgan. *The Shaping of Southern Politics: Suffrage Restriction and the Establishment of the One-Party South, 1880–1910*. Yale Historical Publications. Miscellany 102. New Haven: Yale University Press, 1974.

Kutler, Stanley I. *Judicial Power and Reconstruction Politics*. Chicago: University of Chicago Press, 1968.

———. *The Supreme Court and the Constitution: Readings in American Constitutional History*. Boston: Houghton Mifflin, 1969.

Langston, Joy. "Rising from the Ashes?" *Comparative Political Studies* 36, no. 3 (2003): 27.

———. "La Competencia Electoral Y La Descentralización Partidista En México." *Revista Mexicana de Sociología* 70, no. 3 (2008): 457–86.

Lankina, Tomila V., and Lullit Getachew. "A Geographic Incremental Theory of Democratization: Territory, Aid, and Democracy in Postcommunist Regions." *World Politics* 58, no. 4 (2006): 47.

Lerche, Charles O., Jr. "Congressional Interpretations of the Guarantee of a Republican Form of Government during Reconstruction." *Journal of Southern History* 15, no. 2 (1949): 192–211.

Levitsky, Steven, and Lucan Way. "Linkage versus Leverage: Rethinking the International Dimension of Regime Change." *Comparative Politics* 58, no. 4 (2006): 379–400.

———. *Competitive Authoritarianism: Hybrid Regimes after the Cold War*. Problems of International Politics. New York: Cambridge University Press, 2010.

Lijphart, Arend. *Patterns of Democracy: Government Forms and Performance in Thirty-Six Countries*. New Haven: Yale University Press, 1999.

Lindberg, Staffan I, Ed. *Democratization by Elections: a New Mode of Transition*. Baltimore, MD: The Johns Hopkins University Press (2009).

"Los Malos Pasos En La Interna Del Pj." *El Liberal*, April 1 2004.

Lodola, Germán. "Gobierno Nacional, Gobernadores, e Intendentes en el Período Kirchnerista." In Andrés Malamud and Miguel De Luca, Eds., *La Política en los Tiempos de los Kirchner*. Buenos Aires: Eudeba (2011): 215–25.

Lowe, Richard. "The Freedmen's Bureau and Local Black Leadership." *Journal of American History* 80, no. 3 (1993): 989–98.

Lujambio, Alonso, and Horacio Vives Segl. *El Poder Compartido: Un Ensayo Sobre La Democratización Mexicana*. México, D.F.: Océano, 2000.

Magaloni, Beatriz. *Voting for Autocracy: Hegemonic Party Survival and Its Demise in Mexico*. Cambridge Studies in Comparative Politics. New York: Cambridge University Press, 2006.

Martínez Vázquez, Víctor Raúl. *Movimiento Popular Y Política En Oaxaca, 1968-1986*. Mexico City: Consejo Nacional para la Cultura y las Artes, 1990.

———. *Autoritarismo, Movimiento Popular Y Crisis Política: Oaxaca 2006*. Oaxaca, Mexico: Universidad Autonoma Benito Juarez, 2007.

Martínez Vázquez, Víctor Raúl, and Fausto Díaz Montes, eds. *Elecciones Municipales En Oaxaca*. Oaxaca: Instituto de Investigaciones Sociológicas, 2001.

Marván Laborde, Ignacio. "Reflexiones Sobre Federalismo Y Sistema Politico En México." *Política y Gobierno* 4, no. 1 (1997).

McKitrick, Eric L. *Andrew Johnson and Reconstruction*. Chicago: University of Chicago Press, 1960.

McMann, Kelly M. *Economic Autonomy and Democracy: Hybrid Regimes in Russia and Kyrgyzstan*. New York: Cambridge University Press, 2006.

McPherson, James M. *The Struggle for Equality: Abolitionists and the Negro in the Civil War and Reconstruction*. Princeton, NJ: Princeton University Press, 1964.

———. "Grant or Greeley? The Abolitionist Dilemma in the Election of 1872." *American Historical Review* 71, no. 1 (1965): 43–61.

Mickey, Robert. "The Beginning of the End for Authoritarian Rule in America: *Smith V. Allwright* and the Abolition of the White Primary in the Deep South, 1944–1948." *Studies in American Political Development* 22, no. 2 (2008): 143–82.

———. *Paths out of Dixie: The Democratization of Authoritarian Enclaves in America's Deep South.* Princeton: Princeton University Press, 2012.

Miller, David. *The Regional Governing of Metropolitan America.* New York: Westview Press, 2002.

Ministerio de Justicia, Seguridad, y Derechos Humanos. *Informe Santiago Del Estero.* Buenos Aires: Seguridad Ministerio de Justicia, y Derechos Humanos, 2003.

Mizrahi, Yemilc. "Pressuring the Center: Opposition Governments and Federalism in Mexico." Mexico City: *Documentos de Trabajo – CIDE* (1997).

Molinar Horcasitas, Juan. *El Tiempo De La Legitimidad: Elecciones, Autoritarismo, Y Democracia En México.* Mexico City: Cal y Arena, 1991.

Mora y Araujo, Manuel, and Ignacio Llorente. *El Voto Peronista.* Colección Historia Y Sociedad. Buenos Aires: Editorial Sudamericana, 1980.

Munck, Guillermo, and Jay Verkuilen. "Conceptualizing and Measuring Democracy: Evaluating Alternative Indices." *Comparative Political Studies* 35, no. 1 (2002): 5–34.

Mustapic, Ana María. "Conflictos Institucionales Durante El Primer Gobierno Radical: 1916–1922." *Desarrollo Económico* 24, no. 93 (1984): 85–108.

Nathans, Elizabeth Studley. *Losing the Peace: Georgia Republicans and Reconstruction, 1865–1871.* Baton Rouge: Louisiana State University Press, 1969.

Nohlen, Dieter. *Elecciones Y Sistemas Electorales,* 3rd ed. Caracas: Fundación Friedrich Ebert: Editorial Nueva Sociedad, 1995.

Ochoa-Reza, Enrique. "Multiple Arenas of Struggle: Federalism and Mexico's Transition to Democracy." In *Federalism and Democracy in Latin America,* edited by Edward L. Gibson. Baltimore: Johns Hopkins University Press, 2004: 255–96.

O'Donnell, Guillermo A. *On the State, Democratization, and Some Conceptual Problems (a Latin American View with Glances at Some Post-Communist Countries).* South Bend, IN: Helen Kellogg Institute for International Studies, the University of Notre Dame, 1993.

O'Donnell, Guillermo A., Philippe C. Schmitter, and Laurence Whitehead. *Transitions from Authoritarian Rule: Prospects for Democracy.* Baltimore: Johns Hopkins University Press, 1986.

Oxford English Dictionary. Oxford: Clarendon Press, 2001.

Paddison, Ronan. *The Fragmented State: The Political Geography of Power.* Oxford: Basil Blackwell, 1983.

Powell, Lawrence. "The Politics of Livelihood: Carpetbaggers in the Deep South." In *Region, Race, and Reconstruction: Essays in Honor of C. Vann Woodward,* edited by J. Morgan Kousser and James M. McPherson. New York: Oxford University Press, 1982: 315–47.

Rable, George C. *But There Was No Peace: The Role of Violence in the Politics of Reconstruction.* Athens: University of Georgia Press, 1984.

Raúl Benitez Zenteno, ed. *Sociedad Y Política En Oaxaca, 1980.* Oaxaca: Instituto de Estudios Sociológicos, 1980.

Redding, Kent, and David R. James. "Estimating Levels and Modeling Determinants of Black and White Voter Turnout in the South: 1880 to 1912." *Historical Methods* 34, no. 4 (2001): 141–58.

Reyna, José Luis, and Richard S. Weinert. *Authoritarianism in Mexico.* Inter-American Politics Series, Vol. 2. Philadelphia: Institute for the Study of Human Issues, 1977.

Reynoso, Diego. "Alianzas Electorales Y Contingentes Legislativos En Los Estados Mexicanos (1988–2006)." *Revista Mexicana de Sociología* 72, no. 1 (2010): 113–39.

Riker, William H. *Federalism: Origin, Operation, Significance*. LB Basic Studies in Politics. Boston: Little, Brown, 1964.

Rodriguez Leirado, Pablo. "La Provincia De San Luis. El Eterno Feudo." *Revista Digital Sitio al Margen*, 1998.

Rodríguez, Victoria Elizabeth, and Peter M. Ward. *Opposition Government in Mexico*. Albuquerque: University of New Mexico Press, 1995.

Rokkan, Stein, Derek W. Urwin, and European Consortium for Political Research. *Economy, Territory, Identity: Politics of West European Peripheries*. London: Sage Publications, 1983.

Ross, Michael A. "Justice Miller's Reconstruction: The Slaughter-House Cases, Health Codes, and Civil Rights in New Orleans, 1861–1873." *Journal of Southern History* 64, no. 4 (1998): 28.

Rueschemeyer, Dietrich, Evelyne Huber, and John D. Stephens. *Capitalist Development and Democracy*. Chicago: University of Chicago Press, 1992.

Sack, Robert David. *Human Territoriality: Its Theory and History*. Cambridge Studies in Historical Geography 7. Cambridge: Cambridge University Press, 1986.

Sartori, Giovanni. *Parties and Party Systems: A Framework for Analysis*. Cambridge: Cambridge University Press, 1976.

———. *Social Science Concepts: A Systematic Analysis*. Beverly Hills: Sage Publications, 1984.

Saville, Julie. *The Work of Reconstruction: From Slave to Wage Laborer in South Carolina, 1860–1870*. Cambridge: Cambridge University Press, 1994.

Sawers, Larry. *The Other Argentina: The Interior and National Development*. Boulder, CO: Westview Press, 1996.

Schattschneider, E. E. *The Semisovereign People: A Realist's View of Democracy in America*. Hinsdale, IL: Dryden Press, 1960.

Schedler, Andreas. "The Nested Game of Democratization by Elections." *International Political Science Review* 23, no. 1 (2002): 20.

———. "From Electoral Authoritarianism to Democratic Consolidation." In *Mexico's Democracy at Work: Political and Economic Dynamics*, edited by Russell Crandall, Guadalupe Paz and Riordan Roett. Boulder, CO: Lynne Rienner, 2005: 9–37.

———. "Authoritarianism's Last Line of Defense." *Journal of Democracy* 21, no. 1 (2010): 12.

Schulman, Bruce J. *From Cotton Belt to Sunbelt: Federal Policy, Economic Development, and the Transformation of the South, 1938–1980*. New York: Oxford University Press, 1991.

Scroggs, Jack B. "Carpetbagger Constitutional Reform in the South Atlantic States, 1867–1868." *Journal of Southern History* 27, no. 4 (1961): 475–93.

Seip, Terry L. *The South Returns to Congress: Men, Economic, Measures, and Intersectional Relationships, 1868–1879*. Baton Rouge: Louisiana State University Press, 1983.

Selee, Andrew D., and Jacqueline Peschard. "Mexico's Democratic Challenges." In *Mexico's Democratic Challenges: Politics, Government, and Society*, edited by Andrew D. Selee and Jacqueline Peschard. Stanford, CA: Stanford University Press, 2010: 1–18.

Séptimo Informe De La Intervención Federal Al Honorable Congreso De La Nación. Santiago del Estero: Gobierno de la Intervención Federal en la Provincia de Santiago del Estero, 2004.

Serrafero, Mario. "La Intervención Federal En Argentina. Experiencia Y Jurisprudencia." Unpublished Manuscript. Buenos Aires: Facultad de Ciencias Jurdídicas y Sociales UADE (2009).

Simpser, Alberto, *Why Governments and Parties Manipulate Elections: Theory, Practice, and Implications*. Forthcoming, Cambridge University Press.

Slap, Andrew L. *The Doom of Reconstruction: The Liberal Republicans in the Civil War Era*. Reconstructing America Series. New York: Fordham University Press, 2006.

Snyder, Richard. *Politics after Neoliberalism: Reregulation in Mexico*. Cambridge Studies in Comparative Politics. Cambridge: Cambridge University Press, 2001.

———. "Scaling Down: The Subnational Comparative Method." *Studies in Comparative International Development* 36, no. 1 (2001): 93–110.

Snyder, Richard, and David Samuels. "Legislative Malapportionment in Latin America: Historical and Comparative Perspectives." In *Federalism and Democracy in Latin America*, edited by Edward L. Gibson. Baltimore: Johns Hopkins University Press, 2004: 131–72.

Solt, Frederick. "Electoral Competition, Legislative Pluralism, and Institutional Development: Evidence from Mexico's States." *Latin American Research Review* 39, no. 1 (2004): 155–67.

Spiller, Pablo T., and Mariano Tommasi. *The Institutional Foundations of Public Policy in Argentina*. New York: Cambridge University Press, 2007.

Stepan, Alfred. "Electorally Generated Veto Players in Unitary and Federal Systems." In *Federalism and Democracy in Latin America*, edited by Edward L. Gibson. Baltimore: Johns Hopkins University Press, 2004: 29–84.

Stoner-Weiss, Kathryn. *Local Heroes: The Political Economy of Russian Regional Governance*. Princeton, NJ: Princeton University Press, 1997.

Suarez-Cao, Julieta. "Arquitectura Institucional Del Legislativo: Los Casos De San Luis Y Tucuman." Paper presented at the XXIII International Congress of the Latin American Studies Association, Washington, DC, 2001.

Swain, Carol M. *Black Faces, Black Interests: The Representation of African Americans in Congress*. Cambridge, MA: Harvard University Press, 1993.

Tarrow, Sidney G., Peter J. Katzenstein, and Luigi Graziano. *Territorial Politics in Industrial Nations*. New York: Praeger, 1978.

Tipps, Dean C. "Modernization Theory and the Comparative Study of Societies: A Critical Perspective." *Comparative Studies in Society and History* 15, no. 2 (1973): 199–226.

Tocqueville, Alexis de, Phillips Bradley, Henry Reeve, and Francis Bowen. *Democracy in America*. New York: A. A. Knopf, 1945.

Tuck, Stephen. "The Reversal of Black Voting Rights after Reconstruction." In *Democratization in America: A Comparative-Historical Analysis*, edited by Desmond King, Robert C. Lieberman, Gretchen Ritter, and Laurence Whitehead. Baltimore: Johns Hopkins University Press, 2009: 133–56.

"Un Régimen De Miedo Y Terror Manda En Santiago Del Estero." *La Nación*, November 28, 2002.

Valelly, Richard M. *The Two Reconstructions: The Struggle for Black Enfranchisement*. Chicago: University of Chicago Press, 2004.

Vommaro Gabriel. "La Política Santiagueña en las Postrimerías del Juarismo." In *El Voto Liberado, Elecciones 2003: Perspectiva Histórica y Estudio de Casos*, edited by Isidoro Cheresky and Inés Pousadela. Buenos Aires: Editorial Biblos (2004): 225–52.

Webb, Steven B., and Christian Y. Gonzalez. *Bargaining for a New Fiscal Pact in Mexico*. Washington, DC: World Bank, 2004.

Wiecek, William M. *The Guarantee Clause of the U.S. Constitution*. Cornell Studies in Civil Liberty. Ithaca: Cornell University Press, 1972.

Wiñazki, Miguel, Daniel Malnati, and Gabriel Michi. *El Adolfo: Crónicas Del Fascismo Mágico*. Buenos Aires: Planeta, 2002.

Woodward, C. Vann. *Origins of the New South, 1877–1913*, Vol. 9 of *A History of the South*. Baton Rouge: Louisiana State University Press, 1951.

———. *Reunion and Reaction: The Compromise of 1877 and the End of Reconstruction*. Boston: Little, Brown, 1951.

———. *Tom Watson: Agrarian Rebel*. New York: Oxford University Press, 1972.

Index